DIVE
SOUTH CORNWALL

A DIVER GUIDE

Richard Larn

Underwater World Publications

Above: Some of the many thousands of brass artefacts
recovered from the *Santo Christo de Castello* (Site **155**).
Title page: The new jetty at Polruan, where you can land and
take on fuel.
Front cover: Diver with cannon on the offshore wreck site of
HMS *Coronation* (Site **17**).

Maps drawn by Suzanne Hall

Editorial production by Martyn Yeo

Produced by Diver Magazine

Published by Underwater World Publications Ltd,
55 High Street, Teddington, Middlesex, TW11 8HA

First published 1983
Second edition 1987
Third edition 1996

© Underwater World Publications Ltd 1996

ISBN 0 946020 25 6

Printed in the United Arab Emirates by Emirates Printing Press,
PO Box 5106, Al Quoz, Dubai

Contents

Sennen, near Land's End.

How to use this Guide

The south coast of Cornwall has been divided into eight areas, each based on a major geographical feature. They start just west of Plymouth and continue west to Land's End. Previous editions of this guide have also included the area to Cape Cornwall, but as that is part of the north coast it will be covered in a new guide, *Dive Isles of Scilly and North Cornwall*.

For each area covered by this guide there is a general description. Various coastal wreck and scenic sites are described as they occur, followed by descriptions of coastal dive sites, shipwrecks and offshore sites with recommended launching points for inflatable boats.

Detailed information is given for each area: simplified route instructions, parking facilities, launch sites, the type of diving available, wreck details and much more are included. A list of useful addresses, contact telephone numbers, air sources, servicing, hire and repair facilities will be found in Appendix 1.

The information given was correct and relevant at the time it was written, but nothing stands still and change is inevitable. The author and publishers would greatly appreciate any current information on existing sites, which will be used (with acknowledgement) when this guide is updated. Please also send in details of any new site that you wish to share with others. The use of symbols in the guide has been avoided, so that services and facilities are listed in plain English.

It is in everyone's interest that guides such as those in this series carry current and up-to-date information. After all, you have probably derived some benefit from this guide as it stands, which has only been made possible by the kind co-operation of others – people like you!

Unless otherwise specified, references to Ordnance Survey maps are to the 1:50,000 Landranger Series – sheets 200, 201, 203 and 204. Details of the relevant Admiralty Charts are given for each area, and can be obtained from

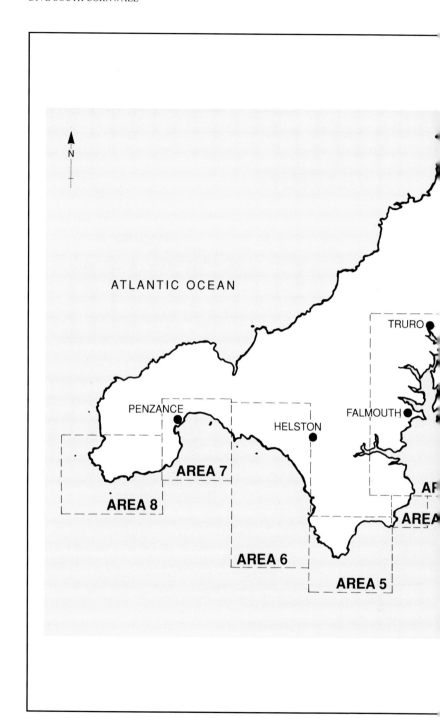

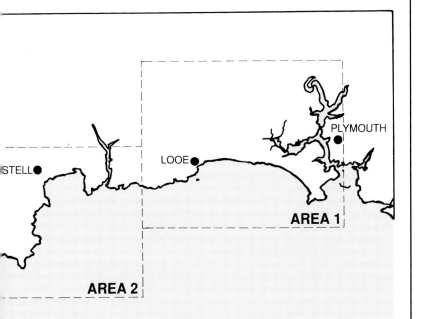

PLYMOUTH

STELL●

LOOE●

AREA 1

AREA 2

The eight chapter areas

ENGLISH CHANNEL

The slipway in the inner harbour at Porthleven.

chart agents A.E. Monsen Ltd at Vauxhall Quay, Sutton Harbour, Plymouth (tel. 01752 665384) or Commercial Road, Penryn (tel. 01326 373581 or 372714).

All readings of latitude and longitude are given in degrees, minutes and seconds, for example: 50 00 25N; 05 05 48W.

Decca positions, derived from special Decca Admiralty charts, are more accurate than latitude and longitude and are given where known. They are marked on the charts with three sets of "lines" coloured red, green and purple. To give a reference you use the colours and numbers, thus Decca (R) 24.7 and (G) 15.6 refers to red line 24.7 intersecting with green line 15.6. More information about Decca positions can be obtained from *Coastal and Offshore Navigation* by T. Cunliffe.

Dive sites and wrecks are numbered consecutively through the guide, and over 200 are listed and described. The site numbers are printed in bold type, and relate to the numbers shown on the detailed map for each area. Depths are given in metres; distances in yards and miles. Ship tonnages are gross unless stated otherwise.

We trust you will enjoy your visit to south Cornwall, and experience good, safe, adventurous, fun diving

About Cornwall

The county of Cornwall has a very long coastline with many miles of inlets, creeks and harbours. The county is bounded by the sea on three sides, and the combination of its temperate climate, clear water, an abundance of shipwrecks, great variety of underwater scenery and plentiful marine life offers sport divers an underwater environment of unusual richness.

In shape, Cornwall's outline represents a booted leg, 75 miles long from east to west, with 50 miles separating the English Channel and Bristol Channel at the widest part, from Hartland Point to Rame Head. Within its boundary lies an area of some 868,000 acres, with a resident population of about 525,000 (including the Scillies). The county town is Truro; the principal tourist towns are Newquay, Looe and Penzance. St Austell is probably the largest of Cornwall's industrialised areas, its largest single employer being the English China Clay Company.

The county has a Celtic origin, and has much in common with the geography and traditions of both the north coast of Brittany and south Wales, to which it was once attached. A strong sense of identity survives, with anyone from the other side of the River Tamar considered a foreigner. Any true Cornishman crossing into Devon considers that he has "gone to England" – an attitude often adopted by even the most recently arrived immigrant from Sheffield or Guildford!

Cornwall's climate is probably the mildest in the UK. The winters see little snow or frost, although they can be extremely wet and windy. Consequently, spring comes early, and the coast will be ablaze with yellow gorse, early daffodils and primroses well in advance of other counties. However, air temperatures and sunshine hours vary little from Kent, since onshore breezes often keep temperatures well down, except in sheltered parts.

The warm Gulf Stream benefits the Isles of Scilly and Cornwall only in that it warms the prevailing south-west winds. Sea temperatures off the far South West

5

will be found, surprisingly, to be far below those off Dorset and Sussex, except in sheltered, shallow bays. Diving without the protection of a full drysuit or wetsuit is not recommended, as it can quickly lead to hypothermia.

Travel

Roads The two main road routes into Cornwall are the M5 and A303. The M5 links with the M4 from London and the M6 from the North. The M3/A303/A30 is a fast alternative route from London, with long stretches of dual carriageway and bypasses. This route is some forty miles shorter than the motorway and is far less congested, with plenty of service stations. There is also the south coast motorway and trunk route (A27/M27/A31/A35).

These routes converge at Exeter, where the motorist has the choice of continuing through Devon and into Cornwall via the A30 or the A38. The A30 goes via Okehampton, Launceston, Bodmin and Redruth to Penzance, and is dual carriageway almost all the way. The A38 is also a dual carriageway. Plymouth has a flyover bridge at Marsh Mills, and a bypass to the Saltash toll bridge; after this the route goes via the Saltash tunnel and right through to Dobwalls. From here it continues west and joins the A30 at Bodmin, or you can follow the more southerly A390 via St Austell and Truro.

Cornwall can also be reached by ferry services to Plymouth from France and Spain.

Do remember that Devon and Cornwall are popular tourist areas with long seasons, and that during the peak holiday periods – from mid July to the end of the first week in September – something like three million visitors will enter the county, outnumbering the locals by some six to one. For six weeks prior to July, and for three weeks after early September, the holiday season continues, but the congestion is far less acute, and apart from Bank Holiday weekends you may well find car parks, coves and beaches deserted.

Travelling on the roads at peak periods should be carefully planned, since queues of caravans, trailers and cars will be encountered around Bristol, at the motorway junctions and at Taunton, and long tailbacks entering and leaving Cornwall at the Saltash bridge at weekends are frequent. You are advised to check with the AA, RAC or Police before departure regarding road conditions and recommended routes. Outside peak periods travelling to the South West

---

MOTORING ORGANISATIONS

The two main motoring organisations may be contacted as follows:

AA 24-hour breakdown service: tel. 0800 887766 (0345 887766 from mobile telephones). Enquiries (Plymouth) 01752 229651.

RAC 24-hour breakdown service: tel. 0800 828282. Enquiries (Plymouth) 01752 669301.

Dive boats on the beach at Porthoustock.

should present no problems, but make allowances for delays when timing your journey.

Until recent years, cynics described the roads through Cornwall as "the longest lanes in Britain", but that no longer applies. The only lanes encountered now are those well off the main roads. However, to get to a great many of the dive sites described in this guide will require negotiation of high-sided lanes of one vehicle width only, with infrequent passing places that may accommodate a single car, but not a car and boat trailer combined. Your reversing skills may frequently be put to the test – but if there is a vehicle in your group that is not towing let that lead the way, to advise other road users that a long vehicle is following.

Many of the launch sites have limited or no parking facilities, and consideration for others must be given. Leaving empty boat trailers blocking slipways, residents' boat spaces, dinghy parks or access is thoughtless and unnecessary, and will only provoke trouble. Where possible, parking places are mentioned throughout this guide. Please use them, and accept that there are few places where you can leave your vehicle alongside a slipway or at the water's edge.

Rail services Cornwall is well served by the railways, with services from London, the Midlands and the North. Seats on Friday afternoons to the South West are almost always fully booked in advance, mostly by commuters, and without a seat reservation you may not be allowed on certain trains leaving Paddington. Details of services may be obtained from the stations at Truro (tel. 01872 76244) or Plymouth (tel. 01752 221300).

Flights Brymon Airways operate to and from London Heathrow to Newquay. The flight time is approximately one hour, and details can be obtained through the information service at Heathrow (tel. 0345 222111) or the Brymon flight desk at Newquay Airport (tel. 01637 860551).

Where to stay

As you would expect of a major tourist area, Cornwall has an abundance of accommodation, ranging from its only five-star hotel (in Newquay) through lower rated hotels, guest houses, bed-and-breakfast at private houses and farms, self-catering houses, cottages, flats, caravans and camp sites. There should be no problem in finding somewhere suitable to stay in each of the areas described.

Booking accommodation in advance at peak holiday periods is strongly recommended. To arrive at peak periods without accommodation may well leave you sleeping in your car or paying more than you had intended.

The coast usually offers more expensive accommodation than somewhere a few miles inland and possibly off the beaten track. There are also many pubs and inns in Cornwall where you can enjoy a pint of beer, have a meal or book bed-and-breakfast. The following guides are recommended:

The Complete Guide to Cornish Pubs, David Guthrie, Half Pint Press, Erith, ISBN 0 9514450 0 6.

Cornwall (Golden Hart Guides), David Franklin and Paul Watkins, Sigwick and Jackson, London, 1983, ISBN 0 283 98912 2.

Where to Go – What to Do, Town and Country Books, Newton Abbot, ISBN 0 9511165 0 9.

The Shipwreck and Heritage Centre at Charlestown.

The slipway at Marazion, with St Michael's Mount in the background.

The Three Tuns pub at St Keverne.

The Cornwall Tourist Board, which has its main office in Truro, will send a free accommodation guide and other tourist information:
   General enquiries (tel. 01872 74057)
   Accommodation (tel. 01872 863946)

Details of accommodation for any particular area can be obtained from the appropriate local Tourist Information Centre:
   Falmouth and Kerrier (tel. 01209 713352 [24 hours], 713360 or 718324)
   Looe (tel. 01503 262071, mornings only)
   Penzance (tel. 01736 62207)
   Plymouth (tel. 01752 264849)
   Restormel (tel. 01637 871345)

The following numbers are also useful sources for accommodation:
   Carrick Amenities and Information Service (tel. 01872 312300)
   Falmouth Amenities and Information Service (tel. 01872 312300)
   Falmouth Holiday Guide Bureau (tel. 01326 318618)
   Lizard Peninsula Tourist Association (tel. 01326 290799)
   Penwith District Council, Resorts Section (tel. 01736 62207)
   Truro Information Office (tel. 01872 74555)

The following places to stay are convenient for diving holidays:

Area 5

Sea Acres Holiday Park, Kennack Sands (tel. 01326 290064) – they re-charge air cylinders, have a selection of diving equipment and spares for sale, and offer a very efficient drying room facility
Chycarne Chalet Park, Kuggar (tel. 01326 290541).
Kennack Sands Caravan Park (tel. 01326 290533).
Kennack Sands Inn and Hotel (tel. 01326 290547).
Brooksea Holiday Park (tel. 01326 290512).
Pinetrees, Goonhilly Downs (tel. 01326 22310).
Gwendreath Farm Park (tel. 01326 29066).

Area 6

Lizard Holiday Village, Mullion (tel. 01326 241111).
Polpeor Holiday Flats (tel. 01326 240315).
Criggan Mill Holiday Caravan and Camp Site (tel. 01326 240496).
Glenhaven Caravan Park (tel. 01326 52734).
Pengersick Caravan Park (tel. 01736 762201).
Praa Sands Caravan Park (tel. 01726 3215).

Areas 7 and 8

Kenneggy Cove Holiday Park, Rosudgeon (tel. 01736 763453).
Penderleath Camping Park, St Ives (tel. 01736 798403).
Wayfarers Camping Site, St Hilary (tel. 01736 763326).
Cheriton House Holiday Flats, Market Place, Penzance (tel. 01736 795083).
Chycarne Farm Cottages, Ashton (tel. 01736 762473).
Tregeseal Holiday Cottages, Mousehole (tel. 01736 731398).

Looking out to sea towards the Manacles reef,
off the Lizard peninsula.

Dive Planning

Cornwall offers possibly the best diving in Great Britain. It has coasts facing in three directions, so unless there is a severe gale from the south-west lasting several days, it is always possible to find a lee shore somewhere. An east wind leaves the north coast unaffected, northerly winds have the same effect on the south coast, while westerlies leave the lee of the Lizard, Manacles Reef and the Falmouth area sheltered. More precise details have been included in the information for individual areas.

Weather

The prevailing wind is from the south-west, which between late October and March will bring heavy rain and strong winds. Severe gales are mostly experienced between January and March but, with what appears to be a shift in weather patterns, strong winds of up to storm force – even hurricanes – can occur from October to March. During the summer months strong winds are infrequent, particularly from north-west to north-east. If the wind settles in the east it will generally last some time, even two or three weeks, bringing dry, cold conditions.

A southerly wind of Force 3 or stronger will generally prohibit diving on the entire south coast, except in small sheltered coves. An east or south-east wind will prohibit diving from Rame Head right through to the Lizard, and from Cudden Point to Land's End, but the eastern part of Mount's Bay, centred on Mullion and Looe Bar will be calm, as will Whitesand Bay and Sennen Cove near Land's End.

Overcrowding and restricted areas

As with Devon, "diver saturation" is no idle expression at some of the more popular dive sites. Porthoustock, Kennack Sands and Mullion are all areas that

WEATHER INFORMATION

Weather forecasts for Cornwall are available as follows:

Radio

BBC Radio 4 – shipping forecast daily at 0033, 0555, 1355 and 1750.

BBC Radio Cornwall – general weather forecast at 0745 and 0845, then after each news bulletin on the hour. Inshore waters coastal conditions at 0715 and 0815. Shipping and tides at 0745 and 0845.

Fax

General 24-hour shipping forecast: 0336 400441 (updated at 0030, 0600, 1400 and 1800 daily).

Two-day South-West region coastal forecast: 0336 400458 (updated at 0700, 1300 and 1900 daily).

Three- to five-day national inshore waters forecast: tel. 0336 400450 (updated at 0500 daily).

Two- to five-day Channel waters forecast: 0336 400471 (updated at 0500 daily).

Telephone

Weather Marine Call (South-West Channel area) 0891 505358.

Five-day forecasts (South-West Channel area) 0891 505358.

The South-West Channel area (No. 458) covers Lyme Regis to Hartland Point.

Marine weather forecast: 0898 500458.

Local weather forecast: 0898 500404.

Three- to five-day national forecast: 0898 500450.

frequently suffer from overcrowding by divers. This has regrettably led to restrictions, but fortunately not to the complete closure of any area except Porthallow (*see* page 102).

The full potential of diving in Cornwall is only to be found using a boat, since few of the interesting sites are accessible directly from the shore. With long stretches of isolated cliffs between launch sites, a passage of several miles may be necessary with no refuge or help available should you break down. Therefore a box of spares, reserve fuel and a second engine are essential additions to the usual boat equipment.

Many of the offshore wreck sites mentioned in this guide will place a diving boat in a shipping channel or a main tidal stream, so you must carry the appropriate equipment to ensure you can be seen by others and can signal distress. If you are moored in a shipping channel, don't imagine for one moment that your A-flag will influence the passage of a 500-ton coaster, or a 100,000-ton container ship. You would probably be too small to show on their radar screens, and they wouldn't see your flag until they were almost on top of you, when it would be too late to take avoiding action. If you feel threatened by a large vessel, then get out of its way as quickly as possible, and worry about recriminations once you are safe.

Summer fog is another frequent hazard of this coast. It can envelop a boat in minutes, so always carry a compass.

From the foregoing it will be evident that this part of the Cornish coast should not be taken lightly, since it is extremely isolated, people on the high cliffs are unable to see what is going on in the shallows directly beneath them, generally the Coastguard lookouts are no longer manned, and it is swept with fierce tides. You can be out there all day sometimes, and hardly see another boat. It is therefore of paramount importance that your dive boat is in good order, with a spare engine, spare fuel, anchors, warps, a VHF radio and distress pyrotechnics. A second engine could well be the best investment you ever made.

There are only two restricted areas of open water along the south coast of Cornwall. These are the Navy degaussing range off Penlee Point near Plymouth, and the gunnery firing range at Tregantle Fort in Whitsand Bay, which may cease to be used in the near future. A new firing range is being established off Dodman Point, but patrol craft and helicopters will warn you if you are in the firing zone.

Readymoney Cove is good for snorkellers and families.

The majority of ports and harbours have local by-laws prohibiting diving in certain areas without permission, particularly Plymouth and Falmouth. At most slipway launch sites there will be a charge, but at Mullion in particular the number of boats and the number of divers in boats is restricted as well.

Finally, the relationship between divers and shell fishermen is fragile, so you are advised not to moor to pot markers or keep-pot buoys, never to dive deliberately on pots, and to keep well away from the keep-pots often found close inshore to a creek or cove, in which the fishermen keep their shellfish alive. The sea is such a large expanse that there is no justification for violating local fishermen's territory. Remember: today's minor incident can become tomorrow's major restriction.

Fishing regulations

Cornwall's fishing regulations are similar to those for other parts of the country, with the exception of the minimum sizes for crabs and lobsters. There are also minimum sizes specified for crayfish. The details are shown in the tables below. The Cornwall Sea Fisheries Officer can be contacted by telephone on 01736 69817.

Shipwrecks

Cornwall was often the seafarer's last sighting of England on departure, and his first on return. Off Land's End is where the shipping routes divide: vessels bound for Glasgow, Liverpool, Ireland, Wales and Bristol all turn north or pass along the north coast of Cornwall whereas those bound for Falmouth, Plymouth, Portsmouth, London, the North Sea ports or Northern Europe take the southern route.

The passage of ships back and forth along these time-honoured routes spans more than a thousand years, and it will come as no surprise that Cornwall, including the Isles of Scilly, has witnessed more than 3600 shipwrecks. Of these, the south coast holds some 1600, which suggests something like 13 wrecks per

Crabs (across broadest part of back)	
Males	16cm
Females (berried females should not be taken)	14cm
Spider crabs (across broadest part of back)	12cm
Lobsters (rear of eye socket to rear end of body shell)	19cm
Velvet crabs	6.5cm
Crayfish (across carapace)	11cm
Scallops (maximum width of shell)	10cm

Minimum sizes for shellfish.

Bass	37.5cm
Black bream	23cm
Blue ling	70cm
Brill	30cm
Cod	35cm
Conger eel	58cm
Dab	15cm
Flounder	25cm
Haddock	30cm
Hake	30cm
Herring	20cm
Lemon sole	25cm
Mackerel	20cm
Megrim	25cm
Mullet, grey	30cm
Mullet, red	15cm
Plaice	25cm
Pollack	30cm
Saithe	35cm
Sea bream, red	25cm
Shad	30cm
Skates and rays	
(from wing tip to wing tip)	35cm
Sole	24cm
Turbot	30cm
Whiting	27cm
Witch	28cm

Minimum sizes for fish.

mile of coastline. Of course, a great many of these were deep water founderings, some distance offshore.

Only the Goodwin Sands, the Thames Estuary and the east coast – the latter with its once vast trade in coal ships between Sunderland, London, and the Naval dockyards – can claim a greater number of shipping losses. Cornwall can certainly claim more large wrecks than any county in the British Isles, since liners, tea clippers, East Indiamen and warships all sailed this coast, many remaining there for ever.

While many wreck sites have been found in these waters, there are hundreds yet to be discovered. New wrecks – perhaps a long forgotten steamship, a sailing vessel, or merely a cluster of iron cannon – are found by divers every year. The advent of the portable magnetometer and satellite (GPS) navigation systems in small boats has revolutionised wreck hunting, with great success.

Each area in this guide lists a number of known wreck sites you can find and visit easily, some shallow, some deep. There are many wrecks yet to be found,

Above: The liner Mosel (Site 124) on Bass Point in 1882.

Below: The wreck of the Cromdale (Site 126) in 1913.

and it is reasonably certain that an organised search of any isolated headland or stretch of coast will reveal something new.

Protected wrecks The south coast of Cornwall has several historic protected wrecks. Others come under the Military Remains Act, and many others have known owners. Buying a wreck is not cheap, and anyone who has bought one will not be very pleased if your club comes along without permission, armed to the teeth with crowbars and explosives, intent on removing what you can. So be warned: there have been many successful prosecutions of divers who have taken items from wrecks. All finds should be declared to HM Receiver of Wreck using Form TCA/ROW 1. Completed forms should be posted to the Receiver of Wreck at The Coastguard Agency, Spring Place, 105 Commercial Road, Southampton SO15 1EG. Blank forms may be obtained from the same address, from Customs houses or Coastguard stations.

If you want advice as to who owns what, have an artefact you want identified, are looking for a temporary or permanent home for a particular piece from a wreck (with suitable public acknowledgement of the group or individual), are looking for advice on treatment or conservation, or just want general guidance, contact the Shipwreck and Heritage Centre, at Charlestown, near St Austell (tel. 01726 69897 daytime or 01726 73104 evenings and out of season) or the Royal Institution of Cornwall Museum, Truro (tel. 01872 72205 – Mr R. Penhallurick, Curator).

Decompression accidents

The procedure to be followed if these occur is laid down in the booklet *Safe Diving Practices* compiled by the National Diving Committee of the BSAC:

Decompression sickness symptoms vary between those so sudden that immediate air evacuation to a chamber is vital, to those which may not become apparent for some hours. Some of these less dramatic symptoms, which may well be delayed, can be more serious and produce greater disability than the excruciating pain associated with a joint bend. Tingling and numbness are included in this category.

At sea Air embolism or severe Decompression Sickness symptoms, occurring at sea, require rapid transfer of the subject to a compression chamber, laid flat on their back and, if possible, the administration of 100 per cent oxygen. Being bounced, rapidly, in a small boat is almost certainly going to worsen the symptoms rather than help the situation. RAF or RN Search and Rescue helicopters will almost certainly be involved and the use of VHF radio is essential.

HM Coastguard, although co-ordinating all rescues at sea, are not medically qualified to diagnose diving-related medical disorders and have to seek advice before activating a "Medivac" air evacuation. The Department of Transport and British Telecom International operate a Radio Medical Advisory Service through the BTI Coast Radio Stations.

If your radio has a "Duplex" operating system, with Coast Radio Station working frequencies, it is advisable to contact the nearest Coast Radio Station where you will be put in direct contact with a doctor, via a telephone link. There is no charge for this service. Once the doctor has given his advice, the Coastguard is in a position to follow up without delay.

If your radio does not have Coast Radio Station frequencies, or has a "Simplex" operating system, it is advisable to contact the Coastguard on Channel 16.

This may take more time, as the Coastguard will have to contact the doctor on your behalf. If the situation is serious enough a "Pan-Pan" call would be necessary.

On land If decompression sickness symptoms arise on land and they are serious, you are advised to dial 999 and ask for an ambulance, explaining the symptoms on the phone. If a helicopter is needed, the doctor will contact the Coastguard (if you are on the coast) who will co-ordinate the rescue. Inland, rapid transport with police escort, can be arranged by the medical emergency services.

With less dramatic symptoms, contact with a GP or hospital casualty department is advisable. Ensure you carry the HMS Vernon phone number – 01705 818888 and ask for the Duty Diving Medical Specialist or Duty Lieutenant Commander – to enable the doctor concerned to get specialist medical advice. Transfer to the nearest available recompression chamber, where necessary, will be arranged.

The following information will be of assistance if you have to deal with any type of diving emergency in Cornwall, if you wish to advise the authorities of your activity or boat movements, or merely want a weather forecast.

HM Coastguard Falmouth Marine Rescue Co-ordination Centre (tel. 01326 317575) is located at Pendennis Point, Falmouth, and is manned 24 hours. It broadcasts weather forecasts on VHF Channel 67 at four-hourly intervals, after an initial announcement on VHF Channel 16 and at two-hourly intervals if wind speeds are likely to reach Force 6 or above. A local weather forecast can be obtained by telephoning the Marine Rescue Co-ordination Centre before going to sea.

Brixham Marine Rescue Services Centre (tel. 01803 882704) carries out the same functions as the Falmouth Marine Rescue Co-ordination Centre, and will respond to radio distress calls from Dodman Point to the east.

Note that very few Coastguard lookouts around the coast are staffed, other than perhaps on a bad weather basis, so that no reliance should be placed on anyone maintaining a visual watch of a particular area or activity, and that attempts to make visual contact with a lookout station may be wasted time and effort.

The Coastguard advise that diving boats should contact them on Channel 16 on leaving the shore, with details of the size of the party, the type of craft and the area

---

EMERGENCY SERVICES

The Police, Fire Brigade, Ambulance Service and Coastguard (including lifeboats) can be contacted through any public or private telephone free of charge by dialling 999 or 112. You will be asked which service you require, and be put in direct contact with them.

The local marine rescue centres can be contacted on VHF Channel 16, or by telephone as follows:

Falmouth Marine Rescue Co-ordination Centre – tel. 01326 317575.

Brixham Marine Rescue Services Centre – tel. 01803 882704.

---

in which diving will take place. Indeed, they welcome such advance information, since in the event of an emergency, boats known to be in the area could be contacted and asked to assist. In the same way, diving boats that call the Coastguard on departure *must advise them on leaving the diving area or on return to shore*, otherwise they could be posted as overdue or missing.

It is also most important that an early radio call is made to the Coastguard Marine Rescue Co-ordination Centre if there is any concern for the safety of a divers who may not have surfaced within a reasonable time or may have gone missing on the surface. It takes time for the rescue services to be alerted and assemble, and the Coastguard would prefer to have rescue services on stand by and then call things off, rather than a last-minute call when a situation has deteriorated to the point of being serious. If a diver goes missing call the Coastguard immediately with the details – do not wait.

Radio information Coastguard Marine Rescue Co-ordination Centres maintain constant watch on VHF Channel 16, which is the distress, safety and calling channel. Always call for assistance on Channel 16. If it is a distress or urgency call, it will have absolute priority. If in a distress situation, when life is in grave or imminent danger, use the distress call MAYDAY MAYDAY MAYDAY followed by your name and/or the call sign of your craft, your present position and the nature of the problem with the craft or divers.

If the situation is urgent, but no imminent danger to life exists – for example you may have broken down, are drifting or have run out of fuel – use the following urgency call PANPAN PANPAN PANPAN followed by your name and/or the call sign of your craft, your present position and intention, and the nature of the urgent problem. Continue to broadcast the message until an answer is received.

Emergency medical advice and assistance Coastguard rescue centres hold details of the emergency hyperbaric (compression) chambers in the area, and have access to 24-hour emergency transport and specialist emergency diving medical advice. If at sea contact the Marine Rescue Co-ordination Centre on VHF Channel 16; if on shore use the same procedure, or telephone 999 or 112 for the emergency services and ask for the Coastguard.

Do not yourself attempt to organise the admission of a diver thought to be suffering from a bend or other compression problems to a compression chamber. The chamber may not be able to accept the patient, the necessary medical backup team may not be available, or an alternative chamber may be nearer, in which case valuable time could be saved. In the South West generally, all compression treatment will normally take place at the Diving Diseases Research Unit (tel. 01752 209999), which moved to Derriford Hospital, Plymouth in June1996.

Cornwall has its own air ambulance service, and the county is well served by the search-and-rescue helicopter service based at RNAS Culdrose, on the Lizard peninsula. The Coastguard Maritime Rescue Centre is in direct contact with all emergency services.

The Military Remains Act

The Military Remains Act 1986 may in the future affect the wreck diver much more than it does at present. Its main drive is to preserve the sanctity of "war graves" – the wreckage of military ships and aircraft known to contain remains of service personnel.

The wreckage of all military aircraft of any nation is automatically protected, but ships will have to be designated by the Secretary of State and will need a statutory instrument to do so. This means that ships to be named as "war graves" will have to be named and approved by Parliament in the same way that ships to be protected as historic wrecks need a statutory instrument passed through Parliament.

There seems no doubt that those who passed the Act had little idea of the number of ships that could fall under its terms, such as a merchant ship with a Navy gunner aboard – was he among the survivors? – and as a result no ships have yet been named under the Act. This does not mean that ships are not covered by the general thrust of the Act and divers should therefore treat all possible "war graves" with total respect.

However, once these ships have been named, the diver commits an offence only by tampering with, damaging, moving, removing or unearthing remains, or by

---

INSTRUCTORS WILLING TO ASSIST

If your club or group wants advice about a particular site, the following instructors are willing to assist:

Kevin Sessions (BSAC South West Area Coach), 16 Croft Road, East Ogwell, Newton Abbot, Devon TQ12 6BD (tel. 01626 56740).

David Crockford (former BSAC South West Area Coach), 8 Munro Avenue, Collaton Park, Yealmpton, Devon PL8 2NQ (tel. 01752 872198).

Fort Bovisand Underwater Centre, Plymouth (tel. 01752 408021).

entering an enclosed interior space in the wreckage. The punishment on conviction of an offence is a fine. Nothing in the Act prevents the wreck diver from visiting the site, examining the exterior or even settling on the wreckage. An offence is only committed if the diver disturbs remains or enters a proper compartment of the wreck. The punishment on conviction is a fine.

This is of course only a brief description, and serious wreck divers should study the Act itself. Your library or H.M. Stationery Office should be able to supply a copy.

The Merchant Shipping Acts

The Receiver of Wreck is responsible for the administration of the Merchant Shipping Act 1894 and the Merchant Shipping Act 1906, which deal with wreck and salvage. It is a legal requirement that all recovered wreck (flotsam, jetsam, derelict or lagan – whether recovered within or outside United Kingdom territorial waters) is reported to the Receiver of Wreck.

Finders who conceal items are liable to prosecution, so any object – even if it appears to have no monetary value – should be declared as soon as possible. The Receiver of Wreck can then make a decision as to the future ownership of the property.

Wreck recovered from within United Kingdom territorial waters that remains unclaimed at the end of a statutory one-year period becomes the property of the Crown, and the Receiver of Wreck is required to dispose of it. This may be through sale at auction, although in many instances the finder will be allowed to keep unclaimed items of wreck in lieu of a salvage award. This, however, is at the discretion of the Receiver of Wreck, and each case is judged on its merits.

For further information contact: The Receiver of Wreck, The Coastguard Agency, Spring Place, 105 Commercial Road, Southampton SO15 1EG (tel. 01703 329474; fax 01703 329477).

The Protection of Wrecks Act

Divers who find a site that might be of historical, archaeological or artistic importance should leave everything as it is and report their findings, in confidence and as soon as possible, to the Department of National Heritage (or its equivalent in Northern Ireland, Scotland or Wales). If appropriate, the wreck can then be designated under the Protection of Wrecks Act 1973, in order to control activities on the site.

Designated sites may only be dived or items recovered if a licence for that purpose has been granted; failure to comply with this is an offence and can result in a fine. All recoveries from designated sites must be reported to the Receiver of Wreck. For further information contact: The Secretariat of the Advisory Committee on Historic Wreck Sites, 3rd Floor, Department of National Heritage, 2/4 Cockspur Street, London SW1Y 5DH (tel. 0171 211 6367/8).

East Looe, with the slipway and lifeboat station in the foreground.

AREA 1:

Whitsand Bay

Whitsand Bay (not to be confused with Whitesand Bay near Land's End) is at the centre of this area, which starts at CREMYLL, inside Plymouth Sound at the entrance to Devonport, and continues for 23 miles round the eastern side of the Sound, taking in Rame Head, Looe and Polperro, to PENCARROW HEAD, just short of the entrance to Fowey harbour.

Most of this area is steep cliff with infrequent access to the foreshore, but there are three sites on the western side of Plymouth Sound that offer boat launching facilities. Within Whitsand Bay there are three more, then Looe and Talland, after which there is nothing for about seven miles until you reach Fowey.

Within the Sound itself, only south or south-easterly winds of Force 4 and above will prohibit diving, since the massive breakwater across the entrance offers considerable shelter. The remainder of this area is affected by any winds from south-west round to south-east. Shallow generally, a depth of 30m can be found only half a mile due south of Rame Head, with that contour continuing west to Pencarrow Head, varying in distance offshore from 2½ miles in Whitsand Bay to half a mile at Fowey.

Rame Head and the Udder Rock off Polperro are subject to a fairly strong tide, as is Cremyll Passage. Otherwise the tide is generally weak. The many rivers and creeks that feed into Plymouth Sound reduce the underwater visibility to an average of 2 to 5m, and the heavy bottom silt is easily stirred up. However, visibility further out in the Sound can be excellent, and improves as you travel west.

Whitsand Bay itself is often ignored by divers as having no potential, but the list of ships that went ashore here in bad weather, having missed the entrance to Plymouth, is legion, and there are many shallow remains. Also, the marine life in the shallows of the Sound and Whitsand Bay is extensive, with a wide variety of flatfish on the sand, and, among the gullies and rock outcrops, many other species suitable for photography.

There are strict diving regulations for the part of the Sound close to Plymouth. Divers should note that Port of Plymouth Order No. 1975 states:

25

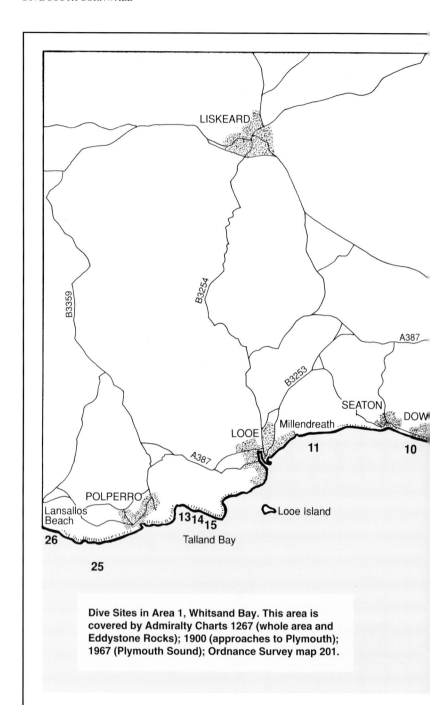

Dive Sites in Area 1, Whitsand Bay. This area is covered by Admiralty Charts 1267 (whole area and Eddystone Rocks); 1900 (approaches to Plymouth); 1967 (Plymouth Sound); Ordnance Survey map 201.

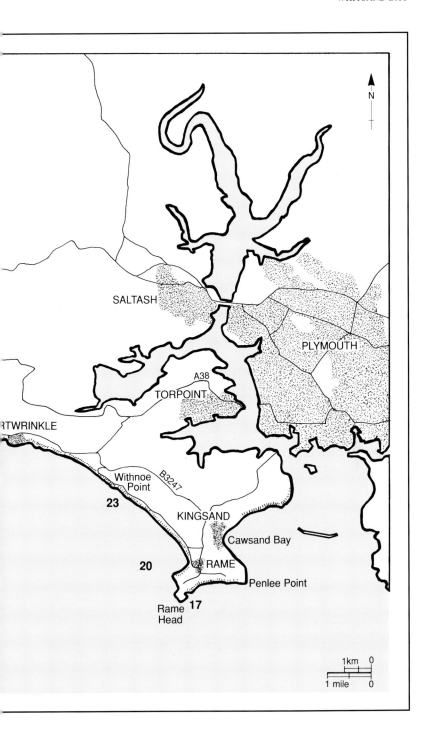

N

SALTASH

PLYMOUTH

A38

TORPOINT

RTWRINKLE

Withnoe
Point

B3247

23

KINGSAND

Cawsand Bay

20

RAME

Penlee Point

Rame **17**
Head

1km 0

1 mile 0

No diving shall take place within 100m of the walls, slipways or boundaries of Her Majesty's Dockyards, floating docks or other Crown Establishments, or within 150m of any of Her Majesty's vessels, or anywhere within the fairways of the Dockyard Port, save with the licence in writing of the Queen's Harbour Master.

While this may sound very formal and restrictive, permission to dive can usually be obtained by contacting the Harbour Master at the Longroom (the Harbour Control Office) – tel. 01752 663225 or call "Longroom" on VHF Channel 16. The Harbour Master will want to know the time you intend to dive and the exact location, the number of divers involved, anticipated duration of diving, and the name and type of surface craft involved. You must dive only in the area you have specified; you must have surface boat cover and use SMBs; ideally you should have a VHF radio on board in case it is necessary to contact you to advise of large vessel movements.

The authorities' jurisdiction covers the entire Sound and seaward to a line drawn from Penlee Point on the western side, to Wembury Point and HMS *Cambridge* to the east. This entire area is regularly patrolled by MOD police launches, and the Sound is monitored by closed-circuit TV cameras located on Drake's Island.

While usually carried out at sea, high-power sonar trials occasionally take place within the Sound itself, and the Harbour Master will normally transmit a warning by VHF radio. Should divers hear loud and possibly painful bursts of high pitched sound, they are advised to leave the water immediately and call the Longroom for information.

Coastal dive sites

Turn off the A38 at the Trerulefoot roundabout and follow the A374 to Antony. If you start from Plymouth, cross the Tamar via the passenger and vehicle chain ferry to Torpoint, take the A374 west to Antony.

At Antony, turn onto the B3247 for Millbrook and the Cremyll ferry terminal. Cremyll is the Cornish end of this small passenger ferry service, used by commuters to Plymouth and the many thousands of visitors to the picturesque Mount Edgcumbe Estate, owned by Lord Edgcumbe. Cremyll is also the southern part of the narrows where the Hamoaze leads into Plymouth Sound. It offer a shingle foreshore suitable for launching small trailed boats free of charge. Parking is available, and there is a café, inn, public telephone and toilets. Family facilities are excellent – there are picnic areas, superb walks along the cliffs overlooking the Sound, or the gardens of Mount Edgcumbe. The ferry trip to Plymouth takes only a matter of some 15 minutes, after which it is an easy and pleasant 1-mile walk to the city shopping centre.

Very strong currents sweep through the narrows here, up to 5 to 6 knots on the ebb, and there is a sharp drop-off into deep water and thick mud. It would be foolhardy to attempt a shore dive from here, and Cremyll is only suggested as a launch site for Barn Pool, Drake's Island, Redding Point or further into Plymouth Sound.

The narrows are the main shipping channel in and out of Devonport Dockyard, which runs north along the opposite shore. Diving anywhere in the fairway of the Naval port is expressly forbidden. However, the area offers interesting diving outside the channel buoys and along the foreshore.

As well as being the mooring site for a Fort Bovisand deep-diving training platform, Barn Pool was the site of the stranding of the 70-gun third rate man-of-war *Harwich*.

1 Harwich On 3 September, 1691, during the same gale that sank the larger second rate *Coronation* off Rame Head (Site **17**), the 993-ton *Harwich* ran aground at Barn Pool. She was so badly damaged that she was broken up for her timbers where she lay.

2 Steel pontoons The shallow rocky area linking Drake's Island with the mainland is known as The Bridge, and holds the remains of some World War Two steel pontoons and barrier material. It has a particularly steep northern face, dropping down almost sheer from 5 to 25m. At 30m, on the edge of yet another ledge, can be found a World War Two military barge.

3 Die Fraumetta Catharina von Flensburg It was along this face, under Raven's Cliffs, that divers of the Plymouth Sound BSAC found a bronze bell sticking up out of the mud at 30m in October 1973. On closer investigation, the partially intact wooden hull was discovered of what is now known to be the Danish brigantine *Die Fraumetta Catharina von Flensburg*. This ship arrived in the Sound on 10 December, 1786, seeking shelter from an increasing southerly gale, while on passage from St Petersburg to Genoa with a cargo of hemp and leather hides. That night, having parted from her anchors, the 53-ton ship drove over The Bridge, tore open her hull and foundered in the dark. Her captain Hans Jensen Twedt and his crew all managed to reach the shore safely.

Her cargo is quite remarkable, both for its nature and condition, since the reindeer hides, six to each roll, include the animals' legs, ears and tail, and often carry Russian markings. Preserved by the tanning they received with willow bark, and birch oil currying, followed by some 200 years buried in deep silt, the hides are generating funds for a continuing excavation programme by being made into bags, holdalls, wallets and belts by a leather worker near Truro.

Divers are requested not to interfere with the wreck, but should contact Ian Skelton at 1 Valley Road, Saltash if they wish to join the team working on the site with airlifts.

Once named St Nicholas Island, DRAKE'S ISLAND was a heavily fortified battery of cannon defending the entrance to the dockyard. Later, Lancaster muzzle-loading guns firing 68-pound shot were installed. The island is still derelict, but it has now been purchased for development, which could utilise the many buildings and storerooms cut into the rock. It will probably become an activity and heritage centre.

4 Conqueror Artefacts covering several centuries are to be found in the shallows, including lead shot and cannonballs from HM man-of-war *Conqueror*. This ship was stranded here on 26 October, 1760, and had to be dismantled.

The B3247, which leads to Cremyll, continues 1¼ miles from Millbrook, to a point directly opposite the western arm of Plymouth breakwater. The historic, picturesque village of KINGSAND has very narrow, winding streets, unsuitable for large vehicles or trailers with anything other than a small inflatable. A large, free car park is sited inland from the two small slipways, the foreshore being sand and shingle, and very popular among holidaymakers and children when the tide is out. The bay itself offers sheltered, safe conditions for beginners, with good visibility and plentiful flatfish.

A short distance south is CAWSAND, a fishing hamlet once renowned for its smuggling and later for its extensive fishing fleet. As with Kingsand, narrow, winding streets, steep in places, do not encourage towed boats. There is a slipway that can be reached through the village square, but congestion by small boat users has led to the requirement to book in advance with the Harbour Master if you wish to launch. There are good family facilities, with public toilets, shops, cafés and a large, free car park on the outskirts.

Offshore, the same conditions apply as for Kingsand. A 10-knot water speed limit is imposed on all craft in Cawsand Bay, and coxswains should keep a sharp lookout for surface swimmers and snorkellers. The maximum water depth out to the fairway buoys is 15 to 17m.

Divers from Plymouth Sound BSAC, who located the wreck of the Danish brigantine Die Fraumetta Catharina von Flensburg (Site 3). They are holding one of many thousands of animal hides carried in the ship, which are worked locally into bags, belts, coasters and other items to generate income to help finance the continuing survey. The project leader, Ian Skelton, is on the right wearing a T-shirt.

The slipway at Downderry.

Dominating the entrance to Plymouth Sound, PLYMOUTH BREAKWATER is a massive structure almost a mile long, with Breakwater Fort just north of its centre, detached so that it could not easily be stormed by troops. There is a safe passage with 7m of water between the fort and breakwater.

5 Self-propelled Hopper Barge No. 42 This 150-ton barge was returning from a dredging contract at La Coruña when she struck the breakwater and sank. Although re-floated and taken in tow, she then sank again in the main shipping channel (50 20 06N; 04 09 30W), where she broke in two. The part to the north-west consists of her boiler and firebox; that to the south-west is most of the rest, upside down, in 15m. Do not attempt to dive this barge without permission from the Longroom authority.

6 Lancaster bomber This World War Two bomber of the RAF's 49 Squadron was returning from a raid on the German U-boat pens at Lorient in a damaged condition on 14 February 1943 and was forced to ditch, striking the breakwater and killing all seven crew. Not much survives, but pieces may still be found at 50 19 58N; 04 09 10W among the boulders on the western seaward end of the structure in 15m. An intact engine and propeller remained until recent years, but are believed to have been salvaged by an aircraft recovery group.

7 Two motor fishing vessels The remains of what are thought to be two wooden motor fishing vessels, possibly Admiralty, stand 4m off the bottom in 15m at 50 19 42N; 04 10 14W. They are covered in fishing nets.

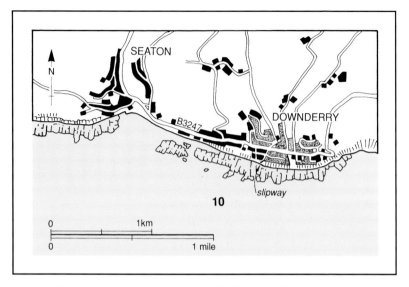

Seaton and Downderry, showing the location of the Gipsy (site 10).

8 MFV Encourage 50 19 25N; 04 09 57W. This wooden fishing vessel of 45 tons detonated a magnetic mine on 25 October, 1940, while leaving for her fishing grounds, and sank in 17m with the loss of all four crew.

9 Taxiarchos 50 19 30N; 04 13 30W. This 300-ton Greek brig was on passage from the Danube to Hull with a cargo of bones, when she ran aground on the south-west corner of Rame Head on 28 January, 1843. The pilot, who had been picked up at Falmouth, had ordered a course of SE when Rame appeared ahead, but due to a misunderstanding the helmsman steered NE instead, straight on to the rocks. The pilot and 14 crew all managed to scramble ashore, spending a wet and cheerless night in the old Rame Head chapel, high up on the headland, before local people took them in and gave them hot drinks and dry clothes.

The bell of the *Taxiarchos* was discovered in 1993 by Dave Peake, a veteran Plymouth diver, lying only a short distance from her two iron anchors, windlass and other wreckage, in some 12m depth.

From the B3247 turn off seaward in the village of Crafthole, following the signs for PORTWRINKLE, once a fishing village. There is a small sand and shingle beach with acres of flat rock exposed at low water, a large, free, sea front car park and the Whitsand Bay Hotel. There is also a small but steep slipway leading to a granite jetty, but the entrance is blocked by posts set in the ground, and it is impossible to launch an inflatable here.

There are public toilets, a telephone, a couple of shops and guest house accommodation. A sewer outfall runs out over the rocks on the eastern beach, and on both beaches public notices state that bathing is dangerous on the ebb of outgoing tides.

Another small village right on the edge of the sea, DOWNDERRY has an excellent concrete slipway suitable for launching large inflatables. Turn off the B3247 opposite the Methodist Church Hall, and down a narrow lane named Beach Hill, past the Wide Sea Nursing Home (tel. 01503 5736). There is car parking off the lane, and it may be possible to obtain permission from the nursing home to leave a trailer and vehicles there.

The foreshore is sand and shingle, with a lot of flat rock and gullies. Offshore, the reefs extend for almost a mile with a maximum depth of 14m, finally ending in the Knight Errant Patch, which is almost two miles off at the furthest point. The Sherberterry Rocks (possibly thus named in connection with the Danish East Indiaman *Wolf* lost just off East Looe beach, which was carrying sherbet, porcelain, indigo and dyewood) offer acres of rock formations with sand patches, and are full of marine life, including fish, lobsters and crabs. Many porcelain shards have been picked up on Looe beach, or uncovered offshore by divers, but the wreck site remains obscure (*see* Site **12**).

10 Gipsy Approximately 180m offshore and 90m west of the slipway in 8m depth can be found the remains of the steel 1447-ton full-rigged sailing ship *Gipsy* (formerly *Rodney*) of Nantes, built as the *Polymnia* of Hamburg, in 1874. On 7 December, 1901, while bound for Plymouth from Chile with a cargo of nitrate, she lost her bearings and was stranded on the rocks off Downderry, without loss of life. Her wreckage includes many recognisable features including wooden dead-eyes, and is strewn over a distance of some 100m. It can safely be reached as a shore dive.

At the western end of the village there is a large, free car park, the Sea View Inn, public toilets, telephone, shops, camping and caravan park, guest houses and other amenities. For an information brochure, contact Looe Town Council, the Guildhall, Fore Street, Looe (tel. 01503 262255), or the Information Bureau, (tel. 01503 262072, May to September).

Continue on the B3247 west along the coast road for Seaton and Looe.

This coastal village of SEATON is smaller than Downderry and three-quarters of a mile to the west. It has a popular, grey sand holiday beach set in a valley and is used by residents of the adjacent holiday village. There is ample car and trailer parking, two beach cafés, public toilets and a telephone, with easy launching for inflatables and other boats capable of being taken across a beach.

Offshore, the same conditions exist as for nearby Downderry, since Seaton is centred on the offshore Sherberterry Rocks. Beware of swimmers, water-skiers, surfers and other activities close inshore, particularly in the summer season. For information, contact Looe Town Council – details as for Downderry.

The B3247 follows the valley north out of Seaton, and joins the A387 at Hessenford. One mile west of this junction, fork left on to the B3253 at Widegates, and continue towards the coast, looking for the Millendreath Holiday village sign on the left hand side, two miles from the A387 turning. This will take you down a narrow, steep lane, an unclassified road with very few passing places and not suitable for large trailers. MILLENDREATH is a small sand and shingle beach, with a great many rocky outcrops and steep cliffs on both sides, and a concrete jetty ideal for loading and unloading boats enclosing a children's swimming area. Colmer Rocks, to the east of the cove, is an interesting reef to visit for marine life.

There is access through a hole in the sea wall to launch trailed boats, but the beach is soft. Millendreath Marine have a beach tractor – during the summer months they will launch and recover your boat on a trailer at any state of the tide, for a nominal charge.

Most of the valley behind the beach is occupied with a sprawling holiday complex and residential bungalows. This offers car parking, a beach café, surfboard hire and instruction, an inn, toilets and public telephone, but is very crowded in summer. One of the car park areas is the home of the Millendreath Marine Water Sports unit, which has a compressor and sells air and basic diving equipment. The complex is seasonal, open from April to October, and enquiries regarding air charging should be made via the Millendreath Holiday Village (tel. 01503 263281).

Looe, showing Looe Island and the location of the Flying Fortress bomber (Site 11).

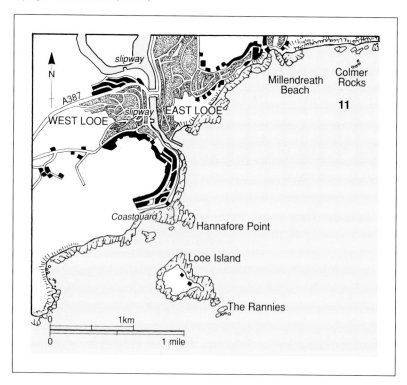

The holiday complex, beach and slipway at Millendreath.

11 Flying Fortress Half a mile offshore in 10m depth are the remains of a World War Two Flying Fortress bomber, believed to have been of the United States Air Force. It has been heavily salvaged. Ask at Millendreath Marine for the marks and current details.

Return to the B3253, then north to meet the A387 leading into Looe, or continue south on the B3253 and take the back road into the town. Either the B3253 or the A387 will bring you down into the Looe valley, and to the bridge that spans the river that runs through LOOE. There are three main car parking areas, two on the river bank in East Looe, and one across the bridge in West Looe, off the main A387 on the right hand side. Looe is a large, bustling town, with a harbour, busy fishing community and fish market, and is very popular with seasonal visitors.

Looe is also the home of the British Shark Fishing Club, but do not let that worry you – they only catch small blue sharks and the odd thresher shark many miles offshore! No diving is allowed in the harbour, nor within 1000ft of the harbour entrance, and there is a speed limit of 5 knots. Since the Harbour Master's office is on the edge of the river, it is a good idea to keep to the speed limit!

Two slipways offer boat launching facilities, one in West Looe, for which you are expected to pay the launching fee at the Harbour Office in advance, but this dries out at low water, as does all this end of the harbour. The other is in East Looe, leading off Church End Lane, next to the RNLI Inshore Rescue Boat house. It belongs to the sailing club, and always has water.

Looe makes an ideal base from which to explore the coastline to east and West, as well as Looe Island, an inhabited rocky island some half a mile offshore from Hannafore Point. Alternatively, provided you stay away from the mouth of the harbour, shore diving from Hannafore Point is popular, close to the Coastguard Station. While reasonably shallow, the abundance of rock provides numerous locations for shell fish and marine creatures to hide. The clear water makes it ideal for photography, with protection from all but south and south-westerly winds. You may even find some remains of the 240-ton iron schooner *Naird*, wrecked on Hannafore Point on 28 March 1931.

12 East Looe beach Similarly, shore diving from East Looe beach could be rewarding. When the *Wolf* was wrecked offshore in the shallows early in the 18th century, it is believed she deposited a large quantity of Chinese porcelain on the sea bed, many fragments of which can be found by beachcombing and diving.

For information contact the Looe Information Bureau (tel. 01503 262255), the Harbour Master (Mr E. Webb) and Water Safety Officer (tel. 01503 262839).

Continue along the A387 out of West Looe, up a steep hill, then either fork left on to an unclassified lane leading to the village of Portlooe, and then via Hendersick to Talland Bay, or follow the signs for Porthallow, which overlooks Talland Bay. (This village of Porthallow should not be confused with another place by the

The slipway at West Looe.

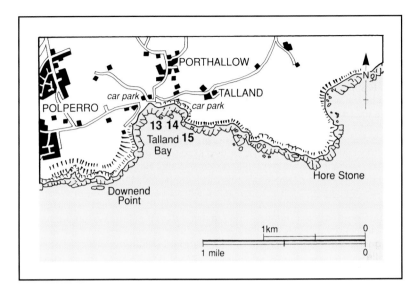

Talland Bay, showing the locations of the Marguerite (Site 13), Ester (Site 14) and Tregothick (Site 15).

same name that overlooks the Manacles Reef, near Falmouth.)

There is a very steep hill leading down to Talland Bay and, although the narrow, single track lane presents no difficulties other than during the busy summer months, it is suitable only for small towed trailers or boats. There is a large car park close to the shore as you turn right at the bottom of the hill, with additional field parking off a small lane to the left of the hill, opposite the telephone kiosk. There are two cafés and a set of public toilets.

At low water the foreshore is an extensive area of sand and pebbles, with Rotterdam Beach to the east (the name surely suggests a long forgotten Dutch wreck) and Downend Point and shoals to the west. Again, there is good snorkelling and swimming in this area, with clear sandy patches ideal for training down to 15m. At high water there is little or no beach remaining dry, and explorers should take care not to get cut off by the tide when clambering across the extensive rocks. The sweep of Talland Bay holds the remains of three known wrecks.

13 Marguerite The 220-ton Boulogne steam trawler *Marguerite* ran ashore here on 3 May, 1922, and her boiler still shows in the shallows.

14 Ester You have to search hard for remains of the Austrian brig *Ester*, lost during an easterly gale in March, 1885.

15 Tregothick The outward bound West Indiaman *Tregothick* of London was reported in *Lloyds List* to have "mistaken a point of land under Talland Manor for Rame Head, and on 10 January 1786 ran on shore, and was so completely dashed to pieces that a horse might have carried away the largest piece of the wreck; Captain Elder, his son and eleven seamen drowned."

Among the best known of the old Cornish fishing ports, POLPERRO has a long history of pilchard seining and smuggling. Fishing is still active from a fleet of small boats, but the entire village is now dominated by the holiday trade.

The main road to Polperro is the A387 from Looe. The unclassified back road that comes in from the east should be avoided, and will not accommodate any sort of trailed boat or craft. Polperro is a place for walking, and its narrow streets, impossibly sharp corners, small bridges and sheer mass of people in the summer strongly discount it as a launching or beach dive site. However, Polperro offers the only haven between Fowey and Looe, and when approached from the sea offers a secure, safe berth to have a break and make repairs or purchases. In winter, the harbour entrance is sealed off with timbers.

There are huge car parks on the outskirts as you approach, but no parking within the village and only one slipway, which is not recommended. There is a new Smuggling Museum, but there are no marine facilities relating to sub-aqua activities.

From Polperro west to Pencarrrow Head (and in fact as far as Fowey harbour) there is no access to the sea, the next six miles being steep cliffs or coastline, embracing Lantivet Bay and Lantic Bay. The next possible launch site is either Polruan or Bodinnick.

Polperro is one of the prettiest of the Cornish ports.
You can call in for supplies or to take on fuel.

Offshore dive sites and wrecks

The entire southward facing area, from Penlee Point in the east to Rame Head in the west, is generally described as The Rame, and consists of shallow, rocky cliffs at the Penlee end, and steep faces of over 45m in the immediate Rame Head area.

A boat ride of 3 miles from Fort Bovisand, or one mile from Cawsand Bay, will bring you to Penlee Point, the start of 2½ miles of rugged, rocky coastline round to Polhawn Cove. Here you will find good diving from 3 to 15m with a rock and boulder sea bed with sand patches, changing to broken shale and silt as you go deeper offshore. Care should be taken with tides off Rame Head, which can be quite strong and sweep close inshore along this face.

There are three good dive sites in the area. Halfway between Penlee Point and Rame Head is Lady Cove – in reality a mere cleft in the rocks. Here, an area of the sea bed covered by a radius of some 150m is protected by a Crown Commission lease of the sea bed, the lessee being Alan Bax of Fort Bovisand (tel. 01752 42570). This lease, taken out prior to the introduction of the Protection of Wrecks Act 1973, gives an alternative form of protection to:

16 Shallow water wreck site There are 54 iron cannon and three anchors at Lady Cove, almost certainly from the wreck of HM man-of-war *Coronation* (Site **17**). No diving or interference with this site should be conducted without the permission of the lessee.

17 The Coronation Centred on 50 18 57N; 04 11 98W. A second, deeper site is also protected, this time by the Secretary of State's Designation Order No. 2, 1978, which recognised the site as being of national importance. As with any designated site, it is an offence even to dive here, let alone carry out any salvage work, unless your name appears on the list of nominated people. This order protects a scattering of some 15 cannon, 3 anchors and other items.

The wreck of the *Coronation*, besides being historically important, ranks high in the league of Naval disasters of the period, since, of its 600 crew and two companies of Royal Marines, only about 22 men were saved. The accident, which happened on 3 September, 1691, was the worst shipping disaster within the Plymouth area.

Commanded by Captain Charles Skelton, this second rate 94-gun man-of-war was part of a fleet patrolling the English Channel under Admiral Russell, hoping to lure the French into battle after the humiliating defeat in June of the previous year off Beachy Head. Against Russell's advice, the Admiralty kept the fleet at sea for too long without repair, until on 3 September a south-east gale forced them back to Plymouth. Twenty warships recorded in their log books that they had seen the *Coronation* founder, the Albermarle's master writing "the Coronation came to an anchor to ye eastward of ye Ramehead about a mile and a half off ye shore; presently after they cutt her mast by ye board & immediately she sunk heeling much to port".

With no written account of what happened after the *Coronation* capsized, we can only presume that all the upper deck guns, anchors and fittings fell to the sea

*A diver measuring one of several iron anchors on the offshore
wreck site of HMS Coronation (Site 17).*

bed, including a magnificent 12-inch diameter silver platter bearing Captain
Skelton's family crest, after which the gale drove the upturned hulk ashore at
Lady Cove, where she slowly went to pieces.

The degaussing range, used by the Navy to remove residual magnetism from
the steel or fibreglass hulls of their ships, extends offshore from the Rame area
for about one mile, its limits clearly marked by permanent buoys. Warships and
other Navy vessels use the range at infrequent intervals, and small boats are
at risk if they remain within the area when it is in use. If a vessel leaves the
Sound and turns into the range area, it is you who are expected to keep clear, not
the other way round!

18 Dockyard Dumping Ground Seaward of the range depths increase rapidly
to 50m, the sea bed changing from rock and shale to a soft ooze or mud, with
shallow rocky outcrops seldom more than 3 to 4m high. An interesting aspect
of this area – which stretches right across to the Tinker Shoal in the east near the
Shagstone, and west into Whitsand Bay – is that it has historically been the
Admiralty Dockyard dumping ground for unwanted material. Commencing at
around a depth of 30m, inspection will reveal a large area of old cable, wire,
steel plate, brass shell cases, brass fittings, bottles and ceramics dumped by
generations of ships – the junkyard of the Royal Navy.

WARNING Extreme care should be exercised in bringing material to the surface, since live bombs, shells and other ordnance can be found here, and seemingly innocent shell heads and cartridge cases may contain explosive materials that become unstable if allowed to dry out in the sun. If in doubt, leave it alone, and certainly do not attempt to dismantle unfamiliar objects under water.

The offshore wrecks of the *Poulmic* (50 19 05N; 04 09 38W), HMS *Elk* (50 18 24N; 04 10 12W), HMS *Foyle* (50 16 42N; 04 10 48W) and the steamships *Claverley* (50 08 37N; 04 10 21W), *Brigitte* (50 08 11N; 04 09 11W) and *Lab* (50 07 39N; 04 10 09W) lie in Devon waters. Descriptions of these sites are included in the companion guide *Dive South Devon*.

Some ten miles off the coast lie the EDDYSTONE ROCKS and Hands Deep. The Eddystone is probably the best known lighthouse and reef in the South West, and certainly the most notorious. The first warning light was built here in 1698, two years after the brig *Constance* hit the rocks. The *Constance* was owned by a merchant named Winstanley, and the first he knew of the tragedy was when two of the survivors knocked on his door in London, in the middle of a party!

Built of stone and tarred timber, the light tower at first appeared well able to withstand storms and heavy seas, and as it had been built at Winstanley's personal expense, he was a frequent visitor. Unfortunately for him, bad weather saw him marooned in the tower on 27 November, 1703, and following a fearful gale that night the entire structure, its builder and keepers, were completely swept away.

For the next three years the reef remained unmarked. Then the Trinity Brethren appointed John Runyerd to design a new tower, and by 1709 a warning light again shone to mark the hazard. Just why he was chosen as the architect is uncertain, since by profession he was the proprietor of a London silk shop.

Nevertheless, Runyerd must have been competent since his lighthouse stood for 46 years, until it caught fire on 2 December, 1755. The flames were so fierce that they were seen in Plymouth, and it was a terrible ordeal for the keepers, one of whom died. He looked up from the rocks as the tower started to collapse, and a quantity of molten lead fell into his mouth, burning its way down to his stomach. The piece of lead, weighing 198 grams, is in a medical museum in London.

John Smeaton designed and built the next lighthouse, which was completed on 8 October, 1759. However, by 1870 it was found that the sea had undermined the structure by eroding the rock on which it stood, and in 1879 James Douglas started work on a new lighthouse on another rock, leaving the stump of the old one still in place. Smeaton's old tower was carefully dismantled, transported to Plymouth, and re-built on the Hoe. The current lighthouse – twice as tall as Smeaton's tower and four-and-a-half times larger in volume – has been in commission since May 1882, but no longer has keepers, since it is fully automatic, maintained by engineers who arrive by helicopter.

19 SS Hiogo Eddystone Reef. Located on the Sugar Loaf rock at the north-eastern edge of the reef, in 14m of water on a natural plateau. A screw steamship of 501 tons, the British-registered *Hiogo*, on passage from London to Falmouth and Japan, was on a course that put the Eddystone light dead ahead. Her second officer called the captain and requested a revised course, voicing his fears if they continued. For some reason the captain refused to make any alteration, even declining to go to the bridge to see the position for himself. Afraid to make a course change without permission, the second officer did absolutely nothing, but remained transfixed on the bridge as the Hiogo plunged on to the Eddystone reef at full speed.

All the crew and passengers were saved, as was the £20,000 cargo of coins she carried, but the sea soon tore the wreck to pieces. Two boilers and part of the engine room are the most prominent remains today, but a word of warning: the Eddystone is not an easy dive. In summer, the thick kelp makes it almost impossible to find the wreck, so it should be a winter or spring dive. It can only be dived at slack water, but even at the slack times given in the tide tables the tide may still be running at full flood over the actual site. Wait until the water is completely slack all round the reef, then dive.

The underwater scenery is fantastic, with huge shoals of pollack, bass and mackerel just hanging in the tide over the reef. If gannets are present, you may even see them under the water, plunging with folded wings to catch their prey. If you fancy searching for one of the many other wrecks on the reef, there were the *Winchelsea* in 1703, *Snowdrop* and *Constant* in 1696, *George Thomas* in 1869, *Paulus Heinkes* in 1880 and *Tellus* in 1887 – all wooden sailing vessels.

WARNING The Eddystone is some ten miles offshore, and no one will see you if you are diving there and get into difficulties.

Transit marks for the James Eagan Layne (Site 20).

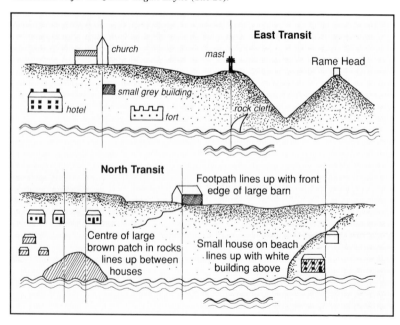

20 SS James Eagan Layne 50 19 32N; 04 04 42W. This 441ft American Liberty Ship of 7,176 tons gross, 10,414 tons dead weight, was one of two leading vessels in the two column convoy BTC-103. She was torpedoed by *U-1195* (Oberleutnant Cordes) between No. 4 hold and No. 5 hold on the starboard side on 21 March, 1945.

The attack took place some 12 miles off Plymouth, the *James Eagan Layne* being on passage from Barry to Ghent, carrying 4,500 tons of U.S. Army stores, plus a deck cargo of military motor boats and timber. With her steering gear out of action, shaft broken, the damaged holds and engine room flooded, her stern sank until awash, but she was taken in tow by HMS *Flaunt* and a minesweeper to Whitsand Bay, where she sank in the shallows.

Until the late 1970s the wreck was easy to find, since her No. 2 mast stuck up above the surface, but this eventually collapsed leaving only her wreck buoy to indicate the approximate area. The stern portion of the wreck lies a short distance to the south, separate from the main hull in 24m depth. The hull is covered in plumose anemones and makes an attractive and interesting dive. The site is exposed to any winds from East, through South to West, but sheltered from the northerly winds, and is about three quarters of a mile offshore.

Tranist marks for the *James Eagan Layne* are shown in the diagram opposite.

21 HM Submarine A-7 50 18 21N; 04 17 52W. This 180-ton Navy submarine, 99ft long with two bow torpedo tubes, disappeared on 16 January, 1914, while engaged in torpedo exercises in Whitsand Bay.

Built by Vickers in 1905, she put to sea under Lieutenant G.M. Welman from Devonport with five other submarines, HMS *Onyx* and HMS *Pigmy*, but failed to surface after making a dummy attack on the *Pigmy*. She was eventually found by Navy divers six days after she went down, her stern buried in deep mud and silt almost up to her forward hydroplanes. Attempts to salvage her continued for a month, but were then abandoned due to bad weather, there being no hope for the eight man crew. Since the *A-7* still holds the remains of her crew, she is listed under the Military Remains Act.

The wreck lies upright in 37m, with the hull buried up to her original waterline, but conning tower and periscope intact, generally in very good condition. [Decca position: SW chain, Red A.2.95; Green D.30.03; Purple B.62.63.]

22 SS Rosehill 50 19 40N; 04 18 25W. This British-owned armed merchant ship of 2,788 tons (formerly the *Minster*) was torpedoed by the German submarine *U-40* on 23 September, 1917, 5 miles south-west by south of Fowey. No lives were lost in the explosion that followed, and she steamed a distance of some 15 miles towards Plymouth before sinking with her cargo of coal in 26m.

For many years the *Rosehill* was thought to lie nearer to Gribbin Head, until John Shaw of Padstow, now the legal owner, positively identified the wreck from the maker's name and number on her emergency steering standard, taken off her poop. Her stern gun has been removed, but shells are still found around the stern. She sits upright on a sand and shale bottom and is still reasonably intact.

23 SS Chancellor A small Plymouth steam trawler of 168 tons, built of steel in 1901, which was wrecked at Withnoe Point in Whitsand Bay, less than half a mile east of Sharrow Point, on 17 January, 1934. Steel frames and a small boiler remain in the shallows. Her approximate position is 50 20N; 04 14W.

24 Looe Island One mile south of Hannafore Point, Looe Island is privately owned and permanently inhabited. It is surrounded by interesting reefs and gullies that harbour a wide variety of marine life in shallow water. Detached and to the south-east is a separate reef known as the Ranneys. Until recently, there were two or three iron cannon on the south-west side, and pewter and brass artefacts among the gullies – evidence of an early shipwreck – but the guns have since been raised. There is a strong tide over the reef and caution should be exercised. The maximum depth is 12 to 14m.

25 SS White Rose The Udder Rock, marked to seaward by a permanent light buoy, shows above the surface only half a metre on an exceptionally low tide, so is covered for most of the time. General water depth outside the reef is 25m, with a strong tide. The distance from Looe Harbour is about 5¹/₂ miles, and 2¹/₂ miles from Talland Bay and Fowey. There are prominent while painted markers on the cliff overlooking the site, and the Udder is in a direct line between the buoy and the marker. The *White Rose* was a small steamship of some 500 tons, carrying grain from La Pallice to the Mersey in December, 1911, part of a fleet of West Country ships known as the Bunch of Roses that went missing on passage. Her lifeboat was picked up in Plymouth Sound the following January, and it was months before her wreck was found on the Udder Rock. No traces of her captain or ten man crew were ever found. Steel from the wreck lies scattered on the seaward side.

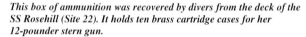

This box of ammunition was recovered by divers from the deck of the SS Rosehill (Site 22). It holds ten brass cartridge cases for her 12-pounder stern gun.

The SS White Rose (Site 25) struck the Udder Rock off Polperro on 5 February, 1901, while in ballast. None of her crew lost their lives.

26 SV Islander A cutter-rigged yacht of only 4 or 5 tons, wrecked in Lansallos Bay, in the centre of Lantivet Bay, halfway between the Udder Rock and Fowey harbour. Her remains are scattered in the shallows of a pebble and sand beach, and she acquired notoriety since a Naval Commodore, a Unionist MP for Paddington, three Naval Captains and a Commander all drowned when she stranded during a gale in August 1930, on the outside of Island Rock. Divers have reported a massive lead keel, weighing several tons, has been found on the site.

27 SS Orchis 50 16 41N; 04 34 26W. This small British coasting steamship of 483 tons, 191 tons net, built in 1917, had loaded 500 tons of china clay at Par and sailed for Dundee and Aberdeen. She sprang a leak off Gribbin Head less than two hours after leaving port, and foundered in a position given as 4 miles off Pencarrow Head, close to the Owen Rock.

Immediately after the crew took to their lifeboat she went down, the men being picked up by a Mevagissey fishing boat and landed at Fowey. The wreck lies at 060/240 degrees in 43m in two sections, upright on a sandy bottom, the highest point above sea bed being 6m. The wreck was positively identified when first located in 1987 by the builders' name plate.

28 SV Beatrice 50 17 42N; 04 20 24W. This 30ft wooden pleasure yacht sank following collision on 8 September, 1988, with the fishing vessel *Gratitude*, and lies in 44m.

WARNING The *Beatrice* lies in an area described on 1940 charts as spoil ground – it was used by the Admiralty for ammunition dumping until 1945 – so beware of what you may find around this wreck.

Portloe slipway, Veryan Bay.

AREA 2:

Gribbin Head

This area, comprising the coast from FOWEY to GULL ROCK, is centred on Gribbin Head. The striking red and white day mark on this headland can be seen from almost anywhere throughout the 23 miles of coastline described (except west of Dodman Point), and acts as a useful landmark.

The port of Fowey is at the eastern extremity of this area. Once spelt Foy – and pronounced that way to this day – it is a working but historic seaport, almost a centre for the china clay industry. Here there are excellent sheltered launching facilities for the diver, and it is recommended as a base from which sites as far away as Looe in the east and Gull Rock in the west can be easily reached.

West of Gribbin Head is St Austell Bay, which has five boat launching sites. These are all adequate, but require the crossing of public beaches or foreshores that can be heavily congested with sun seekers and small children in the holiday season. Generally speaking, an early start will avoid the worst of the problems associated with launching, and ensure a parking space as well.

Par and Charlestown are commercial ports, Mevagissey a centre for tourists and a fishing fleet only. The former both load coasters of up to 750 tons with china clay. There are a few inshore wreck sites off Fowey itself, the majority being offshore from the Dodman Point area: World War One and World War Two victims of torpedo attacks, most of which are deep water wrecks.

Tidal streams in this area are generally weak and predictable, except when off Dodman Point where the tide can reach 3 to 4 knots, and great caution should be exercised if diving more than a few hundred yards offshore. The entire area is open to south or south-easterly winds, but both St Austell Bay and Mevagissey Bay offer some shelter from the prevailing south-westerlies.

Visibility under water anywhere in the Fowey area is dictated by rainfall, since the River Fowey discharges into the sea here. Rain usually brings into spate the many streams that flow through the china clay producing areas.

The spoil tips that grace the skyline above St Austell – and incidentally make good landmarks when fixing the position of offshore wrecks – are known locally

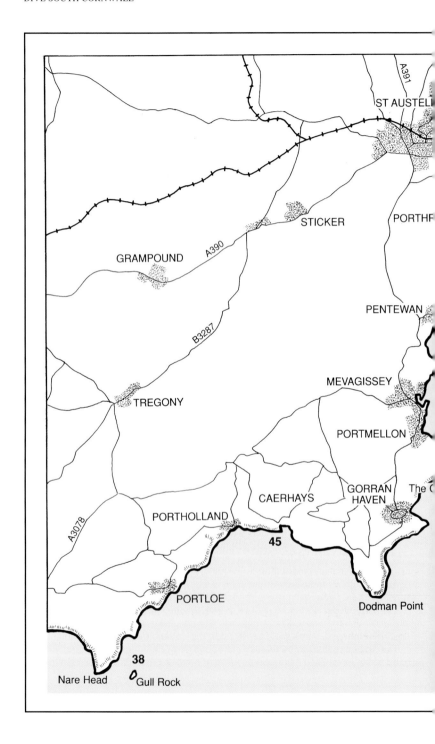

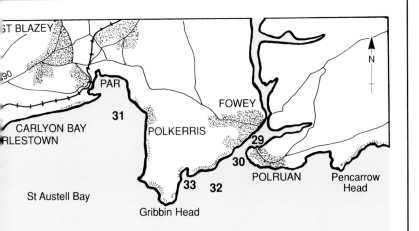

ST BLAZEY

90

PAR

31

CARLYON BAY
RLESTOWN

POLKERRIS

FOWEY

29

30

POLRUAN

Pencarrow
Head

St Austell Bay

33 32

Gribbin Head

evagissey Bay

N

36

Dive Sites in Area 2, Gribbin Head. This area
is covered by Admiralty Charts 1267
(Falmouth to Plymouth, with details of Fowey
Harbour and approaches); 31 (Par and
Charlestown); 147 (Mevagissey); 154 (includes
Gull Rock and Nare Head); Ordnance Survey
map 204.

1km   0

1 mile   0

as the "St Austell Alps". The effect under water of several hundred years of clay waste being discharged into the sea is described in some detail below.

Coastal dive sites

The previous area ended at Pencarrow Head, a short distance east of Fowey harbour entrance, and the last recommended dive site was at Talland Bay, which could be reached by turning south from the A387.

Return to the A387 at the village of Barcelona, which offers two routes west to Fowey: 8¹/₂ miles via the Bodinnick car ferry, or 20 miles via the town of Lostwithiel, taking the main A390 around the River Fowey. Both routes will take you on the B3359 north to the village of Lanreath, where you either turn off left on to an unclassified road for the ferry, or continue on the B3359 to its junction with the A390 at Middle Taphouse.

Of the two, the Bodinnick ferry route is the more scenic. On arrival at the eastern slipway you might have to wait 15 minutes or so for the ferry to unload its vehicles and foot passengers on the western bank and return. The view over the harbour – particularly from slightly higher up the hill – is fantastic. If the wait is longer due to congestion, then there is a very good inn a short way up the hill opposite the slipway. Another advantage of this route is that on disembarking at Fowey you arrive in Caffa Mill car and dinghy park, which has the best launching slipway in the port.

The alternative route involves a drive of some 35 minutes, through the town of Lostwithiel with its historic Restormel Castle, up the steep hill to the west of the town, and off left on to the B3269, signposted to Fowey.

At the mini-roundabout where the A3082 joins from the right, turn left (still the B3269) down a steep hill marked "to the Docks and Ferry". Although narrow and steep this road is suitable for trailers and large vehicles. You are strongly advised not to follow the A3082 into and through Fowey town itself – its streets, tight corners and sharp bends are among the narrowest in Cornwall, and there is very little parking available.

It has already been mentioned that FOWEY is a working seaport, with ships of up to 15,000 tons visiting regularly, which lie at moorings in the main stream awaiting berths, or alongside the loading jetties up-river from Caffa Mill. Diving anywhere within the area of the Harbour Commissioners' jurisdiction is prohibited, unless a request is made at the Harbour Master's Office on Albert Quay, giving the details of the intended diving, duration and location. A conditional permit may then be issued. This covers the entire harbour area, from a line joining St Catherine's Castle and Punch's Cross at the mouth, up the river as far as Lostwithiel.

It is unlikely that any visiting divers would want to seek such permission, other than to dive the wrecks of the *Helena Anna* (Site **29**) or *Mary* (Site **30**). There is constant boat traffic in the harbour, with pilot boats, tugs, two ferries, a lifeboat and

Opposite: The area around Fowey, showing where the Helena Anna (Site 29)
and Mary (Site 30) can be found.

deep sea shipping, and you must not obstruct the fairway, tie up to the big ship mooring buoys, or get in the way of the ferries.

When using the harbour to reach or return from the open sea, keep well to either the east or west bank, observe the 6-knot speed limit and keep a sharp lookout for small boat moorings and running lines. A permanent weather station is maintained with remote readout units of wind speed and direction outside the Harbour Master's Office on Albert Quay for the benefit of the public, and provided the tide is right it is a simple matter to call in there on your way to sea to check the likely conditions. The Harbour Master's Office maintains a listening watch on

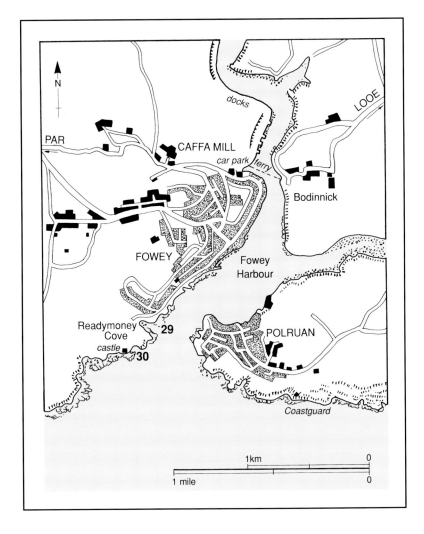

VHF Channels 16, 12, 11 and 9 during office hours only. Brixham Coastguard Marine Rescue Services Centre have recently installed a relay VHF radio aerial high up on the cliffs at Polruan, to assist radio communication with small craft.

Within the Caffa Mill car and dinghy park areas, you must keep to the sections for boats and vehicles, and remember that all the trailer slots will be allocated to local residents who pay for the privilege. Equipment strewn around is likely to get run over, so please be tidy. It is permissible to launch a trailed boat at Caffa Mill – having first bought your launching fee ticket from the machine – and then park your vehicle either here or in the overflow car park about 100 yards away from the town beyond the Customs House, which at the time of writing has been earmarked to be closed.

Compressed air and dive shop facilities are available at Caffa Mill. Toilets, a telephone, café and marine electronics are also available.

Fowey itself is of considerable antiquity, having been granted a charter in 1200, and has been providing ships and men for the Navy since 1226. The two ruined fortifications or blockhouses on opposite sides of the river near the entrance were built following a Spanish raid in 1380, and thereafter were joined by a huge chain, which when hauled taut was an effective boom across the harbour.

St Catherine's Castle, on the west bank of the entrance, was built between 1538 and 1542 and mounted six cannon. Bodinnick and Caffa Mill were both once shipyards, the latter having been a tidal inlet or creek, which was filled in and reclaimed only in recent years. The area on which the new Customs House stands was once a railway station and goods yard; the private heavy goods road and tunnel from here to Par docks follow the route of the old railway line.

On the opposite bank to Fowey, close to the harbour entrance, is the small town of POLRUAN, built up over the centuries on a steep hillside to the extent that it looks as if everything is about to slide into the harbour. It can be reached by road from Polperro (or from Fowey via the Bodinnick ferry) and has a small slipway and jetty, two pubs, cafés, a few shops and a chandler. It is not recommended as a boat launching site due to the narrow approaches, congestion and lack of parking.

Diesel fuel and petrol are available from pumps on the quay, and it is very convenient to go alongside to fill tanks or outboard cans. Ask at the shop.

Just south of Fowey is READYMONEY COVE, historically a place where smugglers came ashore with their goods and sold them on the beach for "ready money". Under the harbour regulations diving in the cove is prohibited without a permit, but snorkelling is allowed. Parking can be a problem, unless you leave your vehicle some distance away, up a side road. Boat traffic in and out of the cove is prevented by a floating boom in the holiday season.

Within the narrow confines of this attractive cove, which is overlooked by St Catherine's Castle, the sea bed is sand with small rocky outcrops. There is a reef to the north side and steep rocky cliffs on the south. The maximum depth is 4.5 to 6m and visibility is usually very good. It has a pleasant sandy beach, with toilets but no other facilities.

29 Helena Anna 50 19 42N; 04 38 33W. This wooden topsail schooner was towed into Readymoney Cove in 1940 and scuttled across the entrance as a

You can buy fuel at Polruan, but you cannot launch here.

block ship, to prevent possible German landings on the beach. Sections of her wooden hull remain buried in the sand, and after rough weather often show just beneath the surface.

30 Mary 50 19 38N; 04 38 34W. This wooden brigantine of Milford was on passage from Woolwich Arsenal to Swansea with a cargo of scrap iron, mostly 12- and 18-pounder cannon and muzzle loading 68-pounder Lancaster guns.

While attempting to enter Fowey harbour without a pilot during a gale, Captain George Jones allowed his vessel to drift to leeward, and she struck the rocks directly under St Catherine's Castle at 1.30pm, in one of the many gullies. The captain managed to jump ashore onto a rock ledge but two brothers, E. and J. Eynon, and the ship's boy, Orial, were all drowned.

Some of the guns were salvaged by the Fowey Tug Company, and the government sent a ship to pick them up and take them to Wales. In August 1967, divers found the ship's bell and recovered a George III cannon, and the author was later involved in the recovery of two other guns. Since then at least six more have been recovered, and there is probably little left except a great mass of concretion, with ship's fittings protruding.

A schoolboy, snorkelling in this area and along the cliffs under the castle in the late 1970s, found a solid silver cast eagle of considerable antiquity and value. Its origin or use remain unknown, and it is unlikely to have come from a shipwreck – it may have been lost over the castle walls at some time.

On the eastern side of the Fowey harbour entrance is a long shallow reef of rocks marked with a wooden cross, known as Punch's Cross. The reason and origin of this is unknown, but when it is washed away in a gale or falls down due to age, it is always replaced by an identical device, maintaining the tradition. There is a shallow sandy bay on the harbour side of the reef, well clear of boat traffic. This has been the site of a number of small wooden wrecks, which have left many interesting pottery shards, pulley blocks and other souvenirs to be found. This area may not be dived without a permit.

Leave Fowey on the B3269 to the mini-roundabout, then follow the A3082 and signposts for Par and St Austell.

Two miles from Caffa Mill on the A3082, where the road bears off right downhill, turn left on to an unclassified road marked to Polkerris and Menabilly/Gribbin. After about 100 yards turn right into a narrow downhill lane with steep sides, leading to POLKERRIS, a disused fishing port but popular cove, beach and village.

The top road, which continues for only one mile to a car park, leads to the manor of Menabilly, the private estate of the Rashleigh family, who own Polkerris village. A track leads to farms and eventually Gribbin Head, well worth the walk for the breathtaking views of the entire area from this elevated position. A public

Polkerris and Par Sands.

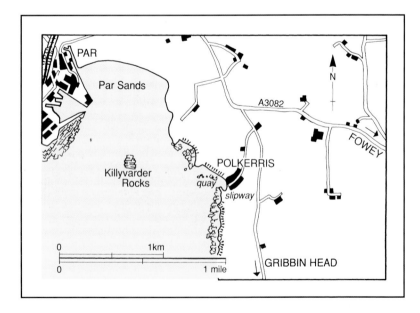

Above: Workmen on the capsized French schooner Capitaine Rémy (Site 31).
The wreck was broken up near Par, but large portions remain beneath the sand.

Below: The main pontoon of the Munton-registered Dutch dredger
Kantoeng (Site 32), which capsized off Fowey in 1937.

footpath on the eastern side of Gribbin Head leads to a small beach and cove known as Polridmouth. At low tide, large sections of shipwreck are still visible among the rocks, part of the *Romanie*, stranded in 1930 (Site **33**).

Although narrow and winding, the road down to Polkerris is suitable for a vehicle and trailer, being less than a quarter of a mile to the foreshore. There is a large public car park on the right, half way down the hill, to which you will have to return with your empty trailer after launching if you are unable to find a space in the pub car park or leave your trailer on the beach in the allocated area.

The road widens at the bottom, and a private slipway leads to the pleasant sandy beach between the Rashleigh Inn and the Old Lifeboat House, now a café and shop. You are advised to unhitch here, and run your boat down to the sea by hand, since vehicles are prohibited on the beach. The entire village, foreshore and quay are privately owned, and there is a small launching fee. Fees are normally collected on the foreshore by the beach warden, who leases the facilities (tel. 01726 815142).

If your group is considering using Polkerris for more than one day, weekly and fortnightly rates are available. These allow you to tie your craft up to the small stone quay overnight, which saves recovery and re-launching. On spring tides the quay dries right out. There are public toilets, a café, and an inn with an excellent restaurant overlooking the sea.

Polkerris is a pilchard fishing harbour dating back to the 16th century. There are a number of iron cannon set in the quay and foreshore, dated to the Tudor period, but there is no record of where they originated. Perhaps they came from a local 16th-century shipwreck – who knows!

Polkerris offers a sandy, safe and shallow foreshore facing due west, leading out into St Austell Bay or the reefs around Gribbin Head and the offshore Cannis reef. Maximum depths within the immediate bay are around 10 to 15m, and there is no significant tidal stream.

31 Capitaine Rémy At 50 20 10N; 04 41 10W this is the only known shipwreck site in the whole of St Austell Bay. This was a composite, five-masted, auxiliary engined schooner, wooden planked on iron frames. Bound from Barry to Nantes with 2,500 tons of coal, she was crippled by a Channel gale on 20 November, 1920.

Abandoned by her crew – who were safely rescued – the vessel capsized and drifted around the English Channel for two weeks, half submerged and a considerable navigation hazard. She was eventually located by the Royal Navy, and tugs took her in tow and got the wreck into the shallows less than a quarter of a mile from Polkerris quay, where she was stripped of her valuable non-ferrous fittings, and holes cut in her sides to give internal access. Iron frames and bits of the wreck lie buried in the sand in less than 6m offshore, and part of the ship's bottom is still used in Fowey as a half-tide grid.

Proceed back up the hill out of Polkerris, and turn left back on to the main A3082 for Par and St Austell.

Continue down a steep hill on the A3082 for half a mile, and turn left off the main road just before the road bridge, opposite the Ship Inn. This is a private road leading to the PAR SANDS. The caravan and beach park are administered by Restormel Borough Council. An entry fee is charged for vehicles and trailers.

Craft can then be taken across the flat sandy foreshore, and the extreme eastern or western ends of this half mile long beach are recommended.

The beach is entirely devoid of rock and so is popular with families in the summer. Outcrops of rock are encountered just offshore, the largest being Killyvarder Rock, near the entrance to Par harbour – the second largest of the Cornish china clay ports. At low tide the beach extends for several hundred yards; it is firm and flat and an excellent point from which to launch and explore St Austell Bay.

Extensive caravan hire and parking facilities, camping areas and every amenity can be found here, with public toilets, a laundrette, showers, shops, amusements, a telephone and pub. The site is seasonal and open for accommodation bookings only from Easter to the end of September, but can be used for launching boats at any time. For further details of accommodation contact the camp office (tel. 01726 812868) or Caravan Association secretary (tel. 01726 813218).

Return to the A3082 and turn left. Follow the signposts for St Austell, past Par docks, through the traffic lights and under the railway bridge. After a garden centre and the English China Clay laboratory, both on your left, turn off left onto an unclassified private road lined with cypress trees marked "to the beach" and "Carlyon Bay". At the first major junction, where you can see the sea on your left opposite a large sign advertising the Cornish Coliseum and Leisure World Centre, turn left down a steep hill. This will bring you down to a large car park at sea level, which serves CRINNIS BEACH, the largest of the Cornish entertainment beach areas, offering big group concerts and band shows, roller discos, skating, a swimming pool, cafés, restaurants and a beach more than a mile long.

The mica sand beach is soft and quite steep. Inflatable craft can be launched

The 340-ton steel schooner Romanie (Site 33) drove onto the rocks at Polridmouth in heavy weather on 16 January, 1930. Parts of the wreck uncover on the beach at low water.

You can launch a boat at Charlestown harbour.

easily down the recently laid stone ramp, but make sure there are sufficient hands for the recovery, which is the hard bit! The only rocks around are the large obvious outcrops, and there are steep cliffs off to the west, leading to Charlestown. Conditions are as for Polkerris and Par, except that the beach faces south. For details of entertainment and facilities, telephone 01726 814004 or 814261.

Return to the road junction by the Coliseum advertising hoarding, and continue straight ahead for CHARLESTOWN. This is well signposted, and there are a number of different routes by which this Georgian seaport and village can be reached. The main road to the harbour is the A3061, which leads off a large roundabout on the A390. The village offers a choice of two pebble and sand beaches (one either side of the harbour mouth), a telephone, village shop and post office, accommodation, toilets, three restaurants and two pubs.

There is also the internationally known Charlestown Shipwreck and Heritage Centre, which was established here in 1976. The Centre is prominently marked by the 37ft Oakley class RNLI lifeboat *Amelia*, which stands within the grounds, and has a Royal Navy diving observation chamber and a 1930s armoured deep-diving dress on display outside. Inside there is an audio-visual theatre offering a 14-minute show concerning the history of the village, followed by other local history displays.

The remainder of the Centre (which is open from early March to November) is devoted to the largest and most comprehensive display of shipwreck artefacts open to the public in the UK. Divided into bays, each has a particular theme such as World War Losses, West Country Shipwrecks, General Shipwrecks or East Indiamen. Many thousands of artefacts are on display, ranging in age from

200 BC to the present day, including the entire collection of recoveries from HM man-of-war *Ramillies*, guns, treasure, concretion, cargo items and the John Bevan collection of historic diving equipment. There is a gift shop offering souvenirs and shipwreck artefacts (tel. 01726 69897), and the Bosun's Diner on the first floor is a licensed restaurant open seven days a week (tel. 01726 67618).

Regrettably, the nearest sources of compressed air are at Fowey (Caffa Mill) and Pentewan. Launching at Charlestown is easy with sufficient hands, from the western beach or the half-tide slipway, which is very steep and unsafe for vehicles. There is a small hand-operated crane on the quay, and provided you have slings or strops, it is only a matter of seeing the Harbour Master for permission to launch by this means (for which a small fee is charged). At neap tides the harbour always has water, but on spring tides dries out completely, and you will be unable to re-enter until the tide turns. The Harbour Master can be contacted either at his office in the Round House on the end of the quay (tel. 01726 73021). Alternatively, telephone 01726 70241 for assistance.

Charlestown offers access to St Austell Bay generally, and the high cliffs east and west of the port. Offshore the sea bed is all sand with some reefs and patches of rough ground, maximum depth within the bay being 18m. The best diving areas are around Black Head, two miles south-west of Charlestown. Underwater visibility is generally good, other than near the strip of china clay slurry that has accumulated on the bottom out from Par harbour. Accommodation is available in the Pier House Hotel (tel. 01726 67955) or the T'Gallants Guest House (tel. 01726 70203).

Charlestown.

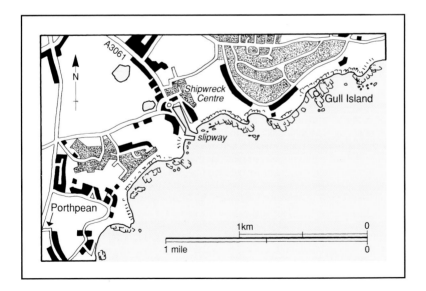

The slipway at Porthpean.

Return uphill out of Charlestown on the A3061 and join the A390 at the roundabout by turning left. After 200 yards turn off left onto the road to PORTHPEAN. Continue for about three-quarters of a mile, taking the third turning on the left, which leads to Porthpean beach. The last part of this road is narrow and single track, opening out into a flat area overlooking the sea, a car park and slipway.

There is a very popular sailing club (tel. 01726 66266) based at the head of the slipway, and vehicles are allowed to assist with launching and recovery. However, you are advised not to put any vehicle on the soft sand unless it has four-wheel drive. Numerous car owners have watched the evening tide lap over their door sills when they have become bogged down.

The beach is flat, with reefs at each end, and popular with families. The immediate offshore conditions are the same as for the other St Austell Bay launch sites, except that Porthpean faces due east, and is totally sheltered from even severe south-westerly winds. Floating lines and buoys segregate areas for use by water-ski boats and dinghy sailors, so make sure you launch and recover at the right place.

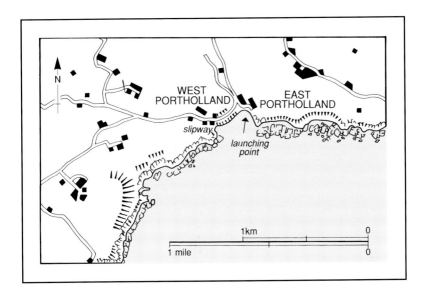

Portholland.

Porthpean is an old pilchard-fishing and smuggling village, with most of the houses clustered around the church at the top of the hill to the south. It has toilets, a shop and some private bed-and-breakfast accommodation.

On leaving the village, return the way you came in. There is an alternative route to the left, up a steep narrow hill, which is not recommended if you are towing a trailer.

On reaching the main Porthpean road again, turn left (south) and continue for 2¹/₂ miles along a steep sided, single-track lane with passing places; the last half mile is down an extremely steep hill. This will bring you into PENTEWAN, with its inn and shops, which was once a thriving china clay seaport, exporting to the world. Pentewan is like a miniature Charlestown, though the inner basin, where sailing ships once lay alongside and loaded clay, is now silted up and home only to a few ducks and swans. The original lock gates survive, as do some of the original capstans and chains, but the once deep entrance channel that gave access to 200-ton ships is almost obliterated by drifting sand.

Parking within the village is restricted, and any diving or beach launching should be carried out only from the adjacent beach caravan site. As you leave the village past the Ship Inn, you will find Oceansports on the right opposite a small car park. This dive and water sports outlet will recharge diving cylinders.

Continue to the main B3273, turn left and then left again into the Pentewan Sands Holiday Park caravan site – several acres of clean and tidy chalets and camping with amenities (tel. 01726 842896).

There are two launching sites here. One is off to the left, nearer Pentewan village, used by the Pentewan Sailing Club, the other (recommended) is straight down the track past the reception and restaurant area. There is a charge for these facilities, and you should call at reception to pay before proceeding to launch. There is a tractor or Land Rover to assist with launching and recovery if necessary. Both launch sites are down wooden ramps and over a popular soft sand beach to the sea, which at low water can be some distance away.

Continue south on the B3273 towards Mevagissey. The road climbs high above sea level and at the top of the hill, at a crossroads, there is the option of continuing on the B3273 into MEVAGISSEY, or turning right onto the road to Gorran and Gorran Haven.

If you are towing any sort of trailer or boat, do not attempt to enter Mevagissey, but take the Gorran road. The impossibly narrow streets, one-way traffic system, sharp corners and sheer congestion of people can only just accommodate cars, and then with frequent traffic jams. The launching of boats into the harbour here is prohibited and totally impractical, so there is no point in attempting to tow any sort of trailer through this way.

Mevagissey is probably the most popular of the old Cornish fishing villages, and its quaint harbour, waterfront, jetties and quays bring in hundreds of thousands of visitors each year. But it offers nothing for divers. No diving is allowed inside the outer or inner basins, there is a speed limit of 3 knots, and it is the somewhat uncommon practice for the local shell fishermen to store their live shellfish in keep-pots inside the harbour itself, instead of outside as is more usual.

Moorings for visiting boats on a short stay are available, or you can lay alongside the outer quay wall, subject to space being available. Permission to remain on the north wall must be obtained from the Harbour Master, whose office is on the quay (tel. 01726 843305, or 842496 after hours) where you can pay the necessary fee.

A number of the Falmouth based dive charter boats use Mevagissey regularly on a short stay basis. Facilities useful to visiting craft include fresh water, fuel, telephone, toilets, shops, cafés, restaurants and chandlers, as well as some engineering support and a boat builder. Care must be exercised on entering or leaving Mevagissey, due to the large number of fishing vessels using the port. There is a small but interesting local history and maritime museum on the quay.

About half a mile south, PORTMELLON is a seaside hamlet situated on the road out of Mevagissey. If you take the route through Mevagissey, you can reach Portmellon by following the one way system and leaving via a steep hill with a magnificent view out across St Austell Bay (as far as Rame Head in good weather). Alternatively, follow the road through to Gorran village but ignore the signs for Gorran Haven, and continue left to Portmellon.

Portmellon is a small cove facing east, with a few houses, the Rising Sun inn, car park, telephone, slipway and sandy beach. The main advantage of this site is that it is seldom used, and is close to the Gwinges (or Gwineas) rocks, an offshore reef with the wreck of the steamship *Ardangorm* (Site **40**), which is a little under two miles from this beach, out of sight round Chapel Point.

To the south there is almost a mile of rocky foreshore, which offers safe shallow exploration and is an underwater photographer's paradise with a wealth of fish, weed and other marine life. During the summer the shallow sandy areas abound in flatfish. The concrete slipway leads directly off the coast road, is public and free, and maintained in good repair.

Continue south out of Portmellon into Gorran village, then follow the signs for GORRAN HAVEN. The road will take you down a long gentle hill into the village, with a public pay car park on your left, to which you will have to return after launching on the beach. Gorran Haven is typical of the old Cornish fishing ports that survived totally on pilchards and agriculture. It has a massive granite breakwater and quay, which shelters fishing and pleasure craft and the original buildings in which the fish were processed, put into casks, pressed and exported to Spain and Italy. Another old building known as the Watch House overlooks the beach. It looks as if it was once a lifeboat house but no lifeboat was ever stationed here, the nearest having been Mevagissey.

The village's original name was Portheast or Porthjust, its inhabitants working closely with neighbouring Mevagissey. It is recorded that in 1740 they processed and exported 35 million pilchards from here. The wide sandy beach, enclosed by the jetty, makes it an ideal launching site in all but easterly winds. The main street runs directly into a gap between two buildings and straight onto the foreshore. There is a small stream running through the beach, cutting it in two, overlooked by a large flat concrete seating area ideal for families and to leave equipment.

The popularity of Gorran Haven beach with families and children has brought about a restriction regarding boat launching. Free access to the beach for launching and recovery and vehicles is permitted at any time except for the last two weeks of July, all of August, and the first week in September. During that period bollards are in place across the entrance to the foreshore between 10am and 5pm, preventing the passage of boats or vehicles. If you wish to use Gorran Haven in the peak months, you must launch early and recover late. Facilities at Gorran Haven include a car park, toilets, a public telephone, cafés, shops and an inn.

The western slipway at Portholland.

Return the way you came in, turn left at the top road junction, then left again shortly, after a bend, for Caerhays. On the road to Caerhays and just a little over three quarters of a mile from the Gorran Haven turning is the village of Boswinger, where you can turn left for HEMMICK BEACH. The large and impressive entrance to the Seaview International caravan and camp site is on the left.

Hemmick Beach cannot be recommended as a launch site, since it is at the bottom of a steep, narrow lane. With large wooden posts set in the ground between the five car parking places and beach, it is obvious that the National Trust, who own the area, do not encourage boats.

The beach is sandy, faces south-west and is overshadowed by the bulk of Dodman Point. Gull Rock can be seen from here, and the area is excellent shallow snorkelling or beach diving territory. It is not suitable for large groups or clubs.

A continuation of the same main road brings you first into view of the lovely Caerhays Castle, set back on your right, high above the surrounding countryside. Directly opposite the castle wall and one of its private entrances is a public car park. CAERHAYS has a large sandy beach, with high rocks and cliffs on each side, forming a cove that faces due south. Sand dunes act as a barrier between the car park area and the beach, but there is a cut through which a trailed boat could be towed and launched.

Even a moderate amount of south or south-west wind will cause a considerable swell, which can make launching or recovery difficult. This is a useful launch site from which to dive Gull Rock, the wreck of the *Hera* (Site **38**), the Middle and Outer Stones – which lie some six miles away – or the wreck of the *Allegrity* (Site **45**). This beach is very popular and care must be exercised in the shallows, which attract small children and swimmers. Facilities at Caerhays are basic but adequate: toilets and a small seasonal beach café.

Continue on the main road north-west out of Caerhays, up a steep hill, following the signs for PORTHOLLAND. The road continues generally in a northerly direction for 1³/₄ miles, where you turn left for East Portholland and continue down a narrow single track lane until you reach the village and waterfront. Ignore for the moment the turning off to the right near the foreshore marked West Portholland.

Portholland is another old fishing hamlet now fallen into disuse, with a dozen houses, a shop and public toilets only. The sea front and small field behind offer car parking for about thirty vehicles, with a shale and pebble beach and a choice of launching sites. One is directly over a concrete-faced ramp leading off the road, where plenty of muscle will be needed; the other through a less steep, stone-filled cut onto the foreshore. These launch sites are not easy but are manageable if there are a few strong individuals in the party. The surrounding steep cliffs make this a cove, with extensive rocks and reefs offshore, and wind and surf conditions are as for Caerhays beach.

Alternatively, drive 100 yards back the way you came, and turn sharp left on the coast road to West Portholland. This will bring you quickly to a second, smaller and less populated cove, with a number of disused fishing industry buildings and lime kilns. There is little parking other than at the roadside, but the cove does offer an excellent, free, concrete ramp from which to launch over a beach.

Dodman Point is clearly visible from here and either of the Portholland locations is ideal if you want to reach this almost undived area. There are no tidal problems in Veryan Bay inshore at this point, but great care should be taken at Dodman Point (see warning on page 47).

Take the road west out of Portholland, climbing steeply for half a mile, then fork left for PORTLOE, another village with a steep downhill approach and very limited parking. Access to the sea is gained by a sharp left hand turn as you reach the village centre. Portloe is the last boat access point into Veryan Bay, and the last in this area before reaching its boundary at Nare Head. This still active fishing village, tucked away and protected by sheer-sided cliffs, is perhaps the most attractive of all Cornish coves, and certainly appears in more calendars than any other! An influx of large numbers of divers or a whole club could well meet with some opposition, mainly due to the lack of space and facilities. However, small and local groups use it frequently.

There was a lifeboat station here from 1870, to give cover between Falmouth and Mevagissey, but it only survived 17 years and closed without having performed a single service – a reflection of the lack of shipwrecks in the area. Although the mouth of the cove is sheltered from all except south and south-easterly winds, one of the deciding factors in closing down the lifeboat station, apart from never being called out, was the problem of launching and recovery when it was at all rough, a situation affecting boat users here to this day.

Local regulations prohibit diving within the harbour, and the Harbour Master's permission must be obtained before use is made of the slipway. There is a launching fee for boats and dinghies at two levels, with or without the assistance of the winch, but this must be operated only by an authorised operator – do not try and operate it yourself. Reduced rates for a week's launching are available.

Facilities include limited parking at the head of the slipway with alternative parking outside the main village area. Public toilets, a telephone, an inn, and the two-star Lugger Hotel and restaurant (tel. 01872 501322) overlook the harbour.

Portloe offers easy access to the offshore Gull Rock and its reefs, and several miles of virtually undived coastline, from Shag Rock in the north-east to Nare Head. From Portloe it is necessary to continue west, uphill out of the village and on to Veryan.

Offshore dive sites and wrecks

The best offshore diving happens to coincide with the few offshore wrecks in this area: the Fowey approaches, the Gwinges rocks, Dodman Point, Nare Head and Gull Rock. The approaches to Fowey can be very busy with shipping, but none of the ships pass so close in as to go over the wreck of the *Kantoeng* (Site **32**).

St Austell Bay offers a few rocky reefs, such as Chugg Reef, which extends for almost a mile. Centuries of china clay deposits, washed down by the streams overlooking St Austell town have discharged into the sea at Par, leaving a white slurry like deposit on the sea bed that extends out level with Gribbin Head and then west towards Black Head. In places this is more than a metre thick and prohibits any marine growth.

From the Gwinges south, water depths increase much closer inshore, as does the tidal stream as you approach Dodman Point. There is a plateau on its southern side almost a mile square where the sea is a uniform 12 to 15m, though it drops off sharply to 50m on the seaward side. Within Veryan Bay itself there are only average tidal streams, with the best scenic diving being Lath Rock, Gull Rock, the Whelps, and of course the well known wreck of the *Hera* (Site **38**).

32 Dredger Kantoeng 50 18 55N; 04 39 10W and 50 19 18N; 04 39 16W. Built at Schiedam in the Netherlands in 1937 by A.F. Smulders, the 3,500-ton *Kantoeng* was the largest bucket tin dredger in the world at the time. She consisted of a huge non-propelled pontoon, measuring 225ft by 75ft, with a massive steel superstructure, holding a great bucket chain that dropped down through a long slot in the hull. On deck were all the electrical generators and motors to operate the machinery, also the rotating drums that separated the tin ore from the mud and spoil.

She sailed from Schiedam on 4 March, 1937, towed by two tugs, the *Humber* and the *Schelde*, heading for Bangka in the Dutch East Indies. Off Land's End

Transit marks for the dredger Kantoeng (Site 32).

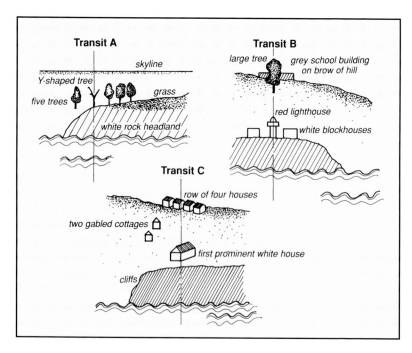

66

during the night of the 7 March she sprang a serious leak and tried to put back to Plymouth for repairs, but off the Eddystone capsized in heavy seas. She drifted closer inshore all the following day until she grounded less than a mile from the harbour mouth at Fowey.

There was great concern that she would drift in even further and completely block the entrance to Fowey, but the wind took her inshore to Coombe. It was then decided that she should be scuttled where she lay, and her 22 watertight compartments were holed in 40 places. The Southampton salvage firm Risdon Beazley undertook some salvage work that same year, and in September 1937 the main pontoon was re-floated and beached on Par Sands in St Austell Bay, where it was broken up.

Today the wreck is in two distinct parts; the remains of the bucket chain, which lie offshore in the first position given, and the scattered remains of the superstructure and machinery close inshore in the second location. At low water, a huge iron gear wheel shows above the surface close inshore, and this is a good marker for the shallow area. The bucket chain was broken by explosives in 1982 and several buckets were landed at Charlestown as scrap metal, but they proved too large and unmanageable to be broken up to go into a smelting furnace, and were of little value.

Both sites are easy dives for beginners, the bucket chain being in only 13m of water. The prolific fish life, and pieces of wreck making tunnels through which a diver can swim, make an interesting and unusual dive.

Transit marks for the *Kantoeng* are shown in the diagram opposite.

33 The Romanie 50 19 18N; 04 40 00W, is not in enough depth of water to be described as an offshore wreck, since it is possible to walk around part of it at low tide, but unless you hike across Gribbin Head to Polridmouth Cove it can only be reached by boat.

A steel, three-masted auxiliary schooner flying the Belgian flag, the 248-ton *Romanie* left Charlestown on 6 December, 1930, loaded with china clay for Nantes, discharged, and was back off Fowey in ballast on 16 January awaiting the tide to enter Par docks.

A strong south-east wind made entry to Fowey difficult, and the *Romanie* was blown into Polridmouth Bay, where the vessel anchored. Unfortunately, both anchors dragged and despite every effort using her engine to keep her afloat, she went on the rocks and became a total wreck on the Shillot Rocks. Her Belgian owner sold the wreck to a Mr Endean of Par, who carried out salvage work, but her bow, frames and bottom plating can still be found among the rocks.

34 Cannis Rock This outcrop about a quarter of a mile off Gribbin Head dries to 4m at low water spring tides and is marked to seaward with a flashing bell buoy. The rock is the centre of a large shallow reef, with an average depth of 8m, which extends right to the shoreline with deep, sand-filled gullies, teeming with marine life, wrasse, pollack, and often bass as well. It is renowned as an excellent spot for underwater photography. There is a degree of tide but nothing exceptional and no known hazards.

35 Chugg Reef Although this reef is not marked as such on any chart, is well known among fishermen and scallopers, who work its perimeter. At the shallowest

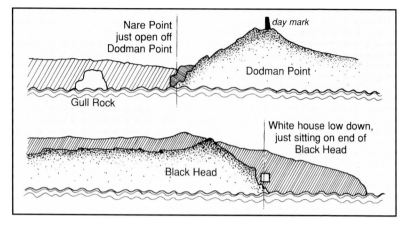

Above: Transit marks for the Eastfield (Site 36).

Below: Transit marks for the Hera (Site 38).

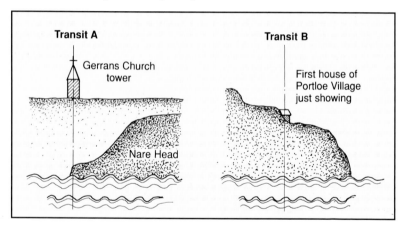

point the reef starts near Black Head in 20m depth and extends more than half way across St Austell Bay. At an average 5 to 6m above the sea bed it makes an excellent drift dive with rock outcrops, gullies and sand patches.

36 Eastfield 50 14 06N; 04 42 08W. This was an armed British steamship of 2,145 tons, 285ft long with a 43ft beam. On passage from Newport to Dieppe in convoy, she was torpedoed and sunk by the German submarine *UB-57* on 27 November, 1917, with the loss of one life only. She carried a cargo of coal.

She was attacked 7 miles ESE of Dodman Point, but her master managed to get close to the coast, attempting to beach his ship in the shallows. She sank in 55m depth, the wreck standing some 8m above the sea bed. All the forward part of the wreck is intact, and her engine and two boilers can be seen through holes in the deck, but the stern section has collapsed. The wreck is owned by the author, and you are requested not to remove souvenirs without prior permission.

Transit marks for the *Eastfield* are shown in the upper diagram opposite.

37 Lath Rock At 50 12 30N; 04 51 55W this rock is seldom dived, since it is difficult to locate without a good echo sounder. It is a spectacular site, with sheer drop-off faces and prolific fish life, and has yielded some sizeable crayfish – a shellfish that seems to be disappearing from Cornish waters.

38 The Hera At 50 12 05N; 04 53 55W this is a shipwreck with a really tragic story to tell, perhaps unique among the many shipping losses on the coast of Cornwall. The *Hera* started her life as the *Richard Wagner* in 1886, a steel, four-masted barque sailing under the British flag. She was then sold to Rhederei Aktien Gesellschaft of Hamburg, who had earlier lost a four-masted sailing ship, the *Pindos*, near Coverack in 1912.

On 1 February, 1914, ninety-one days out from Pisagua with Chilean nitrate, the 1,994-ton *Hera* was nearing the Lizard. With the weather thick and rough, navigation had been a matter of dead-reckoning for days, and the ship's position was uncertain. The crew tried to stand in to Falmouth Bay, where they might sight either the Lizard or St Anthony lights, but hours passed without any sign of land, and the weather steadily became worse.

Without warning, land was sighted dead ahead at midnight, and she sailed

Nare Head, showing the location of the Hera (Site 38).

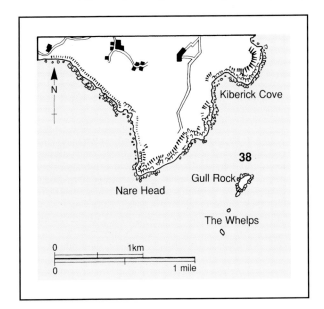

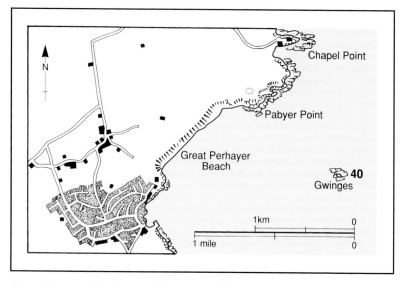

Gorran Haven and the Gwinges. The remains of the Ardangorm (Site 40) lie off the Gwinges, the stern section to the north of the rocks and the bow section to the south-east.

right into the Gull Rock in Veryan Bay. She came off again on the ground sea that was running, and drifted slowly clear, filling fast. Distress rockets were fired and boats were prepared, but the port boat capsized, drowning Captain Lorentz and three seamen, the survivors clambering back aboard. The starboard boat jammed in its chocks, so Chief Officer Muhliesen led the way up the jigger mast to get above the waves.

As the *Hera* sank deeper, so the crew were forced higher up the mast, the cold causing the chief officer to slip away into the sea, followed by the second mate, Petersen. Before he died he passed his silver whistle to Able Seaman Meyer, who blew it until exhausted, passing it higher to Able Seaman Johannsen who continued to use it, hoping to attract attention, which at last it did. After they had been in the rigging for two hours the Falmouth lifeboat – alerted by reports of distress rockets – found them and took off the five exhausted survivors.

A total of 19 men died that night in the wreck, and eight bodies were buried in Veryan churchyard. Captain Lorentz's body was recovered at Portloe. With only her foresail and topmast showing above the surface, the wreck was sold to Harris Brothers of Falmouth for £205. The wreck stands 5m above the sea bed in 17m depth.

Transit marks for the *Hera* are shown in the lower diagram on page 68.

39 Gull Rock and Whelps A prominent offshore outcrop 125ft (35m) tall, about a third of a mile off Nare Head. Average depths around the rock are 10m, with a string of rocks off to the south-west that dry to 4.5m at low tide. Outside the reefs the bottom drops away to 22 to 25m with a sand and shale sea bed, no undue amount of tide and good visibility.

40 Ardangorm 50 14 42N; 04 45 15W. This is the only known wreck on the Gwinges reef off Mevagissey and Gorran Haven. The 5,200-ton, 405ft long British registered steamship *Ardangorm* of Glasgow struck the reef on 4 January, 1940. The navigational buoy marking the hazard had been extinguished as a wartime measure, and during a pitch dark night with a hard ESE gale blowing, the 10-year-old cargo vessel became a total wreck.

Eleven crew were rescued by the Fowey lifeboat, the remainder being saved by Naval tugs the next day, who failed to re-float the vessel. The *Ardangorm* has been heavily salvaged, but there is still a lot of wreckage among which to rummage. Her propeller shafting still remains in a long run, and her boilers and engine lie off the reef in 9m.

41 Part of a huge towed steel barge 50 13 24N; 04 48 36W. This 250ft barge was under tow from Santander to Rotterdam by the British tug *Brittonia*, but she broke in two in heavy seas off the Lizard. The other part of the barge was recaptured some twenty miles south of the Lizard and taken into Falmouth, but the larger part, 150ft long, drifted ashore between Hemmick beach and Dodman Point on 14 October, 1971, and became trapped among the rocks. She is very smashed up, but an interesting dive.

42 Abraham Cove 50 13 30N; 04 27 30W. The *Abraham Cove*, a British registered steel fishing vessel 35ft long, foundered after springing a leak and capsizing on 13 July, 1983. The wreck lies in a general depth of 53m and is reported to be upright and intact, but smothered in fishing nets.

43 Almond Branch 50 12 23N; 04 44 48W. The steamship *Almond Branch* was torpedoed and sunk by the German submarine *UB-57* two miles south-east of Dodman Point on 27 November, 1917, while on passage from London and Port Talbot to South America carrying a general cargo. One member of the crew was killed in the attack. The wreck lies upside down, her stern collapsed, lying north-east to south-west in 54m depth, the wreck 9m above the sea bed. Her 18ft diameter bronze propeller was removed and landed in the spring of 1995.

44 Duen The wooden motor fishing vessel *Duen* (50 14 12N; 04 35 04W) sank while on passage from Plymouth to Barry on 24 February, 1977. The wreck lies in 53m depth. [Decca position: SW chain, Red (A) 10.55; Green (F) 46.75; Purple (B) 66.90.]

45 Allegrity 50 14 00N; 04 50 36W. Built as the MV *Empire Tavistock* in 1945 as a Cadet class coastal tanker of 798 tons. She was sold and renamed *Sobat* in 1951, and *Allegrity* on 13 December, 1961. Eight days after changing hands she went ashore on Greeb Point, near Caerhays, Veryan Bay, carrying a cargo of lubricating oil. Here she defied all attempts to re-float her, later capsized and became a total loss. Much broken steel work remains in the shallows, and it is an easy dive that can be reached from the beach.

*The MV Allegrity was wrecked close inshore near Caerhays on
13 December, 1961, after striking Grebe Point.*

46 Unidentified wreck 50 14 03 6N; 04 41 01 8W. When found initially in 1960 by a Hydrographic Department survey vessel, this was thought to be the SS *Rosehill*, sunk during World War One. When dived in 1981 she was found possibly to have been a wooden sailing schooner, with an intact stern section complete with ship's wheel, standing 4m high in a general depth of 52m. The wreck has yet to be positively identified. [Decca position: SW Chain. Red (A) 11.7; Green (F) 40.7.]

47 Silver Laurel 50 07 45N; 04 39 05W. She was a defensively armed British general cargo ship of 6,142 tons, carrying a crew of 48, 10 gunners and 9 passengers from Douala and Falmouth to Hull. On 18 December, 1944, she was torpedoed 7$^{1}/_{2}$ miles off Dodman Point and sank an hour later. Her cargo consisted of 2949 tons of cocoa beans, 2423 tons of palm oil, 758 tons of timber, 303 tons of lumber, 317 tons of rutile (a mineral), 66 tons of coffee, 30 tons of ramie (a fibre used for making fabrics) and 195 tons of rubber. She lies in 66m, with the top of the wreck at 56m. [Decca position: SW Chain. Red (A) 18.95; Green (F) 39.95.]

48 UB-118 50 09 52 2N; 04 43 04 8W. This World War One German submarine is believed to have been on her way to the breaker's yard when it foundered on 21 November, 1920. When she first sank her stern touched the sea bed leaving her conning tower under water, but part of the bow still above the surface. Average depth in area 55m. [Decca position: SW Chain. Red (A) 16.90; Green (F) 47.00.]

49 Shoal Fisher 50 09 52 2N; 04 48 45 6W. Carrying a British Government cargo of ammunition and machinery, the 698-ton motor vessel *Shoal Fisher* detonated a mine on 23 February, 1941, and sank off Dodman Point in 58m depth, the wreck standing 11m above the sea bed. The wreck is thought to be in two parts. [Decca position: SW Chain. Red (A)17.70; Green (G) 39.15, and Red (A) 17.50; Green (G) 40.10.]

50 Carolus 50 11 00N; 04 48 00W. A Norwegian steamship of 1,041 tons, built in 1900, which was torpedoed by the German submarine *UB-40* on 27 January, 1918, off Mount's Bay. In an attempt to reach Falmouth she sank two miles off Dodman Point in 45m.

51 UB-113 50 11 18N; 04 46 18W. This German submarine broke her towing hawser when under tow from Harwich to Falmouth, and had to be sunk by gunfire from the sloop HMS *Kennet* on 14 November, 1920. The wreck was re-located during the search for the MFV *Girl Rona* in 1977.

52 Butetown 50 12 02 4N; 04 43 18 0W. Built in 1907 as the *Karanja* of 1,829 tons, this armed British steamship was on passage in convoy from the Clyde to Portsmouth with a full cargo of coal when attacked on 29 January, 1918. One and a half miles off Dodman Point she was torpedoed by the German submarine *UB-40*, which killed two crew members, before she sank in 55m. The wreck sticks up 7m above the sea bed, but its condition is unknown.

St Mawes Castle.

AREA 3:

Falmouth Bay

This area centres on the port of Falmouth and Carrick Roads, the largest and deepest natural harbour in Britain and said to be the third deepest in the world. The extremities of the area are NARE HEAD (at the east end of Gerrans Bay) and NARE POINT, approximately 20 miles away.

The Falmouth area generally is very popular with visitors, and so is crowded in the holiday season. Delays on the roads and slipways are inevitable, but if you can plan to arrive at a launch site before 9am you will find little congestion, since holidaymakers seldom go far before 10. Accommodation is abundant, from four-star hotels to bed-and-breakfast, with a lot of hostels and camp sites.

The coastline divides neatly into three sections: Nare Head to St Anthony Head; the Carrick Roads, including Falmouth, St Mawes and Flushing; and the Rosemullion peninsula and Helford River, as far as Nare Point. This part of south Cornwall is extremely beautiful, with the contrast of steep rocky cliffs, wooded valleys reaching down to sheltered sandy beaches, headlands and the utter seclusion of the Helford River.

The first of these divisions includes Gerrans Bay and the Roseland peninsula, which for the most part comprises high cliffs with only two prospective boat launching sites on the 8-mile stretch of coast. While this might appear a disadvantage, in fact it is a bonus, since it makes it an area that for the most part sees very few divers, and is virtually unexplored under water, and offers long stretches of cliff and rocky foreshore.

On a spur of the estuary, PENRYN is Cornwall's oldest town, recorded at the time of the Domesday survey as being a place of importance. But prior to the development of Falmouth, it was the all-important seaport associated with Carrick Roads and handled all the shipping in the area.

Penryn today is a totally different place, consisting of a single small quay, still used by vessels of up to 100 tons, but the approach is badly silted and shallow, and in parts dries completely at low water. A road bridge blocks what was a creek leading to waterfront warehouses and stores, mostly derelict, and it is difficult to imagine the vast numbers of ships from the four corners of Europe that must have traded with this port.

In its heyday, FALMOUTH was one of the most important seaports on the south coast, due to its location and the shelter offered by the Carrick Roads – a corruption of Carrack Roads, which conjures up a mental picture of fleets of carrack-type ships at anchor in the 14th and 15th centuries.

Falmouth's charter is dated as late as 1660, when the hamlet of Smithick or Pennycumquick had its name officially changed. Previously, the county town of Truro, situated some 11 miles up the River Fal, dominated the estuary. In the early 17th century, Sir Walter Raleigh and Sir John Killigrew both saw the location as ideal for a new seaport, much closer to deep water than Penryn. Easily defended, protected from the prevailing south-westerly winds, safe from all but south-easterlies, it was the last deep-water anchorage for ships leaving the English Channel and the first on their return.

For the same reasons, the Post Office later based the mail packet ships here, which communicated with an expanding empire and sphere of influence. Large ocean-going liners collected last-minute mail and passengers before crossing the Atlantic, reducing the suffering of those subject to *mal de mer* by shortening their time on board ship by a couple of days. It was to become a haven of refuge for ships that left foreign ports many months earlier with instructions to call at Falmouth "for orders" as to where to discharge.

In the days prior to radio communication it was a common practice for ships nearing Falmouth to signal to the Lloyd's Station for her owners' instructions. Long sea passages were unpredictable, and a market for a particular cargo could be established only once the owners had the guarantee that the vessel had reached home waters safely. Only then could the ship's captain be advised of the port to which he was to proceed to unload. If no market had been found, or the owners were uncertain, then the vessel would carry on to Falmouth, where it would await its orders through the shipping agent.

The historic potential of diving in and around Falmouth is tremendous. Ships of every nation and size have anchored in Carrick Roads since AD 900 and probably earlier. Sailors today are little different from those of bygone eras; they throw broken and useless things overboard deliberately, lose crockery and utensils accidentally, and have ditched ship's rubbish generally. There must be a vast quantity of artefacts hidden in the mud and ooze of Carrick Roads, together with the remains of vessels that sank at their moorings, were captured by pirates during raids and scuttled, were wrecked in the shallows, or threw their guns or cargo overboard to lighten ship.

Many pitched battles have taken place here, not least one between Spanish and French fleets in Carrick Roads in the early 1500s. Iron and stone cannon shot are often located, ancient hide-shaped tin ingots, weapons, and a host of historic items all await discovery. Similarly, the approaches to Falmouth are littered with shipwrecks from both World Wars, vessels mostly mined close inshore, others torpedoed further out, and there is documentary evidence of many older wrecks in the area.

From Pendennis Point, with its great Tudor fortifications and castle, which offered protection to the anchorage, to the southern bank of the Helford River is an equally ancient and historic stretch of coastline. Again, access is very limited,

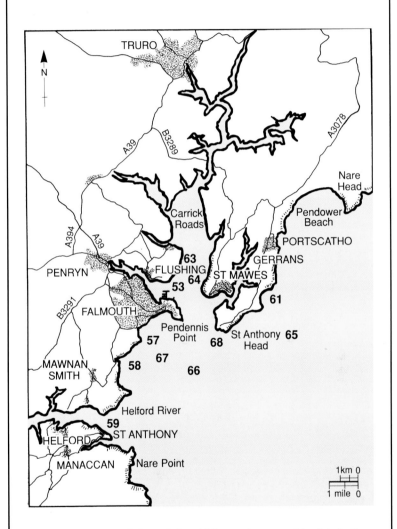

Dive Sites in Area 3, Falmouth Bay. This area is covered by Admiralty Charts 154 (approaches to Falmouth); 32 (Falmouth harbour); 18 (Falmouth inner harbour); 147 (Helford River detail); Ordnance Survey map 204.

but sufficient for any visiting diver to have the opportunity to explore this fascinating stretch of cliff and river estuary.

Overall, the deepest inshore water is inside Carrick Roads, where 40m can be found in certain areas. Otherwise it is generally a shallow sea bed, muddy in the estuaries and a mixture of shale and sand elsewhere. With large volumes of fresh water entering the sea from the River Fal and the Helford River in winter, or following any quantity of rain, the underwater visibility is much reduced but quickly improves when clear of the river mouths.

This stretch of coastline is very sheltered from any wind other than those between south and east, and it is possible to dive around Falmouth Bay in a full south-westerly gale. There are no tidal streams offshore of any great consequence, but within Carrick Roads when the estuary is emptying on a spring tide, you will encounter 2 to 3 knots.

Those wishing to dive in Falmouth Harbour or Carrick Roads area must telephone the 24-hour pilot service in advance, to establish what ship movements are anticipated. Falmouth is a working port and large vessels entering and leaving expect small craft and divers to keep clear. No diving is allowed within the Falmouth Docks area without special permission from Falmouth Harbour Office. Those wishing to dive the River Fal, or further up river to Truro should contact Truro Harbour Master.

Vessels wishing to berth in the Visitors' Yacht Haven are advised that this consists of 172m of floating pontoons that allow some forty average-size vessels to berth at one time. There is sufficient water depth to allow vessels with a maximum draught of 6ft to remain afloat. During the peak season (the end of June, July and August) petrol and diesel are available on the barge adjacent to the pontoons. Fresh water is available on the pontoons, and shower and toilet facilities are located at Custom House Quay within easy reach.

One of the slipways at Portscatho.

This slipway at Portscatho is rarely this clear, although the other slipway there (see opposite) is used even more.

Visitors should seek availability of berths on arrival, call the Harbour Office on VHF Channel 12 or 16. Should a berth not be available, vessels may use a Visitor's mooring or may anchor in the designated areas. The yacht haven is normally open from April, until September.

There are a number of deep water moorings available for visitors, the largest of which is capable of taking a yacht or other vessel up to 80ft. These are marked with green buoys, and located nearest the Falmouth side of the main channel between Greenbank Quay and Prince of Wales Pier and may be booked in advance by contacting the Harbour Office, or the Harbour Patrol on arrival. Vessels may also anchor off Custom House Quay, though may be asked to move at short notice to facilitate commercial shipping movements.

Craft are allowed to berth temporarily alongside Custom House Quay to load and unload, but remember there is a landing fee.

Coastal dive sites

The previous area suggested a route from Portloe through the village of Veryan. At the junction in the village, where the main road goes on to join the A3078 for St Mawes and Tregony, take road signposted to Pendower.

Take the second turning left down this long, narrow lane (towards the hotel), and at the bottom you will find easy access to CARNE BEACH, the eastern end of

Pendower. At this eastern end of the long sandy beach there is ample roadside parking, with an additional car park just back from the foreshore.

The advantage of this location is that it is not well known, and has a very good concrete slipway, free of charge, leading to the beach, which is overlooked by Nare Head. Facilities here are minimal, but there are public toilets at the car park, and non-residents are welcome at the Nare Head Hotel (tel. 01872 501279) for snacks and drinks. Vehicles are allowed on the beach for launching and recovery, and parking is by a courtesy pay scheme.

An alternative to the eastern end of Pendower is the far western end. Access to this can only be gained by taking the St Mawes and Tregony road out of

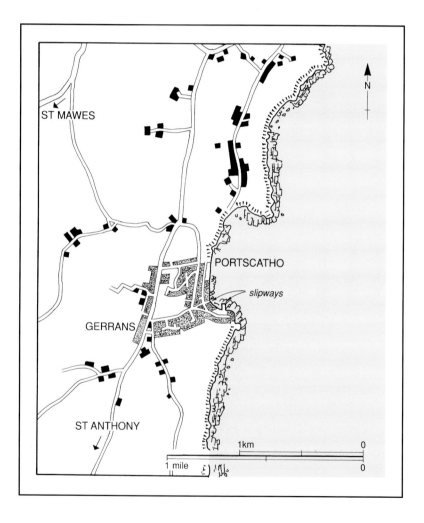

Veryan village to the main A3078, turning left and in a little under one mile turning left for Pendower Beach and the Pendower Beach Hotel (tel. 01872 501241). The hotel has an annexe serving snacks, drinks and meals; the main hotel is open to visitors in the evenings.

A long narrow downhill lane will bring you within sight of the sea on your right, then a wider section with parking for some two dozen vehicles, with a County Council sign that reads "No cars beyond this point". From there a stretch of about 130m of tarmac road, which bears round to the right and out of sight, will bring you to the head of a small beach slipway. PENDOWER is a long stretch of sand and shingle, popular with families and those staying at the Pendower House Hotel. With the prior permission of the hotel management, it is possible to use the short length of restricted road to launch and recover small boats and inflatables. Do not take cars down to the slipway, because of the risk to pedestrians.

Boats manhandled on this roadway and slip present very little difficulty, although it is fairly steep. Launching will take place across a reasonably firm foreshore and is ideal for reaching Gull Rock and Nare Head, with a pleasant beach and some sand dune areas for those left ashore.

This is generally a very shallow area with some reefs on the western end, but is all fine sand offshore for some distance. Care must be exercised in summer when leaving or approaching the beach using an outboard motor, since there will be children in the shallows, and surfers and snorkellers who may be difficult to spot.

Return via the same route to the A3078, and turn left. Continue for a little over one mile to the village of Trewithian, then fork left for PORTSCATHO and left again further on where indicated. This will take you through the outskirts of Portscatho, into a sort of square, with free but limited parking, shops, cafés, an inn, hotel and toilets.

From this pretty fishing village there are two possible launch sites – down the road towards the sea, either to the left or right of the pub. That to the left side (north), leads down between buildings to a concrete ramp with a considerable slope, but manageable by three or four people. The other is the Portscatho harbour slip proper, which in the summer may be partially blocked by local dinghies, who are supposed to leave a clear gangway down the centre, but often do not! For that reason alone, provided the tide is right, the other slipway is preferable. If using the main slipway take care not to damage other boats, crab pots, nets, etc.

Parking is allowed on the top road overlooking the harbour, which is much nearer the launch site than the village square. The wreck of the *Andromeda* (Site **61**) can be easily reached from here.

Leave Portscatho on the road to Gerrans, and on entering the village take the main road left. Three-quarters of a mile further on, in the village of Trewince, where the road takes a sharp left turn, there is a narrow, private lane ahead marked "St Mawes Ferry". Continue down this lane to Porthcuel creek, where there is a landing stage for a foot ferry to St Mawes. This is all part of a private

Opposite: The area around Portscatho.

Mylor Churchtown slipway.

estate, overlooked by the manor house and gardens, but it is possible to launch an inflatable down a good slipway here, providing the tide is right. Parking for some three vehicles is possible, but it is unsuitable for anything other than a small group and one boat. This will give easy access into St Mawes harbour, Carrick Roads and the offshore dive sites and wrecks. Return through Gerrans to the A3078 at Trewithian, turn left and continue to St Mawes. The A3078 forks outside the town: the road to the left will take you directly into the town, waterfront, harbour and parking. The road to the right follows a more scenic route overlooking Falmouth and Carrick Roads, past the historic St Mawes Castle on the edge of the sea, and down to the harbour.

St Mawes is an ancient smuggling and fishing port, with a castle built by order of Henry VIII in 1540, following a sea battle within Carrick Roads in 1537, which was fought all the way up the River Fal as far as Malpas. There is a passenger ferry to Falmouth and up river to Porthcuel (marked "Percuil" on Ordnance Survey maps), and the creeks and harbour of St Mawes are very popular with the yachting fraternity.

The town has all the usual amenities: toilets, cafés, restaurants, pubs, hotels, guest houses, shops, fuel and parking, but all on a limited scale. There are two slipways available, both leading into the harbour, which is protected by a single arm breakwater.

The large concrete slipway at the head of the pier is controlled by the Harbour Master, who also controls parking in this area. Do not attempt to use the slipway without first calling at the Harbour Master's office, which is at the entrance to the quay. There is a launching fee, which varies depending on the length of the craft. The slip is tidal in that it may be unsuitable to launch and recover at very low tides.

The second slipway is situated opposite the main car park, in a gap between the harbour wall and a hotel. This one is cobbled and not as wide as the former and entails taking craft over the sandy beach and foreshore, but it is free and no permission is needed for its use.

Within the confines of St Mawes harbour, creek and estuary out to a line joining the castle with Carricknath Point, there is a water speed limit of 5 knots, and care should be exercised due to the large number of moorings and boats generally, with a lot of marine traffic in the summer months. Out to the mouth of St Mawes creek there is only a maximum depth of 7m, with a shale and silt bottom, patches of mud and sandy patches plus all the litter usually found in a mooring area.

At the mouth of the creek will be found a red and white buoy marking the Lugo Rock, and in a direct line with the very end of the opposite headland will be seen the buoy that marks the eastern edge of the main shipping channel leading to Falmouth docks and Carrick Roads. Diving is forbidden in the shipping channel (*see* Falmouth Harbour Regulations).

St Mawes should be considered a suitable launch site from which to explore offshore wreck sites or the waters around St Anthony Head, Porthmellin Head and Killigerran Head.

Leaving St Mawes by the A3078 going north, there is a choice of two routes to reach Falmouth or the Flushing area. Two miles north of St Mawes, there is a

Mylor Harbour.

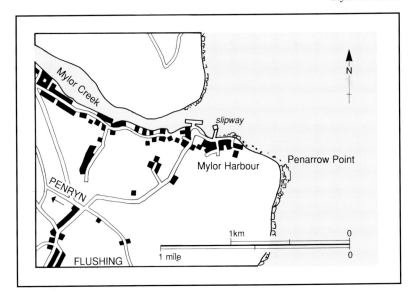

junction with the B3289. This left fork offers a route to Falmouth via the King Harry car and pedestrian ferry – a journey of 6 miles to the main A39. Alternatively, continue on the A3078 via Tregony to join the A39 at Tresillian, which involves a distance of 21 miles to arrive at the same point and takes you through Truro, where you should keep to the A39.

Both routes lead to Carnon Downs; from here follow the road to Devoran and Perranworthal. About a quarter of a mile after the well known and prominent Norway Inn, turn left off the main road for Mylor Bridge. Follow signposts for MYLOR CHURCHTOWN or the harbour, which is 1½ miles further on, on the south bank of the Mylor Creek.

The road will take you past Mylor churchyard and graveyard on the right, along a short stretch of waterfront to the miniature harbour, jetty and slipway, and a complex of marine buildings, yacht club and services. There is a small charge for using the slipway here, which is very wide and well maintained.

Diesel and petrol are available from the end of the jetty, and chandlers, outboard motor servicing and boat repairs are available generally. The area has all the services one would expect at a busy marina, including public toilets, a telephone, restaurant, and self-catering holiday flats, all overlooking Mylor Creek. Car parking unfortunately is difficult and, having launched your craft, if the roadside spaces are all taken and the boatyard cannot help, you may be obliged to park back up the hill, past the church.

This area is known as the Trefusis peninsula. The best shallow diving will be found between Penarrow Point and Trefusis Point, since the vast expanse of Carrick Roads north of Penarrow has a bottom of deep mud. The two steel wrecks of the *Stanwood* (Site **63**) and the *Mitera Marigo* (Site **64**) can be reached easily from Mylor Creek, but the shallows of Trefusis Point also offer a few wreck sites.

53 Queen No less than 250 people lost their lives in the shallows here when the transport vessel *Queen* went ashore on 14 January, 1814, and became a total loss. She had left Lisbon only a few days after Christmas with over 300 people on board, including her crew, invalid soldiers wounded fighting in Wellington's army, women and children who had accompanied the troops, and some prisoners-of-war.

On reaching Falmouth on the 10 January she anchored in Carrick Roads, but three days later started to drag her anchors. Due to an indifferent look-out, this went unnoticed for some time, and when finally the captain was advised it was too late to set sail and clear the rocks, since she was already in the shallows.

She struck during the early hours, with a strong easterly gale blowing – the very worst for Carrick Roads – and huge waves were breaking over her deck, pouring down hatchways and into the hold, causing total panic below decks. Then heavy snow started to fall, blotting out all hope that anyone in Falmouth would see their plight or distress signals, and Captain Carr and his crew were left to save themselves as best they could.

He ordered all three masts cut down, but in falling these smashed down the bulwarks and caused carriage-mounted guns to become loose. These guns careered around the deck, so that men were crushed to death or fearfully injured.

Others were drowned in trying to swim the short distance to the shore, and less than 20 minutes after striking the *Queen* was a broken, half-submerged wreck.

Those who witnessed the scene next day said the foreshore was an unforgettable sight, with dozens of bodies washing about, draped across the rocks, or entangled in rigging. Of the 300 who had been aboard, only 85 soldiers, nine women, one child and four prisoners survived – and of the crew, only the bosun and cabin-boy remained alive. Of the dead, 136 were laid to rest in a mass grave in Mylor churchyard. Now much weathered, the memorial stone can still be read, and is inscribed "To the memory of the warriors, women and children who, returning from the coast of Spain, unhappily perished in the wreck of the Queen, transport, on Trefusis Point."

Falmouth, showing the location of the Ponus (Site 57) off Gyllyngvase Beach.

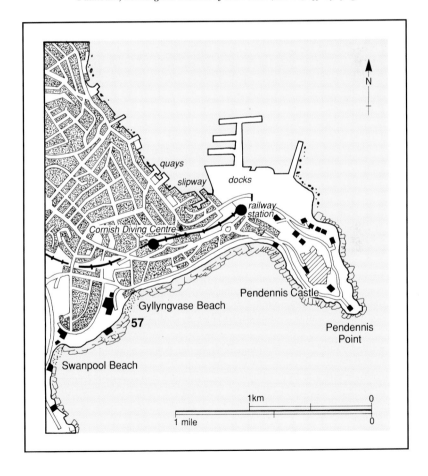

Grove Park slipway at Falmouth is the best launch site in Cornwall and has a car park beside it.

Although no tangible remains that could be identified as the *Queen* are to be found, there are some massive timbers at 50 09 45N; 05 03 00W, which are thought to be part of her keel. A few hours searching in the shallows might well reveal some artefacts.

The whole of the Trefusis foreshore area is broken rock, grey sand and shale, but it has seen many wrecks and the relatively shallow depths of 4.5 to 6m are ideal for the less experienced, or as a shallow second dive after exploring one of the deeper offshore wrecks. Of the many victims of Trefusis, it is worth looking for the Dutch brig *Nautilus*, 1887, or remains of HMS *Torrid*, an old R-Class destroyer broken up on the rocks in 1937.

North up Carrick Roads out of Mylor Creek there are two areas that might prove interesting shallow diving. On the west bank by Porthgwidden, and on the opposite side a little further north, just past Turnaware Point, is where landing craft for the D-Day assault on Normandy in 1944 lay at anchor and were loaded.

54 Landing craft Concrete ramps and mooring posts set in the bank show the areas concerned, and here tank landing craft were run ashore, and American troops embarked with their vehicles and weapons. Since practice loading and disembarkation went on for some time, it is likely that there are relics to be found here: ammunition, helmets, or even weapons dropped overboard accidentally.

55 King Harry Ferry Further up river still, into the narrows, you will come across this car and pedestrian ferry crossing. A ferry has worked across this stretch of river for hundreds of years, and again, there must be artefacts lying on the bottom in this area – but do not obstruct the operation of the ferry.

A small waterfront town once well known for its many shipyards, and its large houses owned by captains of the packet vessels, FLUSHING is on the south side of the Trefusis peninsula, less than a mile from Mylor. The entire waterfront overlooks Falmouth town and docks. (There is another place named Flushing in the Helford area.)

Approaching from Mylor, at the bottom of a hill where there are hotels and an inn on the left, the road swings round a bend and levels off at the shore line. Right on the point of that bend is the only public slipway in Flushing, which is free to use, but restricted and cannot be recommended other than for a small inflatable with 4 divers at the most.

Splendid harbour views and a sheltered position make Flushing very popular with holidaymakers, who fill the waterfront and jetties, watching the boats, watching fish being landed, and generally enjoying the location. You can pay to park on one of the jetties, which also has a seasonal café, public toilets and telephone, but there are other places to eat and limited free parking areas. Any diving from the waterfront area would be unwise and probably against the regulations, since there is considerable small boat traffic here all year round, and a passenger ferry from Falmouth calls at the western jetty at regular intervals. While Flushing is a useful place from which to reach Trefusis Point, Mylor is advisable in preference.

Take the road out of Flushing and follow the signs for Penryn and FALMOUTH, joining the A39 on the outskirts of Penryn close to a pedestrian crossing. The main A39 passes through Penryn's Commercial Road area, to a large roundabout, and then goes off left following the waterfront itself into the town, but this route is

Carrick Roads, the deep water mooring area off Falmouth for countless thousands of ships in the past, is a rich ground for divers seeking odd crockery. Some items have already been claimed by marine squatters.

not recommended. At the roundabout take the second exit, go up a long hill and continue straight ahead over a set of traffic lights, over two more roundabouts. After a left hand fork turn sharp left under the railway bridge at the third roundabout. Follow this road round, past the entrance to Falmouth Docks, Port Pendennis marina, past Cornish Diving Services on your left, and just past a large public car park on the right, is the Falmouth Boat Park and slipway, which is huge, able to take a dozen boats launching and recovering all at the same time.

Parking on the premises is not allowed, but you can unload, launch, change, and then put the car and trailer in the adjacent pay and display park, which has a public toilet alongside. Until recently, this slipway was the headquarters of an RAF torpedo recovery unit. The gates are locked at night, but the times of opening and closing are displayed on a board.

USEFUL TELEPHONE NUMBERS

24-hour pilot service – tel. 0836 661668.

Boat Park Supervisor – tel. 01326 312285, extension 29.

Falmouth Harbour Office, Leisure Services – tel. 01326 312285.

HM Customs and Excise – tel. 01326 314156.

Penryn Harbour Office – tel. 01326 373352.

Pollution Control Officer – tel. 0800 378500 (all calls free of charge).

Port Health Authority – tel. 01326 313423.

Truro Harbour Master – tel. 01872 78131.

Daily and weekly rates are available, and this is the best all-tide slipway site in the whole of Cornwall. Very large inflatables can be launched from here easily, and the Manacles and Lizard areas are the within easy reach, the latter only 40 minutes away. For details, contact the Boat Park Supervisor. With Cornish Diving Services so close at hand, re-charging cylinders during or at the end of a diving day is made easy.

The large and active ship repair docks at Falmouth are obvious from anywhere in the town, since they dominate the southern end of the waterfront. They also support the offshore exploration of the Western Approaches, and may soon become a terminal for ferries to Ireland and Spain. There are frequent and numerous arrivals and departures of very large ships, usually accompanied by tugs.

By Harbour Commissioners' Order "no diving shall take place in any fairway, under any circumstances". This means all the buoyed channel area, from a line joining Zone Point and Rosemullion Head in the south, to Penarrow Point joining St Just Creek in the north, which is the extent of the Commissioners' authority.

North of the Penarrow–St Just limit, the authority becomes Carrick District Council, who have a Maritime Officer who controls the river all the way to Truro.

In short, no diving should take place in or around the commercial docks area, nor within any of the buoyed channels or the approach to the docks from the channel, or the immediate approach to Carrick Roads between Black Rock and St Anthony Head at the entrance.

Diving is permitted outside these areas, with the exception of the main Truro River channel, in which case the Carrick Maritime Officer should be contacted first, since very large ships are laid up from time to time in the narrows below King Harry Ferry, and nothing must obstruct the tricky operation of getting them in and out of the river. Otherwise the only restriction is a 5-knot speed limit, which you are advised to observe – the Maritime Officer has high speed patrol boats and can impose fines.

Carrick Roads, apart from the dredged deep-water channels and very deep areas, is generally shallow and silted. In the centre of the harbour entrance is Black Rock, an aptly named outcrop, once said to have been joined to the west bank by a reef, so that it was possible to walk right out at low water, but that must have been a very long time ago! Diving takes place around the rock, and in the western gap (a small boat channel), and cannon balls are regular finds, probably fired from St Mawes Castle or Pendennis Castle, using the rock as a target.

Outside the harbour area, to the west and past Pendennis, which houses the Coastguard Maritime Rescue Co-ordination centre, is an area known as Gyllyngvase, the area of the larger Falmouth hotels. There is a clockwise one-way traffic system running round Pendennis Point. Almost under a small seaward side car park area, well round from the point is an excellent shore dive on World War One submarines.

One of the German submarines (Site 56) that were brought to Falmouth for gunnery trials shortly after World War One. The U-118 sank of Dodman Point on passage, two were used and sunk in trials and six drove ashore in a gale in 1921.

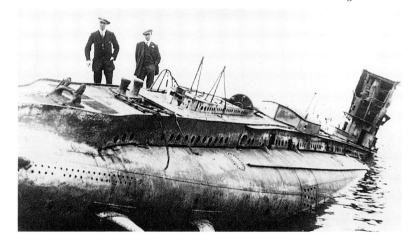

89

56 World War One submarines At the end of World War One, when the Allies allotted the surviving German Navy ships to different countries, to do with what they liked, a total of seven U-boats were allocated to Falmouth for Royal Navy gunnery trials. These were duly towed here from Harwich in 1920 and – except for one that sank off Dodman Point – moored off Gyllyngvase beach.

Some of the submarines were taken to sea and sunk by shells, and the numbers were slowly whittled down until a November gale drove the remaining five vessels onto the rocks, where they were declared total wrecks. Sold to a succession of scrap merchants, they have been slowly reduced over the years to piles of rusting iron, but interesting brass valves, nameplates, taps and gauges are still found in the shallows. The site by the car park was the last resting place of two submarines close inshore, with others further west. Average depth is 7 to 8m, with good visibility.

Between Falmouth and the Helford River there are three public beaches from which shore diving or boat launching is permitted. Take the unclassified road that follows the sea front past the hotels, towards GYLLYNGVASE BEACH, which is at the end of the promenade. This is a flat, sandy public beach, run by Carrick District Council. Facilities consist of pay-parking, public toilets, a café and abundant accommodation. There is a tarmac strip suitable for trailers leading from the road to the beach – in the summer this is often chained up, but there is a Beach Warden on duty who has the key and can advise when launching is permitted. A very shallow, sandy foreshore, with rock outcrops at each end.

Situated one mile further south on the Maenporth road is SWANPOOL BEACH, similar to Gyllyngvase, usually more shingle than sand, and less restricted. There is access to the beach directly from the main road, and launching boats is a matter of negotiating a trailer down a long gentle slope to the waters edge, but must be by hand – no vehicles are allowed on the beach.

Out from the beach, with its rocky sides and shallow cliffs, is identical to Gyllyngvase. There is a large car park just across the road from the foreshore, two cafés and a public telephone, with numerous camping and caravan sites within half a mile. The wreck of the *Ponus* (Site **57**) can be easily reached from here, or from the next beach, Maenporth.

Continue out of Swanpool heading inland, fork left at the main road junction, and continue for about one mile. MAENPORTH BEACH is similar to the previous two – sandy, flat, popular with holidaymakers and surrounded by low cliffs. Cars and trailers can be parked on the beach or across the road in a car park (there is a charge for either). Boats must be manhandled across the beach, but the Falmouth Underwater Centre based here has a Land Rover, which for a small charge will assist with launching and recovery. The Centre's dive shop can supply or hire equipment, as well as re-charge cylinders, and is attached to a pleasant beach café, under the same management. One of the attractions of Maenporth is the wreck of the *Ben Asdale* (Site **90**), which can be a shore dive, a boat dive, or you can just look down on it from the cliff above the beach.

57 Ponus 50 08 27N; 05 04 00W. In a most dramatic incident this 5,077-ton tanker caught fire and burned like a torch for three whole days. During World

The abandoned wreck of the Aberdeen-registered stern trawler Ben Asdale (Site 68) off the cliffs at Maenporth. She was driven ashore in a gale in 1978 after a complete hydraulic failure of her steering gear. Although it is now much damaged and stripped of valuable material, the wreck can be explored on foot at low water or by divers at high water.

War One a number of ordinary merchant vessels were converted to oil carrying, and consequently had their bridge and accommodation amidships. The *Ponus* was one such vessel, which had been launched in 1902 by Russell's of Port Glasgow as the *Kennebec*, but undergone a change of ownership and name.

On 2 November, 1916, she arrived off Falmouth from Trinidad at 7pm, and with no pilot available, she anchored some three quarters of a mile offshore. During the night the wind increased to gale force, and despite a second anchor the ship dragged ashore between Swanpool and Gyllyngvase. Blasts on her siren for assistance must have woken half the population of Falmouth, and with distress rockets soaring up, hundreds came to the beach to watch the tug *Victor* attempt to tow the Falmouth lifeboat round Pendennis to the rescue in heavy weather.

Heavy seas forced them both back, and acutely aware that he must take some action himself, Captain Collins risked the lowering of two lifeboats, both of which managed to reach the shore safely. One of those boats returned to the ship and managed to take off the captain and remaining crew members. About an hour later smoke was seen curling up from the ship, which quickly became dense. Onlookers were at first amused when a man then appeared on deck, wearing nothing more than a very short vest!

As the fire took hold, so the sole crew member – asleep in his bunk until then and quite oblivious to the fact that the ship had been abandoned – suddenly realised his predicament, and promptly set about making a small wooden raft. This he threw overboard and leapt after it – still wearing only his vest. Raft and

91

Maenporth Beach has a good diving centre, just visible in the background of this photograph.

occupant were then pinned under the stern by the tide, and only the timely action of an onlooker with a dinghy to hand saved his life.

By evening the entire amidships section was well alight, and at 5.30am on 4 November, a terrific explosion sent burning oil pouring out across the sea. There were further explosions as the day wore on, and soon the fire was a real threat to property ashore. One of the remaining lifeboats on board, afloat but full of oil and on fire drifted away spreading the flames, and by 7pm the fabric of the ship was glowing red hot in the dark.

The fire did not die down until 6 November, and still structurally intact, the ship remained untouched until November 1918 when the stern was cut away, re-floated and scrapped in the docks. The remainder was sold and resold, slowly demolished and reduced to her bottom plates, but a great deal still remains in the shallows.

58 Ben Asdale 50 07 40N; 05 05 00W. A British steel stern-trawler of 422 tons, built in 1972, which anchored off Falmouth on 29 December, 1978. She dragged her anchor as the wind got up and when her engine was started to get her clear her steering gear broke down; she drove ashore the following day. Attempts were made to re-float her but she fell on her port side at low water and became a total loss. Some attempts were made to cut the wreck up, but failed. The wreck currently belongs to the proprietor of the Maenporth Hotel.

The road out of Maenporth leads to the village of Mawnan Smith; fork left here for Helford Passage. From here on the lanes are very narrow and steep, and it would be advisable not to take a very large vehicle or boat trailer to Grebe Beach.

Larger vehicles should go on through Mawnan Smith towards Penryn, picking up the B3291 to Gweek and St Keverne, or the main A39 to Helston.

Few maps indicate GREBE BEACH, but the hamlet of Durgan will be marked, which is at the bottom of a very narrow, winding lane turning off the Mawnan to Helford Passage road one mile from Mawnan Smith, on the left.

Durgan is nothing more than a cluster of houses on the edge of the north bank of the Helford River. It has a rough stone and cobble slipway giving access to the sand and pebble foreshore, but no parking or other facilities on site. The National Trust have provided a large car park well back up the hill, but no camping or overnight sleeping is allowed. Durgan is no place for a large diving group, but a small party with a small inflatable could manage easily. Shallow rocky fingers encompass the foreshore and in the river a maximum depth of 10m will be encountered, with coarse sand, rock and silt bottom. Visibility is seldom better than 4 to 5m. There are the remains of a steamship wreck out in the river.

59 Rock Island Bridge 50 05 52N; 05 05 56W. This was an American registered steamship of 3,545 tons, which was in collision with the SS *Kenosha* some ten miles east of the Lizard in dense fog on 22 March, 1920. The ship was ripped open and leaking badly, and her crew immediately abandoned ship, thinking that she was about to sink, but re-boarded two hours after when she stopped going down, got her radio going and transmitted an SOS signal. This brought out two tugs from Falmouth.

As it was feared that she might sink within Carrick Roads and block the port, the tugs towed the *Rock Island Bridge* into the shallows at Porthallow, where it was found a bulkhead had collapsed. She was then taken round to the mouth of the Helford River, where she fell onto her starboard side. Every attempt was made to save her – huge concrete anchor points were built into the cliff to which were attached steel wires to pull her upright, but the attempt failed, and she later was reduced by explosives to lay half awash for years. The entire bottom of the ship is still there, but has gone down into the riverbed, so that very little shows.

The steel barque Andromeda on Killigerran Head in 1915. All except one of the crew were rescued.

93

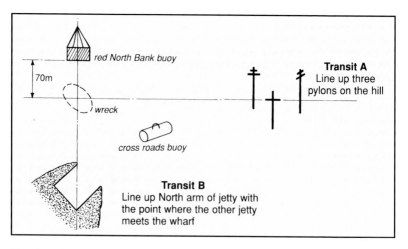

Transit marks for the Stanwood (Site 63).

60 Unidentified wreck The 1952 edition of chart 777 (St Ives to Dodman Point) shows a beached wreck just inside the August Rocks, between Rosemullion Head and Mawnan Church. Exactly what this was is something of a mystery, and the wreck has not been identified.

A passenger ferry operates across the HELFORD RIVER from here, but despite a foreshore and short concrete ramp, launching a diving boat from here should not be considered. The approach roads starts off wide enough, but narrows down sharply, with no parking and no turning space, as well as being a dead end. A beach dive would be possible, with conditions as for Durgan, but care must be taken not to get in the way of the heavy small boat traffic, mostly outboard motors.

In the Helford River, just clear of the ferry line and to the east, is a 16m hole known locally as the Conger Pit, into which rubbish from the river drops. Divers have recovered trading tokens, coins and old bottles from here.

The road from Mawnan Smith via Port Navas to Constantine is narrow and torturous, and should not be taken towing a trailer of any sort. It is advisable to return to Mawnan and join the B3291 at Gweek. Continue around the head of the river, through Gweek, and fork left on to the B3293 to St Keverne. Three miles from Gweek, at the point where the huge Goonhilly Downs satellite communication station aerials come into sight ahead, turn left onto a side road for Newton-in-St-Martin and Manaccan. Continue through Manaccan village, and follow the signs for ST ANTHONY. This gives access to Gillan Creek or Gillan Harbour, once an active pilchard fishery, but now given over entirely to boating activities, under the protection of the National Trust. The foreshore is rough stone with a wooden ramp/slip, boat and trailer park, with car parking just across the road, but apart from a small yachting chandlers right on the beach, there are no facilities at all.

Although the approach road is narrow, it can be a satisfactory launch site for a small party. Within the creek there is less than 15ft (4.5m) of water and diving within the harbour confines is not recommended. St Anthony offers a good start point to dive the *Bay of Panama* (Site **83**), or deeper water out from the Helford estuary.

On leaving St Anthony, the road follows the creek and narrows to 6½ft, with appropriate warning signs. These should not be taken lightly; it is better to go back through Manaccan and follow the signposts for Porthallow, via Carne. The Ordnance Survey map will show what appears to be a launch site at the small village of Flushing, but while there is a beach and slipway, it is all private property and should be avoided.

Offshore dive sites and wrecks

Lying 1¼ miles due east from Killigerran Head and centred on 50 09 28N; 04 57 05W, THE BIZZIES is a large rocky reef with an average 6m depth, dropping off to a sand and gravel bottom in 15m. It extends out from the shore opposite Greeb Point and its one mile length offers plenty of places to find the shellfish that inhabit the reef, including the occasional crayfish.

61 Andromeda 50 09 00N; 04 58 53W. This four-masted steel sailing ship arrived off Falmouth in February 1915 after 116 days at sea, from Portland, Oregon, with 3,000 tons of wheat. Wartime regulations stated that ship's captains were not to bring their own ship into port, but had to make use of a pilot.

Due to heavy seas and a SSW gale, none of the pilot boats or tugs could reach the vessel, and at 4am she dragged her anchors and went ashore. Her crew took to the rigging, from where they were rescued by the Portscatho Rocket Brigade, although one apprentice lost his life when he fell overboard. The wreck was auctioned for salvage on 3 March, and raised just £170. Much of the wreck survives in the shallows, the photograph of her showing the exact location.

The southernmost point of the Roseland peninsula, close to St Anthony lighthouse, ZONE POINT is overlooked by the old Coastguard station. A number of wooden vessels were lost here in the 18th and 19th centuries, and in any case it is an interesting, rough, rocky bottom with heavy kelp in summer.

62 The Captain A British man-of-war, the 3rd rate *Captain*, 74-guns, found herself in trouble here in the early 19th century, shortly before she was gutted by fire at Plymouth in 1813. She drifted so close inshore there was no room to either tack or wear and she went aground. All her guns were thrown overboard to lighten the vessel, which was then hauled clear and saved. Most of the guns were recovered, but several were left on the sea bed.

63 Stanwood 50 10 18N; 05 02 06W. Neither this wreck nor the *Mitera Marigo* are offshore wrecks since both are within Carrick Roads, but their access and depth cannot classify them as shore dives either.

The SS *Stanwood*, launched as the *Hesione* at Hamburg in 1915, was taken as

Previously used as the Isles of Scilly mail steamer, the Lady of the Isles lies half submerged in Lamorna Cove in 1904. She was raised and became a salvage steamer until World War Two, when she was taken into Navy service for cable-laying. She was finally sunk by a mine in 1940 (see Site 65).

a prize ship, placed under the Controller of Shipping for the remainder of World War One. It then passed into the ownership of the Elder Dempster Line, and finally the Stanhope Line in 1937.

On 10 December, 1939, the 240ft long vessel, on passage from Leith to Dakar with a cargo of coal was alongside one of the jetties in Falmouth Docks when a fire was discovered in No. 2 hold forward. Unable to get access to the seat of the fire, the authorities had her towed to the North Bank where she anchored, where she was scuttled in order to extinguish the flames. Unfortunately, she slipped part way off the bank into both deeper water and mud, from where it proved impossible to re-float her. One man, the radio officer, died in the incident.

Extensive salvage work was carried out, and most of the cargo was recovered, but part of the propeller shafting and boilers remain, and part of the superstructure still stands facing towards the north-west with 12m of clear water over her in a general depth of 20m. Her bow section lies in shallow water.

Transit marks for the *Stanwood* are shown in the diagram on page 94.

64 Mitera Marigo 50 10 12N; 05 01 47W. The most recent large shipwreck in the Falmouth area, the *Mitera Marigo* was a Greek owned but Liberian registered motor vessel of 9,200 tons, employed as a general freighter and carrying iron ore when lost. During the early hours of 29 May, 1959, she was in collision with the German-owned SS *Fritz Rhysen* in dense fog off Ushant.

The *Mitera Marigo* suffered so much bow damage that it was thought she would founder before tugs could reach her, but two Falmouth vessels managed to get her into Carrick Roads by 8pm that same day. With No. 1 hold flooded and her forepart very low in the water, it was just possible for onlookers to see the extensive damage to her bow in the fading daylight, as she was secured to a buoy for the night just across the channel from where the *Stanwood* had gone down.

The Falmouth tug *Englishman* stood by the wreck all night, but she was sinking fast, and at about midnight the Falmouth lifeboat was summoned to save the crew. A Customs officer, the last man off, stepped from the ship's rail as the vessel sank beneath his feet!

After settling on the bottom, the wreck remained upright, masts clear of the surface. Her bunker oil was pumped out to avoid pollution of nearby oyster beds, after which the wreck was flattened by explosives to prevent it from remaining a navigational hazard. With parts deeply buried in mud or iron-ore cargo, large sections of the wreck remain visible in 27m with the top of the wreckage at 22m and the cargo mound 20m of dark turbulent water.

65 Lady of the Isles 50 08 48N; 04 54 16W. Originally used as one of the mail packet ferries between Penzance and the Isles of Scilly, this 166-ton steamship was well known in the South West.

While on an excursion trip in 1904, she struck a rock and sank in Lamorna Cove on 1 September, but was raised, sold to the Western Marine Salvage Company of Penzance, and remained with their salvage business until 1940, when she was requisitioned by the Admiralty.

On 3 October, 1940, she was under tow of a tug, on passage from Falmouth to Plymouth, when about 3 miles east of St Anthony Point she detonated a magnetic mine that had been laid by a German aircraft. Of her 19 man crew, 16 died in the explosion and sinking of the vessel, which was carrying cable at the time, although she was not a cable-laying vessel. The 131ft wreck lies in 44m depth on a sand and shale bottom, but is well covered with fishing nets. Her bell, recovered in the late 1970s, identified the wreck. [Decca position: SW Chain. Red (A) 19.66; Green (H) 33.42.]

66 Caroni River 50 06 56N; 05 01 51W. This large oil tanker of 5,807 tons put to sea on 20 January, 1940, for machinery trials, following repairs in Falmouth Docks. Unfortunately for her, either a German submarine or an aircraft had come in close during the night and laid magnetic mines in the swept channel. The tanker caused one of these to detonate and she sank one and three-quarter miles due south of Pendennis Point in 20m.

Due to her position in the channel, the *Caroni River* had to be demolished using explosives, and the wreck lies in three parts, close together with a least depth of 17m. A second section lies at 50 07 00N; 05 01 52W, and the third at 50 07 04N; 05 01 54W. The second section is interesting since mixed up with the wreckage is an unidentified trawler – and at least two live depth charges containing 750lb of high explosive.

97

67 N. G. Peterson 50 07 06N; 05 03 01W. This wreck lies some three quarters of a mile west of the *Caroni River*, in roughly the same depth. She was a Danish steamship of 1,282 tons, 239ft by 36ft by 19ft, built in 1898. She was carrying 1,900 tons of iron ore from Bilbao to Newport, when she collided with the Norwegian SS *Siri* on 13 March, 1918. Her remains, which were flattened, lie in 19m, the highest point being 3.5m above the sea bed. [Decca position: SW Chain. Red (A) 22.24; Green 33.58; Purple 71.71.]

68 Leon Martin 50 08 00N; 05 01 06W. The *Leon Martin* was a casualty of a magnetic mine on 13 November, 1940. This British motor tanker of 1,951 tons was on passage from Swansea to Hamble with 2,300 tons of diesel oil when there was a massive explosion beneath her bow, 202 degrees and 1,050 yards from the St Anthony Light. She sank with the loss of 16 of her 25-man crew.

69 Jersey Queen 50 06 02N; 04 58 21.5W. An armed British merchant steamship of 910 tons, the *Jersey Queen* was sailing from Blyth to Plymouth carrying 1,158 tons of coal. She detonated a mine in the approaches to Falmouth Harbour, and sank 1½ miles and 160 degrees from St Anthony light. She went down on 6 October, 1940, killing two of her 14 man crew. The wreck lies in 60m depth, standing 5m off the hard shale bottom. Her bell was recovered in the early 1980s, confirming the identification. [Decca position: SW Chain. Red (A) 23.1; Green (H) 43.1.]

70 Endeavour 50 05 57N; 04 57 51W. This was a 36ft wooden fishing vessel, which snagged a wreck in 58m on 12 November, 1981, capsized and went down 3.6 miles from St Anthony Point.

71 Unidentified coaster When investigated by divers, the *Endeavour* was found to be lying close to a steel coaster of about 150 tons, which was presumably the cause of the accident. The coaster remains unidentified, but lies in [Decca position: SW Chain. Red (A) 23.44, Green (H) 42.22.]

72 Lord Snowden 50 05 44N; 04 57 12W. A steel steam trawler of 444 tons, built in 1934 as the *Tamura*, requisitioned by the Navy in August 1939 as an armed anti-submarine escort, which was lost following collision on 13 April, 1942, that cut her in two. The wreck stands 20ft (6m) proud of the sea bed in 196ft (60m). A bell, bearing her old name of *Tamura*, was recovered by divers in the 1980s. [Decca position: SW Chain. Red (A) 23.37, Green (H) 40.80.]

73 Rinovia 50 05 50N; 04 58 57.5W. Another hired Admiralty trawler of World War Two vintage, a 429-ton steel steam trawler built in 1931 and requisitioned as a minesweeper in August, 1939. She was lost after detonating a mine on 2 November, 1940. Least depth is 48m in 56m. The wreck is owned by K. Dunstan, is said to be covered in trawl nets. [Decca position: SW Chain. Red (A) 23.58, Green (H) 43.5.]

74 HMS Torrent 50 05 41 5N; 04 58.3W. A steel hulled steam yacht of 344 tons, built in 1930 as the SY *Anna Marie*, she was requisitioned by the Navy in September 1939, converted into an anti-submarine yacht and renamed *Torrent* in

1941. On 6 April, 1941, she detonated a mine off Falmouth in 57m and sank. She is reported to stand 5m clear of the bottom, but there are no known reports as to her condition.

75 Unidentified wreck 50 05 36N; 04 55 22W. Known locally as the *Big Eastern*, this is a large wreck lying in 60m. The site has been dived, but few details are known, except that rows of square ports have been seen, suggesting a small liner.

76 Unidentified wreck 50 05 36N; 05 05 32W. Some sort of steel vessel or wreckage measuring 76ft in length, standing 2m proud of the sea bed in 9m depth. It was discovered by accident in May 1986, when a boat fouled its anchor, which had to be cleared by a diver, and may be part of the *Rock Island Bridge* (Site **59**).

77 Spital 50 05 00N; 04 58 20W. This British steel screw steamship of 4,718 tons, built in 1907, was on passage from the Tyne to Savona with coal. She was torpedoed and sunk by the submarine *U-93* on 15 January, 1918. The wreck stands 14m above the sea bed in a general depth of 61m, and has been dived several times.

78 Unidentified wreck 50 04 37N; 05 01 09.5W. A large, as yet unidentified wreck lying in two parts, standing 11m off the sea bed in a general depth of 56m.

79 Unidentified wreck 50 04 37N; 04 52 07W. Another unidentified wreck, located by magnetometer search in 1965, and shows as a large vessel on an echo-sounder; lies in 216ft (66m) depth.

80 Unidentified wreck 50 04 27N; 05 00 34W. The remains of a steel wreck thought to be of about 4,000 tons lying in two parts in 55m – possibly a World War One cattle boat, as animal bones are trawled up around the wreck. Her stern lies on its side, showing twin-propellers, the remainder of the vessel is upside down. A brass engine-room telegraph of British manufacture was recovered from her in the mid 1980s, but the face carries French engine-room markings.

81 HMS Almond 50 03 11N; 04 54 42W. A Tree Class steel trawler, 164ft by 27ft by 10ft, built by the Ardrossan Dockyard Company and launched on 22 May, 1940. Of 505 tons, she was immediately requisitioned as a minesweeper by the Royal Navy and armed with a 12-pounder gun. On 2 February, 1941 she detonated a magnetic mine laid in the Falmouth approaches and sank. [Decca position: SW Chain. Red (B) 27.46, Green (H) 37.62, Purple (B) 60.63.]

82 HMS Tulip II 50 08 43N; 04 56 23W. The remains of a very small, 88-ton armed drifter, built in 1907, requisitioned by the Royal Navy in 1915 and armed with a 3-pounder gun for general anti-submarine duties. Built as the *Tulip*, she had her name changed to *Tulip II* in 1916. She sank 2³/₄ miles west of Zone Point following a collision on 23 August, 1918.

Porthoustock is a good base for exploring the Manacles.

AREA 4:

The Manacles

One of the best diving areas on the south coast of Cornwall, the Manacles, an area of reef approximately one mile square, is bounded by Polnare Cove, just south of Nare Point, and Black Head, just over a mile south of Coverack, and offshore for one mile (except for a few deeper shipwreck sites).

As the name suggests, the Manacles have an evil reputation, since some 110 ships and over a thousand lives have been lost in this relatively small area. There is no comparable reef on the entire south coast of Britain that has caused such a loss of shipping. Its proximity to Falmouth, lying as it does to one side of the southern approach, has been the direct cause of the majority of losses – but even large ships, which should have been many miles offshore, seem to have become entangled with this sprawling and quite lethal mass of rock. Without doubt the Manacles have become extremely popular with diving clubs, for good reason, since the area offers some of the most exciting diving in the county.

To the north of the Manacles, the coastline is of high granite cliffs, broken by three small bays. These high cliffs then give way to the lower ground of Lowland Point, and continue round Coverack Bay, before climbing to present the solid face of rock that runs through to Black Head, the Lizard and on to Mullion.

Because of the cliffs, boat launching places are few and far between, there being only two opposite the Manacles, and one at Coverack that is not always available. However, the position and size of Porthoustock more than compensate, since anywhere around the Manacles is within a 15-minute boat ride of the outer rocks, and the Lizard is only some 40 minutes away. Generally it is an area of deeper water, with very strong tidal streams, protected from any wind between south-west and due north. It is possible to dive on the Manacles or anywhere in its associated area during a full south-westerly gale without discomfort.

Warning Diving the Manacles should not be taken lightly; boats should be well equipped with an engine of sufficient horse power to combat what can be vicious tides. Regrettably, more than ten divers have lost their lives here – it is no place for beginners or the inexperienced.

Coastal dive sites

The previous area ended at Flushing, a small hamlet in the Gillan Creek, just north of Nare Point. Leave Flushing for Roskorwell, then continue down a steep hill into PORTHALLOW, the village overlooking Porthallow Cove.

An old Cornish pilchard fishing village, Porthallow is home of the well known Five Pilchards inn, run by David Tripp, which has been frequented by sport divers since the mid 1950s. Its walls are hung with wreck photographs, artefacts and models relating to the Manacles area generally. Not so many years ago Porthallow was *the* diving spot, from where it was possible to launch and recover boats easily, being well sheltered, and there was a compressor and dive shop on the beach for some time.

Unfortunately, its great popularity and the increase in the number of divers in the early 1960s was its undoing. A number of clubs and groups grossly abused the use of the beach by holding late night parties, playing loud music, lighting bonfires among the fishing boats, and even burning boat rollers when they ran out of firewood. They often departed leaving a dreadful mess for someone else to clean up.

Requests that they behave sensibly and with some consideration for the residents fell on deaf ears, and in retaliation the local residents eventually bought the beach, totally banned any diving activities, and closed down the compressor. Let that be a sober lesson to everyone – all Cornish beaches have an owner, and abuse of other areas frequented by divers could lead to the same treatment, especially at Porthoustock beach.

Having possibly enjoyed half a pint and a pasty at the Five Pilchards, continue on the road out of Porthallow towards St Keverne, and at the top of the hill take the left hand fork for Porthoustock. At the point where the narrow lane to Porthoustock makes a sharp right hand bend, turn off left on to an unmarked tarmac-surfaced lane, towards PORTHKERRIS.

Having taken what is in fact the back road to Porthoustock, at the point where this narrow lane makes a sharp right hand bend it is necessary to turn off half left on to an unmarked, tarmac lane where a sign indicates the way to the Porthkerris Diving Centre, the newest and best equipped such centre in the whole of Cornwall. As you continue down a gentle hill towards the sea, you have the option of continuing down a steeper winding section to Porthkerris beach, which has another entrance off the foreshore to the Centre, or turning off where indicated to the Dive Centre itself at the higher level.

Opposite: Dive Sites in Area 4, The Manacles. This area is covered by Admiralty Charts 154 (approaches to Falmouth); 32 (Falmouth harbour); 18 (Falmouth inner harbour); 147 (Helford River); Ordnance Survey map 204.

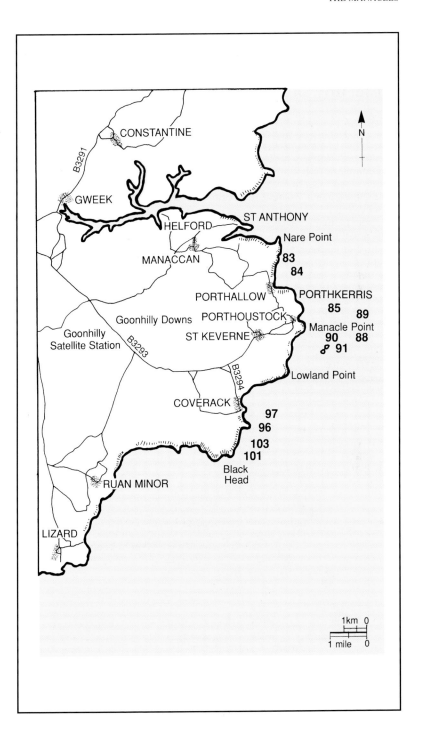

Until World War Two, Porthkerris was an active stone quarry, part of the granite quarry workings that extended from Porthallow through to Porthoustock and then south almost to Lowland Point. The beach area is divided by a large rocky outcrop, now with vehicle access along its full length. Until the late 1970s the large, two storied block building within a security fence was a monitoring station manned by Royal Navy personnel of the Torpedo Trials Unit, based at RNAS Culdrose, near Helston. Anti-submarine air-launched weapon trials were conducted offshore here in the Manacles area for over 30 years, and the remains of a number of old torpedoes remain on the seabed. As far as is known, only inert dummy weapon trials took place here (that is, that the torpedoes and other weapons were fully operational but carried no explosive warheads), it is recommended that any such finds are left alone and reported to the Royal Navy Ordnance Disposal Team at Plymouth. The monitoring station is now a Joint Services Water Sports Activity Centre. Service personnel are allowed access to the Centre's private beaches.

The cove itself was once a BSAC National Diving Site, but since 1993 has been owned and developed by the Anselmi family, who have made a huge investment in its development. Embracing some two miles of coastline, they have created a first class diving facility, with just about every possible amenity, even a children's play area, and local bed and breakfast accommodation can be arranged. Parking is available at any number of sites, with plenty of room for trailers, boat parking, and up to 300 spaces for caravans, mobile homes, and tents, all of which are welcome. It is now also possible to walk along the coastline

Porthkerris.

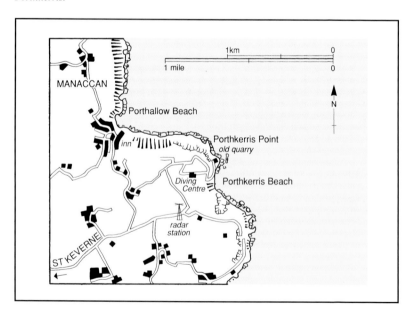

The beach at Porthkerris, where there are good diving facilities.

to Porthallow and Porthoustock village and beach. There is a nominal parking and camping charge, backed up on the beach by an all-day fast-food service and a tracked vehicle that will launch and recover your inflatable down a new slipway created across an otherwise pebble beach, with some sand.

Other facilities include the Porthkerris Farm Kitchen Restaurant, which offers all-day breakfast, snacks, drinks or main course meals; compressed air to 4000psi, cylinder testing, and a workshop maintenance and repair facility covering diving equipment, outboard engines, trailers – even your car if it will not start! A wide range of diver training is available, with a fully-equipped class room that clubs can hire to run their own training sessions. Qualified first-aiders and a diver medic are available on site, and the Centre is planning to install its own compression chamber for dry-dive experience and commercial hire. Haskell tri-mix pumps have been installed for nitrox cylinder charging, and nitrox training courses are available. An emergency 999 telephone is situated on the beach and a public telephone is available inside the complex, as well as public toilets and heated changing room facilities. A retail shop sells a wide range of diving equipment, books, charts, gifts, sweets etc as well as equipment hire, including lanterns for night diving. RIB and hard boat charter are available, also a shuttle service to wrecks and reefs. For details of the Centre contact Mike Anselmi (tel./fax 01326 280620, 280877 or 231339, mobile 0831 820820).

Regarding restrictions, no private compressors are allowed on the beach, nor the carrying of explosives in vehicles or boats, and diesel or petrol fuel will have to be purchased in St Keverne village, some two miles away. Visitors are requested to be considerate to others regarding noise and obstruction. Porthkerris is an area of outstanding natural beauty, much of the nearby coastline being owned by the National Trust. The beach is literally the gateway to the Manacles

Reef, with its many shipwrecks and magnificent underwater scenery. The wreck of the liner *Mohegan* (Site **88**) can be reached within 5 minutes of the slipway, and the well known SS *Volnay* (Site **84**), *Bay of Panama* (Site **83**) and dozens of other exciting wrecks lie within a mile radius. The immediate waterfront beach area offers beginners and snorkellers alike terrific visibility, marine life and safe reasonable depths.

Return uphill to the public highway and turn left at the sharp bend for Porthoustock. Return to the main road. Only a half a mile from the Porthkerris turning will bring you to a very steep and narrow downhill lane leading into the village and cove of PORTHOUSTOCK (pronounced "Proustock"). This was once a pilchard fishing village, and the old lifeboat house still stands at the back of the beach. Until the 1920s, when stone quarrying for road stone became big business here, the sea came right up to where the road runs in front of the lifeboat station. The circular stone structure to one side once held the RNLI flagpole, and the capstan was used to recover not only the lifeboat, but fishing vessels as well. The quarrying caused a great deal of small material to enter the sea, which became ground down by sea action, and slowly caused the cove to silt up completely. This in turn affected the two berths created for small coasters of up to 400 tons to load the granite, and they have been disused since the 1970s, but may be rebuilt and extended, since the quarries are still very active.

The slipway and harbour at Coverack.

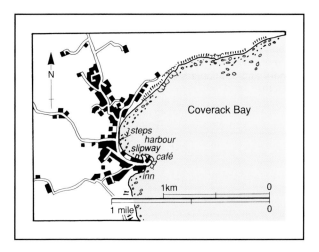

Coverack.

The foreshore of flat, grey stones has created a large vehicle parking area, capable of taking a hundred or more cars. In order to keep some control over the private beach, the area to the north (left looking out to sea) is solely for the use of local residents and local boats. Visitors and divers must keep to the south – do not encroach into the other section, interfere with the fishing boats, their gear, winches, buildings – or take the rope that forms the barrier, which has happened in the past!

In 1992, Cornwall County Council held a meeting with representatives of the different communities on the Lizard Peninsula, to discuss the problems associated with visiting divers. As a result, a number of signs have been put up at popular beaches, including Porthoustock, which read as follows:

Divers – this beach is your gateway to the Manacles. To keep it open, please follow these simple rules.

Do not park cars, trailers, boats or yourselves on the left hand side of the beach as you face the sea. This is reserved for Porthoustock fishermen to launch and winch up their boats.

Do not run compressors on the beach and, before you leave, please put some cash for the beaches upkeep in the box provided.

Other requests are:

No night diving please. Porthkerris is a good alternative location, close at hand.

The roads approaching Porthoustock are narrow and winding. Please drive carefully and slowly.

107

Porthoustock is an easy beach from which to launch and recover, and is very close to a great many offshore wrecks, and of course the Manacles Reef itself, the outlying rocks and Lowland Point – even the Lizard, which is only 30 to 40 minutes away. Clear of the jetties, the maximum depth is 10m, with a grey sand bottom, rocky outcrops, weed and often incredible visibility. At low water, to the right of the mouth of the cove, a small reef is exposed, known as the Veryan Rocks, which offers an abundance of marine life of all sorts, and is excellent for photography.

Round the small headland to the south is the Shark's Fin, a rock named for its obvious resemblance to a dorsal fin, and it was here that the sailing vessel *Andola* came to grief.

A new diving facility based at Porthoustock and Coverack is Lizard Diving Services. They offer a shuttle service using a 5m RIB from Porthoustock beach to anywhere on the Manacles, or special charter trips as far as the Lizard for groups booked in advance. Hard boat charters are also available, and if diving is impossible on the Manacles due to wind conditions, a RIB dive in Mount's Bay, starting from Porthleven, can be arranged instead. The organisation runs a compressor at the back of the Three Tuns Inn at St. Keverne, offering air charging facilities to 4000psi. They also have a lecture and drying room, with wash-down and boat storage facilities at the Little Trevothan Caravan Park, Coverack (tel. 01326 280038).

Take the road going left out of Porthoustock, up a short hill that then levels off, and into the village of St Keverne. Continue on the B3293 from here, then turn off left on to the B3294, which will bring you to the edge of Coverack Bay – a wide sandy bottomed sweep with Lowland Point off on the far left, and the village of COVERACK huddled under the lee of high ground to the right. This is another old Cornish fishing village, with a miniature harbour and quay, disused lifeboat station, thatched cottages, extremely narrow streets and very limited car and trailer parking. Coverack has is a superb launching slip, with water at all states of the tide.

A great many local fishing boats remain afloat on running lines extending from the harbour, and there is still a very strong feeling against "skin-divers" in general, due to countless incidents with crab and keep-pots, and diving gear left strewn everywhere around the quay. It is therefore no surprise that in the window of the Harbour Master's office you will find a notice reading "No skin-divers". Experience has shown that this is not a blanket refusal – but it does require sensible, diplomatic negotiation on the day, face-to-face and not over the telephone. Do not attempt to beach dive or launch a boat at Coverack without first getting permission. Contact the Harbour Master, Vivian Carey (tel. 01326 280583).

The size of Coverack prohibits a large diving party, but one inflatable with a small group, depending on the fishing season, congestion, weather and circumstances on the day, may be given permission to launch and recover. As an alternative, a number of local divers make use of a set of steps to the foreshore part way along the sea front road, clear of the houses, but opposite some gift shops. Inflatables have been launched here over the guard rails and down the steps, but it is practical only with a small boat and engine.

Coverack Bay is shallow with a maximum depth of 10m, but is a good starting point from which to explore either Lowland Point, or the high cliffs towards the

*The Paris Hotel at Coverack was named after a liner
shipwrecked nearby. It has excellent beer.*

Lizard. Chynhalls Point, the wrecks of the *Pindos* (Site **96**), *Veritas* (Site **125**), *Plantagenet* (Site **99**), *Briel* (Site **100**), *Godolphin* (Site **101**), *Clan Alpine* (Site **102**) and *Dispatch* (Site **103**), as well as deeper wrecks, are all accessible from here.

Facilities include shops, hotels, accommodation and the Paris Hotel, named after the liner *Paris*, which stranded on Lowland Point in May 1899, and remained ashore for two months before being re-floated and saved. There are also public toilets, a free but limited car park behind the lifeboat station, and a pay car park at the approach to the village before the road reaches the waterfront.

Leave the village via the B3294 to join the B3293, continue for 2¹/₂ miles and, where the Goonhilly satellite aerial dishes come into view, take the left hand turning for Kennack and Cadgwith.

Offshore dive sites and wrecks

83 Bay of Panama 50 04 18N; 05 04 31W. A most tragic shipwreck, in which some of the crew were found frozen to death in the rigging, on the morning after the Great Blizzard of 1891. A four-masted, steel square-rigged ship of 2,282 tons, built by Harland and Wolff at Belfast in 1883, she was often described as one of the finest sailing ships ever built.

She left Calcutta on 18 November, 1890, with 13,000 bales of jute, destined for the mills at Dundee. By 9 March the following year she was close to the Lizard, caught in a north-easterly gale accompanied by driving snow. This storm was to become the worst remembered in the West Country, when hundreds of animals froze to death in the fields, the railway was blocked for days, and four ships were lost around the Manacles alone.

At just after 1 o'clock in the morning of 10 March, a huge single wave swept her deck from end to end, taking every boat with it, and minutes later the *Bay of Panama* plunged into the cliffs just south of Nare Point. As she struck she swung to starboard, her bow pointing almost east; one mast came crashing down, and the second mate managed to get off one distress rocket before a wave swept him overboard to his death.

The same wave also flooded the cabin, and carried the captain, his wife, the cook, steward and four apprentices into the sea where they drowned. The mate ordered the remaining crew into the shrouds, to get above the freezing sea, where they remained for some time. The bosun went out of his mind and jumped into the sea, and the extreme cold took the lives of many of the men, who were soaked in spray and ill dressed for such terrible exposure. Six died from the cold where they were and remained frozen in the rigging, others fell into the sea. She

The magnificent four-master Bay of Panama (Site 83) in the shallows off Porthallow, a few days after the she drove ashore in 1891 with the loss of twenty lives.

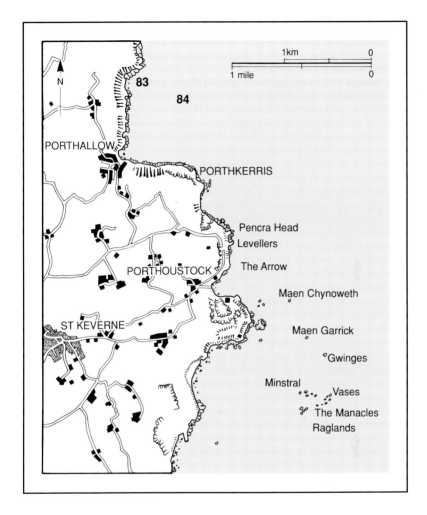

The Manacles, showing the locations of the
Bay of Panama (Site 83) and the Volnay (Site 84).

was found at daybreak by a farmer out looking for sheep, the bowsprit of the wreck less than 50ft from the cliffs.

A breeches buoy was rigged and 17 survivors out of the original crew of 40 were brought ashore, taken to St Keverne and thawed out. The cargo was salvaged and the wreck broken up, but there is still much to be seen, with bottom plates, an anchor, the rudder and mast fittings. The ship's bell, which hung for many years in the belfry of the Helford Church, is now in Manaccan church.

The bell from the SS Volnay (Site 84), sunk off Porthallow in 1917, hangs outside the front door of a retired solicitor in Helston, following its recovery by Martin Vinnicombe. The Volnay is a popular dive because of the large number of brass shell fuse heads and pieces of lead shot that can be found at the wreck site.

84 Volnay 50 04 21N; 05 03 26.2W. Many shipwrecks have brought benefit to the locals around the Manacles in different ways, but this British steamship of 4,610 tons outshone them all. Homeward bound from Canada with luxury goods and ammunition, she detonated a contact mine off the Manacles on 14 December, 1917, and was brought into Porthallow Bay. Thinking she would remain afloat, she was anchored a quarter of a mile off Porthkerris beach, where she sank in 21m.

An obliging wind blew her floating cargo into Porthallow, where it piled up, and soon the beach was stacked with coffee, tea, butter, potato crisps, cigarettes, jam, peanut butter and tinned meats. The wreck, 365ft by 52ft, was abandoned until 1919, when salvage work took place, but the presence of the ammunition precluded the use of explosives, so she could not be flattened. It was not until after World War Two that many thousands of 3.5-inch 8-pounder shells were recovered for their brass cases and Mk. V (L) No. 80 shell caps. These were anti-personnel ammunition, which on detonation ejected a large number of small lead balls rather like a huge shotgun.

While the wreck has been picked over by thousands of divers, shell cases and noses are still found, all of which should be treated with caution – they may contain high explosive. Her bow is still intact with her anchor windlass upside down, the highest part of the wreck being her two boilers at 13m depth.

Transit marks for the *Volnay* are shown in the upper diagram opposite.

85 Lady Dalhousie 50 03 21N; 05 02 54. Just why this British steamship, registered in Greenock, was wrecked will never be known. Only three years old,

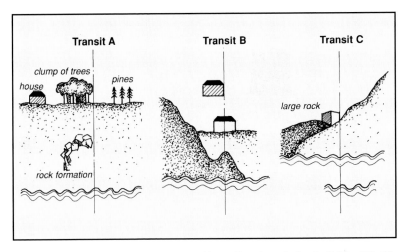

Above: Transit marks for the Volnay (Site 83).

Below: Transit marks for the Lady Dalhousie (Site 84).

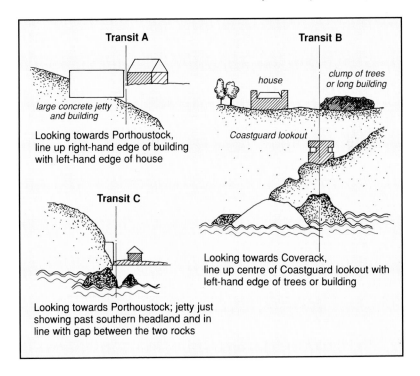

the 1,291-ton ship was on passage from London to Newport in ballast to load coal, when at midnight on 12 April, 1884, in bright moonlight and a calm sea, she crashed into the Maen Chynoweth rock (also known as the Morah). Captain Murchie put her engine to full-astern but failed to move her, and soon it was realised her bow and forward hold were full of water.

Several local tugs went out to assist, but she was impaled on the rocks, and became a total wreck. Her stores and materials were sold off, the hull going to a Mr Edward Trerize for £175, who in turn sold her to the Western Marine Salvage Company of Penzance, who recovered her engine, boilers, and main components.

This is a pleasant beginner's dive, subject to some tide. In summer there is not much to see, as the wreck is blanketed in weed, but a spring time dive shows vast areas of steel still.

Transit marks for the *Lady Dalhousie* are shown in the lower diagram on page 113.

86 Andola 50.03.12N; 05.03.13W. The bow of this 2,093-ton, full-rigged, steel sailing vessel almost touches the Shark's Fin rock. Carrying 2,100 tons of wheat between Puget Sound and Falmouth (for orders), she had suffered terrible sea conditions during her Atlantic crossing, taking 180 days to reach England, and was two months overdue when she reached Falmouth.

Tugs brought out much needed fresh water and food, but there was to be no rest for the hard pressed crew, since they received instructions from the owners to sail at once for Hull. Within an hour of leaving Falmouth on the evening tide, they were off the Eddystone, but a change in the wind forced them to tack south-east, until they sighted lights on the coast of France. Another long tack, and the next thing they saw was the Lizard light – they were back where they had started!

At 7.30pm, during a snow storm, when visibility was reduced to a few yards, one of the apprentices reported he could hear a bell tolling to seaward. Realising he must be inside the Manacles buoy and in grave danger, Captain Passmore ordered the topsails furled and attempted to stand off. Fifteen minutes later the crew were thrown off their feet as the *Andola* crunched into the north side of the Shark's Fin rock, only a short distance from Porthoustock beach.

Signals of distress were made, some unintentional, since a burning flare was accidentally dropped in the magazine, setting off some bomb-rockets, one of which burst up through the deck from below, injuring the young lad who had first heard the Manacles bell-buoy. All 28 crew were taken off by the local lifeboat. As her cargo absorbed sea water through holes in her plates it swelled, her deck and side plates split and she was declared a total loss.

The wreck is an easy, pleasant dive, in about 10m, with large areas of steel plates and the bottom of the ship, among which interesting pieces of brass and copper are still found. An anchor chain survives near her bow, where at least three 8-inch brass letters from her bow plates have been found. The A is displayed on the wall of the Five Pilchards inn at Porthoustock, and the D in the Charlestown Shipwreck Centre – both found by the author in the 1960s.

87 The Manacles Reef This was once an extension of the granite cliffs extending from Porthoustock south to Lowland Point, which at some time in the past was

The Andola (Site 86) aground on the Manacles in 1895.

eroded and then drowned, probably during the last ice age. The reef covers an area roughly one mile square, out to the Voices (or Vases) rocks, which has left a great many peaks and troughs, with a plateau in the south-east corner.

Many of the rocks come to within 0.3m on a low spring tide, but never break the surface except in rough weather. Others dry to a considerable height, but on high water spring tides there is almost nothing to see except for the top of Carn-du, and this can be very deceptive. Depths range from a few metres to 35m, with many spectacular walls, drop-offs, caves and tunnels, falling off into very deep water outside the Voices.

WARNING Unless you are familiar with the Manacles or have someone aboard with local knowledge, great care should be taken when navigating around the reef, otherwise you will find yourself aground with a great hole in your boat, or short of some propeller blades. Take care to navigate around the Manacles carefully and slowly, with someone standing in the bows to look for obstructions. The tidal hazards of the Manacles Reef are severe, and can even be fatal for a diver. Diving should not take place on the outer Manacles during spring tides except at slack water, since they reach 2 to 2½ knots, depending on the wind. The tide table for Porthoustock beach or Falmouth will not give the time of slack water. On the outer rocks of the Manacles slack is 4.5 hours prior to high water at Falmouth, and 2 hours after slack water at Porthoustock. If you intend to anchor on the Manacles anywhere, especially over any of the steel wrecks, make sure that the last 10ft of your anchor line is good solid chain, otherwise your mooring can easily chafe through in a single tide – you will lose your anchor and go adrift.

If you merely wish to pass inside the Manacles on your way south, to Lowlands, Coverack or the Lizard, there is a safe deep water inside channel, which basically follows the coastline with almost no obstructions. There are also safe channels through the Manacles themselves, but these will have to be learned from experience or local knowledge. One will take you southward of the Maen Chynoweth, Little Morah and Maen Garrick, out to the Voices – the most seaward rocks, which cover at high water spring tides but at low water present three distinct peaks. On the outside of these rocks is where the liner SS *Mohegan* (Site **88**) was lost, and just inside the SS *Spyridion Vagliano* (Site **89**).

A large fairly flat plateau of reef is indicated by the Carn-du rocks, which show at all states of the tide, and on the south-west side you will find the remains of the SS *Juno* (Site **91**). Still on the Shallow Ground, as it is known, to the north-west you will find the remains of HMS *Primrose* and her carronade guns (Site **90**), and between the two a boiler and engine of an unknown steamship wreck. Evidence of shipwreck exists all over the Manacles – more than a hundred vessels have ended their days in the area, extending down to Lowland Point, and many new sites have yet to be found.

One mile along the inshore channel following the coastline, past Godrevy Cove, is another patch of shallow ground known as Maen Land, which dries to about 0.8m. Inside this area, between the rocks and the shore you will find anchors and traces of the emigrant ship *John* (Site **92**).

Continue down the coast towards Coverack, and the last point of land is Lowland Point, the southern extremity of the Manacles, consisting of a series of shallow rock reefs stretching offshore for a considerable distance, with the Little Wrea rock, which dries to 5m. The Lowlands area offers much potential but is seldom dived much, because it is so shallow, but it holds many shipwreck remains, mostly jumbled together. Here you can find the sailing ships *Port Chalmers* (Site **93**) and *Glenbervie* (wrecked in 1901), the French collier Gap (Site **94**), the SS *Mina Cantaquin* (Site **95**) and the MV *Fauvette*.

Transit marks for the Mohegan (Site 88). Aligning St Keverne church spire with the easternmost rock in the Manacles at low water and then diving 60 to 70 metres further east is claimed to be the easiest transit.

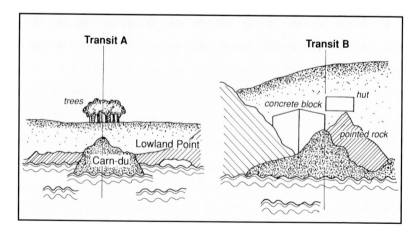

Above: A brass letter N and a ventilation grille recovered from the wreck of the Mohegan (Site 88).

Below: A range of pottery and brass items also recovered by the author from various Cornish wrecks. The dinner plate is from the Mohegan.

88 Mohegan This is the best known and most dived wreck on the Manacles – on Bank Holiday weekends up to 32 inflatables have been counted moored over the site at one time, perhaps 96 divers on one wreck! Her loss was a major tragedy. Owned by the Atlantic Transport Company, this 7,000-ton liner had started life on a slipway of Earle's Shipbuilding Company at Hull in 1897, to be launched the following year as the *Cleopatra*.

Just prior to launch she was purchased by the new owners on 29 July, 1898, and sailed on her maiden voyage. Her completion had been rushed to avoid a late delivery penalty clause, and there were many defects, not least of which were several leaks. She had to enter dry dock at New York on her maiden voyage to have them repaired, and other work was done on the Tyne on her return.

A luxurious modern ship of her day, she carried sixty first-class passengers, a crew of 97, and cattlemen to attend animals on deck in pens. Four-masted, with a single funnel amidships, her four boilers and triple-expansion engine gave her 5,500nhp and a maximum speed of 14-knots. With an overall length of 482ft (147m), a beam of 52ft (16m) and depth of 36ft (11m) she was huge; eight watertight bulkheads and steam pumps were capable of emptying each compartment in turn. An enclosed bridge extended the full width of the ship, reaching back over the engine room, above which were a music saloon, a smoking room and staterooms decorated in the latest Victorian fashion.

She sailed from Tilbury under Captain Griffiths on 13 October, 1898, this time as the *Mohegan*, with 53 passengers, 97 crew and 7 cattlemen. A general cargo included spirits, beer, lead, tin, antimony, artificial flowers, church ornaments, glass, seed and other items. Off Plymouth, the Coastguard signalled her 10 miles offshore, but from there her course and the cause of her loss remains a mystery, since the truth died with the ship – every deck officer going down with her.

Four people saw the liner in her last few moments – boatman Snell of the Falmouth Coastguard, Mr Fooks, Customs Officer and Receiver of Wreck at Falmouth, James Hill, coxswain of the Porthoustock lifeboat, and Charles May, boatman to the Coverack Coastguard. All saw the brilliantly lit liner as she entered Falmouth Bay, and knew instinctively that she was going to hit the Manacles, since no vessel that size should have been so close inshore. Coxswain Hill called out his lifeboat crew and had the boat almost ready to launch before the *Mohegan* struck, an action that saved many lives.

When the ship hit the rocks, the passengers were sitting down to dinner, and the first minor shock and rumble almost went unnoticed, which was almost certainly the moment when she lost her rudder on Penvin Rock. Her engines were stopped, but, presumably incapable of being steered, she crashed full into the seaward face of the Voices.

Several compartments and the forward hold filled with water, and at that moment a design fault in the construction showed up – her generators, located down on the deck plates of the engine-room, were immersed in sea water and drowned, before the level reached the boiler fires – and all the lights went out. She sank within ten minutes of stranding, listing heavily to starboard.

There were many tragic stories told over the following months, and the press reported little else for weeks but the loss of the *Mohegan* and 106 lives. The headless corpse of Captain Griffiths was washed ashore in Caernarfon Bay three months later, still wearing his uniform jacket. A mass burial of some of the victims took place in St Keverne churchyard, the site marked today by a simple cross.

The wreck is an unforgettable dive, with her bow in some 15m and the remainder in 26m. Souvenirs abound, with china plates, portholes, brass letters from her name, toilet fittings, and ingots of tin and lead all still being recovered.

Transit marks for the *Mohegan* are shown in the diagram on page 116.

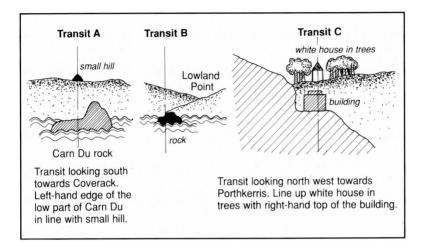

Above: Transit marks for the Spyridion Vagliano (Site 89).

Below: Transit marks for the John (Site 92).

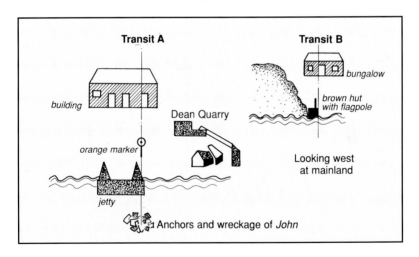

89 Spyridion Vagliano 50 02 75N; 05 02 06W. A Greek owned steamship belonging to the Vagliano Line and built in Sunderland in 1883, this vessel of 1,110 tons was approaching on Falmouth with a cargo of barley from Novorossiysk on the Black Sea, when the struck the Manacles at midnight on 8 February, 1890. Her crew managed to launch two lifeboats, but Captain Cambitzio drowned just off Godrevy beach attempting to get ashore with eight seamen, when the boat capsized. Thirteen other crew in the second lifeboat were never seen again, and it is presumed that they capsized in deep water.

By daylight, the eight survivors having raised the alarm, the lifeboat was out looking for the missing men and the wreck, but found nothing, no part of the vessel showing anywhere. The wreck lies a little to the north of the Voices, and it is an easy swim from the *Mohegan*, since it is in shallower water. Nothing much remains except her double bottom, plates and boiler, lying on a sandy bottom. Her bell is believed to hang in the Southsea BSAC clubroom.

Transit marks for the *Spyridion Vagliano* are shown in the upper diagram on page 119.

90 Primrose 50 02 42N; 05 02 58W. One of so many tragic shipwreck stories concerning the Manacles, HM man-of-war *Primrose*, like the transport vessel *Dispatch* (Site **103**), had been used to transport men and equipment to the Peninsular War. The 18-gun warship, captained by James Mein, carried 126 officers and men plus six passengers. She was on her way to La Coruña to bring back elements of the army, but struck the outer Manacles on 22 January, 1809, in a fearful hurricane, accompanied by snow.

Six local fishermen from Porthoustock put out in the largest rowing boat in the village, reached the wreck on Dolly Lay, and brought back the sole survivor – a young lad named John Meaghen. Some 110 bodies were recovered, of which 104 were buried in St Keverne churchyard.

Two 32-pounder iron carronade guns recovered from the wreck of the brig Primrose (Site 90), which was lost on the Manacles in 1809. The guns are 4ft 6in long and each weigh about a ton.

The Norwegian steamship Juno (Site 91) was wrecked near Carn-du in fog in 1915.

Her guns were 18-pounder carronades, all of which have been recovered except for three that still lie part buried in sand in the shallow area north-west of Carn-du. Her 10ft rudder, complete with gudgeons, has been raised by Northampton BSAC and stands in their clubhouse. Brass and copper hull fastening pins are still found, also copper sheathing and nails.

91 Juno 50.02.33N; 05.02.54W. A small Norwegian steamship of 611 tons, which struck on the southern side of Carn-du on 3 July, 1915. On passage from Le Tréport to Partington (on the Manchester Ship Canal) in ballast, she encountered fog and at 7.50am became a total wreck. The 13 man crew launched their two boats, but as their ship was firmly aground and not going to founder under them they returned several times to recover belongings, instruments, stores and the ship's papers, before being taken to Falmouth on board the tug *Perran*.

Built at Sunderland as the *Munroe* in 1877 by A. Simey and Company and owned by B. Stolt Nielson of Norway, the 176ft vessel was heavily salvaged by a Falmouth company, but her engine and boiler still can be found among scattered steel plates, which lie on the edge of a shelf that drops to 23m.

92 John 50.02.45N; 05.03.40W. On 3 May, 1855, the 486-ton Plymouth barque *John* left the Sound carrying 149 adults, 98 children, and 16 babies, all emigrants for Quebec, plus 16 crew – a total of 279 people, under Captain Edward Rawle. Twenty-four hours later, 193 of them were dead, drowned when she was wrecked off Godrevy beach, and her captain under arrest for deserting his charge, for which he received a prison sentence.

Worried because they had not sighted the Lizard light, the mate of the *John* expressed his fears to the captain several times, but received only the reassurance "You'll see it fast enough when we get there." In fact the vessel was so close inshore that the Lizard was obscured by Black Head, and the mate had every reason to be worried.

The ship struck the outer Manacles just before midnight, was swept over the shallow ground, and sank about half a mile offshore in 9m, from where the modern Dean Quarry buildings stand. Two large anchors and several pieces of wreck still survive among the jumble of rocks and gullies.

Transit marks for the *John* are shown in the lower diagram on page 119.

93 Port Chalmers 50.02.35N; 05.05.50W. One of the earlier sailing ship wrecks near Lowland Point, this 1,495-ton iron barque of Glasgow had been at anchor in Falmouth's Carrick Roads for over two months awaiting sale of her sugar cargo from Semarang in Java, when on 20 March, 1886, Captain Hamilton received instructions to proceed to Liverpool and discharge.

The *Port Chalmers* left port at 11am in tow of the tug *Emperor*, cast off, and headed down towards the Lizard. At 8.30pm breakers were sighted ahead, she struck twice and ground to a halt just to the north of the Davas Rock. Salvage tugs attempted to get her clear, but in very shallow water and badly holed, she was eventually abandoned. The wreck was sold on the beach for scrap, and either as a shallow dive, or a wrecker's walk at low tide, much of the remains can still be seen.

94 Gap 50 02 20N; 05 04 00W. This wreck, the remains of which are somewhat mixed up with those of the *Port Chalmers*, lies a little further south. A French collier of 22,160 tons, on passage from Rouen to Barry in ballast, was another victim of the shallows around Lowland Point, on 24 February, 1928. Bollards, a winch and other remains are to be found among the rocks.

95 Mina Cantaquin 50 02 00N; 05 04 06W. This 662-ton Spanish coaster was homeward bound to Gijón from Newcastle-upon-Tyne with a cargo of pitch when she struck a rock off Chynhalls Point, Coverack, in a south-west gale. She was badly holed forward and taking water; distress signals were fired and her captain attempted to get her into the shallows of Coverack Bay, on 4 November, 1951.

The crew of 17 were rescued by the lifeboat, leaving the abandoned vessel to drift ashore on Lowlands, the only life on board being the ship's dog, Pedro. Efforts were made to save him, but he drowned when the wreck broke up. The 1952 edition of Admiralty Chart 777 marks the wreck with a "stranded" symbol. As with the others here, she is very broken, but parts are still identifiable.

96 Pindos 50 00 58N; 05 05 14W. Launched in June 1890 by Williamsons of Workington as the *Eusemere*, this was a four-masted steel barque of 2,512 tons, originally owned by the firm of Fisher and Sprott of London. In 1896 she was sold to B. Wencke of Hamburg, and in late February 1911 left Hamburg for Port Talbot to load coal briquettes for Mejillones in Chile. She arrived back at Falmouth on 1 February, 1912, then left for Hamburg under tow of the tug *Ancona*.

The two vessels were hardly clear of Falmouth Bay when the wind changed round to the south-east, forcing both ships down the coast towards the Lizard. The *Pindos* went ashore on Chynhalls Point, less than half a mile from Coverack village. It was but a short distance for the Coverack lifeboat to reach the wreck, and under the glare of her acetylene searchlights, she rescued the crew by breeches buoy.

On 20 February, 1912, the wreck was sold for £225. Assisted by salvagers and gales she was reduced to a heap of steel plates and girders, which still lie on the reef in shallow water.

97 Veritas 50 00 45N; 05 05 00W. A Norwegian steamship of 672 tons net, registered at Bergen, the *Veritas* was en-route from Norway to south Wales with pit wood when a collision forced her to enter Portland harbour for repairs. Following temporary work to cure several leaks, Captain Tollefsen sailed again, but off the Lizard on 4 August, 1907, she started to take in a lot of water.

The leaks soon became serious and her pumps were unable to prevent the depth of water reaching her boilers, which were soon extinguished. Leaving the ship in some haste, Captain Tollefsen, his wife and 14 crew rowed to Coverack, leaving the *Veritas* at anchor. Three Falmouth tugs attempted to take her in tow, but with two anchors down and no steam to power the windlass, she could not easily be moved. Both cables were eventually slipped, and she was taken in tow, but off Coverack, on her way to Falmouth she lifted her stern high in the air and her bow plunged down to hit the bottom. This left her standing almost vertical, and she remained in this strange position for two whole days, finally losing the buoyancy of her stern and foundering. She landed on the sea bed

The four-masted steel barque Pindos (Site 96) was stranded off Chynhalls Point in February 1912 while carrying a cargo of nitrate between Chile and Germany.

upside down, and there was hope that the salvage steamer *Etna* – brought down from Lundy where she had been salvaging the battleship HMS *Montague* – could get her into shallow water using pontoons and lighters, but the attempt failed.

The wreck lies in some 27m, still upside down, broken to a certain extent, her engine room blown open in recent years by explosives to extract her condenser. Owned by the author between 1969 and 1991, she now belongs to John Ellis, of Seaways, Penryn, so please do not remove anything from her.

98 Rose 50 00 50N; 05 05 30W. Built by Blackwell of London in 1845, the *Rose* was a three-masted, 150-ton, 119ft schooner rigged steamship owned by the London and Limerick Steamship Company. She left London for Ireland with 15 crew and 30 steerage passengers, as well as a general cargo of agricultural implements, wheat and flour, and stranded on the Suthens rocks at Merys Point during the morning of 10 July, 1866. After she struck her boats were got ready, and passengers and luggage were landed at Coverack within the hour.

Captain Sweetland and crew remained with the ship, removing all her cargo except for the perishable goods, then stripped the wreck of her gear and fittings. On 16 July she broke in two, and was sold by auction for scrap. As with the other shallow water strandings here, she can be found in the 9m zone, very broken but identifiable as a steamship.

99 Plantagenet 50 00 45N; 05 05 30W. This 648-ton steamship joined the other wrecks between Black Head and Coverack on 20 March, 1897, when she ran headlong onto Chynhalls Point in dense fog, drifted clear of the rocks and sank. Bound for Runcorn from St Valéry with a cargo of flints, at high tide her masts were said to be under water, but that seems unlikely bearing in mind she lies in only 13m, so it is more likely they broke off.

Launched in 1883 by Allsop and Sons, Preston, her owners were J. Bacon of Liverpool, who sold the vessel for scrapping where she lay. The wreck can be identified by the large amount of flints lying on the bottom, but there is surprisingly little iron work remaining.

100 Briel 50 00 25N; 05 05 48W. This must have been a magnificent ship, a Dutch 36-gun frigate carrying 350 crew and troops. On her maiden voyage, bound for Lisbon and Demerara (now in Guyana), she struck the coast "half a cable's length from the land, about a mile to the westward of Coverack" on 22 December, 1791.

A local boat rowed out on hearing her distress guns, found the wreck and brought a Dutch lieutenant back to the village. There he explained the predicament, that there was 10ft of water in the ship's hold, and requested every boat available to save his men. Although laid up for the winter, all the seine fishing boats were launched, saving all on board except six, who drowned. The locals did well out of the *Briel* – an agreement with the Dutch gave them one third of the value of anything saved, but they cheated by throwing much of the valuable cargo overboard into the shallows before they reached the harbour, which others recovered and hid on shore. They also plundered the wreck at night of everything they could carry off, and when after five days on shore the upper deck parted from the rest of the ship and came into the shallows, hundreds of people descended on the ship and hacked what they could to pieces.

Divers preparing for action on the beach at Porthoustock.

The wreck was discovered in the late 1980s, a few iron cannon and cannonballs, plus brass fittings and some coins confirming the identification. There are bits and pieces left still, but they are deep in crevices and gullies in less than 6m. A single iron cannon a little way offshore may mark the main part of the wreck.

101 Godolphin 50 00 20N; 05 05 55W. Carrying a cargo of iron ore from Bilbao to Newport, the iron steamship *Godolphin*, of Cardiff, 235ft by 33ft by 16ft, 1,140 tons, built in Sunderland by William Pickersgill and Sons in 1881, ran ashore on the rocks under Black Head on 9 January, 1888. It was nearly low water when she struck at 5pm, and looking down from the overhanging cliffs, the local Coastguard reported "a two-masted vessel, fore and aft rigged, with a black funnel, is on the rocks directly under the point of Black Head, heading westward. She is partly under water, and appears abandoned."

Captain McStewart and his crew had abandoned ship in their boats as soon as she struck, but when advised that it was safe to return they went back, recovering their belongings and the ship's papers. The vessel was a near wreck by 15 January, her mainmast and funnel having collapsed, only her foremast left standing. She was sold as a wreck where she lay, and the Western Marine Salvage Company took off her engine block, boilers and winches, leaving the remainder of the ship to the sea.

102 Clan Alpine 50 00 15N; 05 06 00W. Owned by the River Paraná Steamship Company and launched in Glasgow in 1862, this steamship of 1,538 tons was sailing from South America to Liverpool via Antwerp when she ran into a blizzard

125

off the Lizard on 2 February, 1873. The crew were blinded by the snow and uncertain of their position, and the *Clan Alpine* blundered into Black Head, where Captain Nelson and 13 crew members drowned, the remaining 17 crew and one passenger getting away in a lifeboat.

Her cargo was rich, and included timber, silver ore, copper bars, hides, potatoes, rapeseed and flour. Extensive salvage work was conducted to save as much of it as possible, after which the Penzance based Western Marine Salvage Company took away the engine, boilers, winches and other heavy items, leaving the sea to break up the hull. She is a shallow dive, but interesting, and closer inshore among the rocks there is a single iron cannon, some marble and brass bits and pieces, probably from the *Dispatch*.

103 Dispatch 50 00 15N; 05 06 00W. Lost during the same night as the HMS *Primrose* (Site **118**), on 22 January, 1809, the transport vessel *Dispatch* was not driven ashore near Lowland Point as has often been reported, but drove into the high cliffs close to Black Head.

Commanded by Captain Barclay, the 7th Dragoons were but a shadow of the fine unit that had left England to fight in the Peninsular War, where Sir John Moore's army met a superior French force commanded by Napoleon. A retreat turned into a rout (they were reduced three officers, 72 men and 36 horses) that ended at La Coruña, where the 7th Dragoons embarked on the *Dispatch* and made for Falmouth, to end their days under Black Head, near Coverack.

Only seven survived the wreck, among the dead being Major Cavendish, the 25-year-old son of Lord Cavendish of Eastbourne, and Lieutenant the Honourable Edward Waldgrove, third son of the 4th Earl of Waldgrove. The bodies were identified by fellow officers due to have been aboard the Dispatch, but who at the last moment changed to the transport *Barfleur*, which arrived home safely.

104 War Tune 49 59 00N; 05 04 00W. A British Standard ship of 2,045 tons, built in 1917, which was torpedoed and sunk by the German submarine *U-53* on 9 December, 1917, one and a half miles SSE from Black Head. She was carrying a cargo of coal from Barry. No diving details of the wreck are known, but the wreck is 261ft long, and lies in 40m.

105 Cape Finisterre 50 02 09.5N; 05 01 40W. Torpedoed and sunk by the German submarine *UC-17*, commanded by Kapitänleutnant Branscheid, on 2 November, 1917, about one mile SSE of the Manacle buoy. The 4,380-ton, 385ft ship was carrying a cargo of steel ingots from New York to Falmouth, and claimed the lives of 35 of her crew, including her master.

Extensive salvage was conducted on the wreck after World War Two by an Italian diving company, who recovered hundreds of tons of ingots, but nothing of the wreck's present condition is known. She lies in a general depth of 61m, the least depth being 51m.

106 Bamse 50 02 26.5N; 05 01 51.5W. Built as the SS *Thomas Coates* in 1881, this 1,001-ton, 226ft British vessel fell victim to a torpedo fired by the German submarine *UB-112* on 2 October, 1918. She was carrying a cargo of patent fuel from Swansea to Falmouth, and ten men died in the explosion. She went down in a position given at the time as "5.5 mile East, three-quarters N. from the Lizard", in a depth of 61m, the top of the wreck being at 50m. She was located in 1971 by accident, when Vickers were testing their submersible *Venturer-Pisces*, so the position is accurate.

107 Krosfund 50 02 30N; 05 01 00W. Another victim of World War One, this 1,737-ton Norwegian steamship, built by Svithun Linjen A/S in 1904, was on passage in convoy from Newport to Rouen with coal, when she was torpedoed and sunk by a German submarine on 22 November, 1917 off the Manacles. At 259ft in length, with a 37ft beam, she makes a very substantial target in a maximum depth of 62m.

108 Lydie 50 03 00N; 05 00 40W. One of the Natal Line ships, the 2,559-ton *Lydie*, built in 1899, was torpedoed and sunk by the submarine *U-53* one mile east-by-south of the Manacles Buoy on 9 February, 1918. Carrying coal from Cardiff to Brest, the 313ft armed collier lost two crew in the explosion. Her wreck lies in 62m.

109 Ben Rein 50 03 30N; 05 00 30W. A British steamship that detonated a mine 3½ miles east of the Manacles, but managed to steam closer to the land before sinking. Of only 156 tons, of her seven man crew, two were killed when the mine exploded beneath her hull, while on passage from Plymouth to Falmouth alone, in ballast. She sank north-east of the Manacles in 60m.

110 Sommeina 50 00 45N; 04 56 35W. Built in 1899 as the *Tanagra*, this Cardiff-registered steamship of 3,317 tons gross, 330ft in length, was torpedoed and sunk by the submarine *UC-69* on 15 September, 1917. She was on passage from North Shields to Livorno with what was described as "Admiralty stores" – which could be anything from coal to ammunition. No lives were lost, and the wreck lies 4 miles south-east of the Manacles in over 50m.

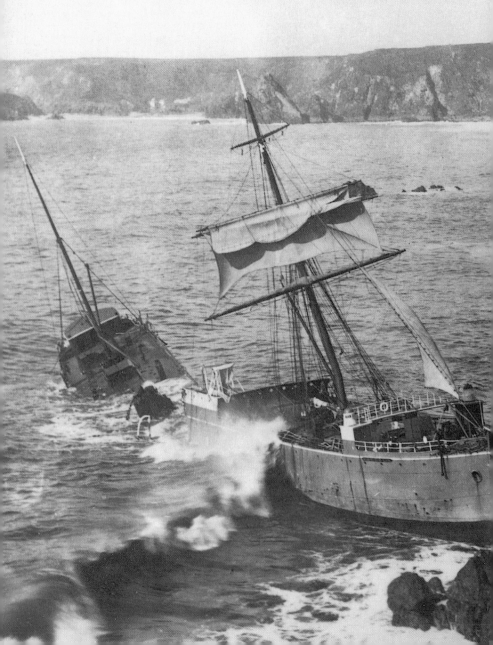

The wreck of the Suffolk near Polpeor Cove is not difficult to find.

AREA 5:

The Lizard

One of the most prominent features of the coast of the South West, the Lizard peninsula is dominated by its great headland, which is the most southerly point of the British Isles. This area includes the coast from BLACK HEAD to THE RILL.

With its double lighthouse towers and prominent white buildings, the Lizard is an unmistakable mark for ships at sea, and can be seen from a considerable distance by day. At night its warning light has a range of 25 miles. The marking of the Lizard headland by a light, first by a wood-burning beacon in an iron cresset, took place almost four centuries ago, though this was not where the light stands today, but on what is now known as the Old Lizard Head.

According to Sir John Killigrew of Arwennack Manor, Falmouth, in his petition to the Queen in 1570, there was a dire need, due to the great many ships lost there every year. His case had a ring of truth, since shipwrecks were frequent and the merchants that owned them frequently complained, but Killigrew's motive was personal and financial. His real reason was that having built his beacon, he could then station a privateer in Mount's Bay, which would extract – by force if necessary – a suitable "light fee" from every passing ship. On the basis that they had only survived being wrecked as a direct result of his philanthropy, Sir John felt that sailing masters and captains would be grateful to pay the few shillings! To reinforce his case to the Crown, Killigrew cited two examples: "the one of 1589, a prize of my Lord of Cumberland in value one hundred thousand pounds cast awaye in Mount's Bay for want of seeing the Lyzard; the other the Gibson, amounting to moore than £6,000, which a light had saved."

When his first application was refused by the Crown, whose decision had been influenced not by objections from ship owners, but the locals who complained it would reduce the number of shipwrecks (of which the Crown took its share). In response, a frustrated Killigrew wrote in December 1619: "they complain that I take away God's grace from them, their English meaning is that they now shall have nor receive no benefit from shipwreck. They have been so long used to reap purchase by the calamity of the ruin of shipping as they claim it hereditary."

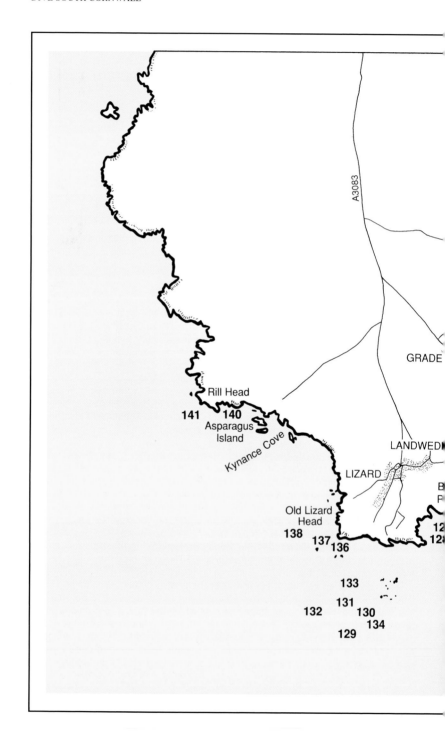

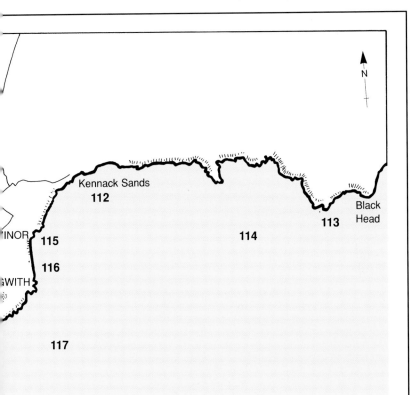

Kennack Sands
112

INOR
115

116

WITH

113

Black
Head

114

117

5

Dive Sites in Area 5, The Lizard. This area is
covered by Admiralty Charts 154 (approaches
to Falmouth and all the Lizard except Kynance
Cove and The Rill); 2565 (Trevose Head to
Dodman Point, including Kynance Cove and
The Rill); Ordnance Survey maps 203, 204.

142

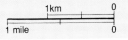

Technically the Lizard headland includes a vast area bounded by Coverack in the east, round Lizard Point, to Gunwalloe in the west, some 15 miles of coastline, but this section of the guide will concern itself only with the ten miles between Black Head and The Rill. It starts under the shadow of the high cliffs at Black Head which, apart from a number of small coves, has only the quarter-mile stretch of sand at Kennack as a relief in its entire length. For this reason, there are only two potential boat launching sites in the entire area, both of which are under considerable pressure due to increased commercial use, and diver saturation at peak season. Other launch sites that were available have now been closed to the public, though they will be mentioned in case this situation changes in the future.

From Black Head to the Lizard Point is a deep bay facing south-east, which offers considerable protection from south-westerly winds, with a maximum depth of 38m. Lizard Head is the remains of a once much larger bluff, which has left a great many offshore reefs and rocks, stretching for almost half a mile due south, which offer tremendous diving conditions and many wreck remains. Within this reef the water is very shallow, and seldom, except at high-water spring tides, will you find more than 14m. On the edge of the reef the bottom drops away quickly, especially on the south-eastern corner where it reaches 45m.

West of the Lizard Point is another shallow bay, smaller and very exposed to the south-west. Within this area, and sheltered because they are so close inshore, are the huge outcrops known as Gull Rock and Asparagus Island. The high cliffs are broken here for a short stretch by Kynance Cove, a small sandy area, then the cliffs rise again and continue well into Mount's Bay.

The main features for this area are therefore high cliffs with very few launching sites, reasonably deep water (often right up to the face of the cliffs), an extensive offshore reef, an abundance of shipwreck sites and very fierce tides.

WARNING Tides of this strength will only be found elsewhere in Cornwall off the Runnel Stone, and they far exceed those found on the Manacles. They will be mentioned in the text where appropriate, but great care should be exercised not only by divers but also by their surface cover if operating in or near the Lizard "race", which can exceed 4 to 6 knots. The worst situation (as elsewhere) is on the ebb, particularly a spring ebb, which brings on overfalls and a great surge of rushing water that will last for two hours or more. The area is thinly populated, with few properties on the cliff edge, and while any craft operating here should have a VHF radio to summon assistance if required, it could be a very long time before anyone ashore would spot your distress signals if you relied on hand signals or smoke flares only. Even if you could reach the shore, you could be faced with 300ft cliffs, which would be extremely dangerous to attempt to climb. With the Lizard Coastguard lookout now manned by volunteers only, in weather conditions when perhaps no one would be diving anyway, you can no longer rely on their visual watch. Like the Manacles, the Lizard has already claimed the lives of too many divers.

The majority of the shipwrecks are regarded as offshore rather than coastal, since few are sufficiently close to the launch sites. In general, the wreck sites are in shallow water, many close to cliffs, and few recognisable, being torn to pieces by the sea. The last major shipping loss in the Lizard area was the MV *Citrine* off Cadgwith in 1956 (Site **117**).

Kennack Sands is used a lot by divers. The gap in the wall allows you to launch a boat.

Coastal dive sites

Drive across Goonhilly Downs with its dozen or so satellite communication dish aerials on your right, and an interesting visitors' centre. Two and three-quarter miles after leaving the B3293, the road reaches a T-junction with the sea ahead. The road leading off to the left carries on to Kennack Sands; to the right leads to Ruan Minor and then Cadgwith.

111 Kennack Sands Take the left hand fork, past several large camping and caravan parks and the Kennack Sands Hotel, where the road becomes very narrow as it leads downhill to the beach and public car park. Kennack has become a very popular site from which inflatables can be launched, giving easy access to the Lizard or Black Head areas.

Generally sheltered, Kennack Sands has a double pressure placed on the resources, since it becomes crowded with holidaymakers *and* divers, usually at the same time. As with Porthoustock beach, things got out of hand, and the BSAC have had to publish a code of conduct and erect a public notice for divers. The problems have all been associated with diving boats leaving and approaching the beach too fast, and the abandoning of trailers on the beach after launching. Present arrangements at Kennack Sands include buoys offshore to indicate the extent of the voluntary speed limit. Trailers must be kept in the car park when not in use.

There are extensive camping and caravanning facilities near Kennack Sands. There are no boats for hire or charter, and although it may be possible to come to an arrangement with a fisherman at Cadgwith, none advertise a boat hire service and they are usually out at sea fishing for a living. Porthoustock and the Helford River offer the nearest hire service, and while both are only 40 minutes from the Lizard, your own craft would obviously be preferable.

The beach here is over a quarter of a mile long, backed by cliffs and sand dunes. A large rocky outcrop breaks the beach into two at low water, but cuts the smaller section off at high water. Reefs extend for some distance offshore, with large sandy patches and usually very good visibility. The depth increases quite rapidly and within less than a quarter of a mile it is over 16m. At the eastern end (the extreme left hand side of the beach looking seaward), a small boiler shows at low water, which marks the grave of the *Normand*.

112 Normand 50 00 18N; 05 08 30W. This 100-ton French steamship, of Bayonne, was on passage from Nantes to Fowey in ballast when she ran aground in fog on 2 April, 1914.

To the south of Kennack Sands, or right hand side looking seaward, the shoreline swings in to Carleon Cove and then out again to form Enys Head. It is here, some 50ft from the rocks known locally as the Criscans, on the edge of the reef area, that you will find remnants of the stranding of the *Highland Fling* (Site **115**) and the *Socoa* (Site **116**). Facilities at Kennack Sand are limited to a car park, café and gift shop, and public toilet. There are extensive camping and caravanning facilities in the immediate area.

Return to the main road, and at the T-junction keep straight on for Ruan Minor village. CADGWITH is well sign posted from Ruan Minor, but the approach lane is narrow and very steep, only just wide enough for an average inflatable or a

Cadgwith.

smaller hard boat on a trailer. Since parking close to the foreshore is almost impossible, a quick assessment of the situation with a single vehicle would be a prudent move. If you descend on Cadgwith in a large group you may receive a less than friendly welcome, since more than six divers is saturation as far as the facilities are concerned. As you negotiate the last part of the approach, you will pass the Cadgwith Hotel, after which the road flattens off opposite the beach area. After another 100ft the road follows another hill up and out of the village.

Cadgwith is a very old and historic fishing village, and is totally unsuitable for anything for than a small group with one boat. If your behaviour is unacceptable, then be ready for some very blunt comments, as the boatmen will not be slow in stating their mind. The original pilchard cellars are now a café and tea room, and there is one small shop in the village, but little else other than a telephone and public toilets. Parking spaces on the higher part of the beach are usually occupied by hotel guests or fishermen, who pull their boats up by winch, and frequently are unable to leave any opening for a diving boat to be trailer launched – conditions vary with the season. A large public car park may be found on the outskirts on the Lizard side, and if you can launch here, unload, get the boat in the water soonest, and take car and trailer out of the way.

In the early 1980s the fishing industry here seemed to be in decline, and the number of boats dropped dramatically, but their number has increased again, and about a dozen large boats work from here all summer. Ask before acting – a friendly approach to the local boatmen usually results in co-operation. There are no formal restrictions on divers using the beach, but as with Porthoustock and Kennack Sands, you are requested to observe the BSAC Code of Conduct.

WARNING Do not under any circumstances attempt a beach dive here, into the narrow approach cove. You will put yourself at risk physically, hold up boats entering and leaving, and because shellfish keep-pots are anchored just off from here, your reasons for shore diving will become suspect.

From Cadgwith, THE LIZARD is as accessible as from Kennack, only a little nearer. Outside Cadgwith, the bottom is quite deep (20m) and very rocky, with sand patches. All along this coastline close in or out to the Craggan Rocks, you will find good visibility and very little tide. The area is particularly good for shellfish, but remember that these are the mainstay of the local economy: do not take more than is reasonable for your personal consumption, and be discreet. Monofilament and tangle nets are used a lot around the Lizard, and caution should be exercised when diving on wrecks in the area or fishermen's marker buoys. Three additional shipwrecks lie close to Cadgwith – the *Citrine* (Site **117**), *Bellucia* (Site **118**) and the *Brest* (Site **120**) – as well as a Beaufighter aircraft (Site **119**).

A large black and yellow buoy will be obvious towards the southern end of the bay, some distance out to sea. This marks the seaward end of the local sewer outfall, which runs out from Lizard Church Cove, close to the lifeboat station at Kilcobben Cove. It makes an interesting dive to swim its length, observing the marine life, including the great profusion of fish at the discharge end.

A quick glance at an Ordnance Survey map of the Lizard would suggest that there is a boat launching facility here, but despite three potential sites, none are suitable or possible. The Lizard Church Cove slipway, which once housed the

You cannot launch a boat at Church Cove slipway on the Lizard, but there is excellent access for snorkelling.

original Lizard lifeboat is private; Polpeor Cove has a wide but steep concrete slipway, leading down to the remains of the second Lizard lifeboat station, which once had a massive turntable. The recovered boat was hauled up the slipway, through its house, out onto the steel turntable, moved through 180 degrees, and put back in its house with its bow pointing seaward.

Unfortunately, there have been difficulties here with divers in the past, with the result there is a notice stating quite bluntly "No Divers". The third possible launch site is Kynance Cove, reached by a long toll road off the A3084, about a mile before you reach the Lizard village, on the right hand side as you enter, but one look from the cliff at the 500 steps you will have to negotiate to reach the beach, and you will see that carrying a boat down would be out of the question. Generations of divers have carried their personal gear down, to reach Asparagus Island by shore diving, but it is hard work. If you feel it is worth the effort, there are basic amenities: a seasonal café, gift shop and toilets.

If you have the determination and stamina to carry your gear this far, diving is permitted and can be well worth the effort, with superb visibility in summer and all the beauty of the islands. Certainly the effort of snorkelling here is well worth the effort of carrying the necessary equipment, and despite the countless thousands of visitors to this National Trust gem, very few make it all the way to the bottom, which makes it such an ideal family beach.

Access to the Lizard from Cadgwith is via the road leading south through Grade. At the junction with the A3083 turn left and continue into the village. Facilities here are good, with fuel, cafés, hotels, an inn, shops and public toilets.

A narrow road leading south out of the square, with the newsagent on the corner on the right, will take you out to the car park on the very top of the headland. Ignore a small turning left part way down to the Lizard lighthouse – the road goes nowhere, and the lighthouse is not open to the public. Carry on down the hill to the parking area, where there are cafés, gift shops, and the old concrete road leading to the disused lifeboat station. If your visit to the headland should coincide with low water, the extent of the diving here will be something of a surprise, but at high water almost all the offshore rocks will be covered.

On the A3083, halfway between the Kynance Cove turning and the village of Mullion, is Predannack Holiday Village, in which you will find Dive Action Watersports (tel. 01326 240042). This centre offers a range of diving facilities, including compressed air, nitrox and tri-mix refills. Also available are RIB and hard boat charters, diving holiday packages, equipment sales and rentals and regulator servicing; the centre has a hyperbaric chamber and offers diver training. There is a restaurant and licensed bar on the site, as well as parking and accommodation.

Offshore dive sites and wrecks

Any of the shipwreck sites that follow are easily accessible from Cadgwith or Kennack Sands. If you are launching from Coverack, Porthoustock, or even Mullion, it is just a matter of time and distance, but make sure your boat is well equipped before you set out. Be aware of the potential hazards of this area.

There are so many wreck sites in a relatively confined area, that you will be spoilt for choice! The sites start in the east, near Black Head, and progress in order through the Area to The Rill.

113 Gunvor 50 00 19N; 05 06 07W. The largest sailing ship wreck in the vicinity, this 1,491-ton steel barque registered in Fredrikstad, Norway, was on passage from Caleta Buena in northern Chile to Falmouth, with a cargo of guano – seabird droppings that make an excellent nitrate fertiliser.

At 8pm on Friday 6 April, 1912, the Gunvor was close to the Lizard, in fact the crew saw the flash of her powerful light and heard the mournful warning blasts of seven seconds followed by two seconds. Setting course for Falmouth, Captain Tobiassen felt relieved to see what he thought was a small steamship running parallel just off his starboard beam, on an identical course, presumably also bound for the same port.

Without warning the barque ran headlong into the 220ft cliffs at Pedn Boar, close to Black Head, tore open her bottom plates, swung parallel with the coast, filled and sank. Fortunately, her steel bowsprit overhung the rocks, and the crew were able to clamber to safety down a rope ladder. At low water the crew were able to return for their belongings, the captain for the ship's papers and instruments. The only casualty was the ship's cat, a black female, who disappeared and presumably drowned. The men managed to climb the steep cliffs, and arrived at Treleaver Farm to give the first news of the wreck.

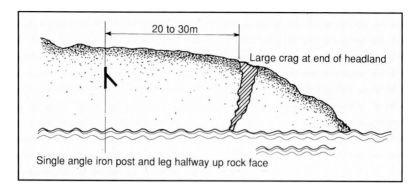

Above: Transit marks for the Gunvor (Site 113).

Below: Transit marks for the Carmarthen (Site 114).

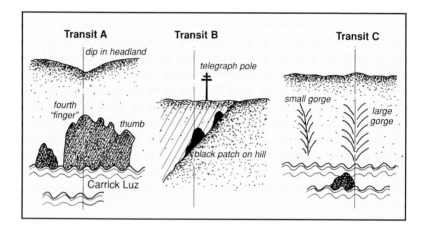

Today the wreck lies spread out just off a rock ledge, her bow and one anchor lie in 5m, her masts reaching out seaward. Her stern just catches the tide, which on the ebb can reach 2 knots.

Transit marks for the *Gunvor* are shown in the upper diagram above.

114 Carmarthen 50 00 07N; 05 07 27W. Belonging to the Cardigan Steamship Company and launched under the name *Arlington* in 1916, this armed steamer of 4,262 tons was in convoy from Genoa to the Tees in ballast, having called at Falmouth, when she was torpedoed by the German submarine *UC-50* off the Lizard on 26 July, 1917. Despite extensive flooding of her No. 1 and No. 2 holds, she managed to reach the relative shallows off Kennack Sands before she sank in 20m.

The *Carmarthen* proved impossible to save; her gun and other fittings were recovered, and she was abandoned. While collapsed, the wreck is intact, but was heavily salvaged during the 1960s for non-ferrous metals.

Transit marks for the *Carmarthen* are shown in the lower diagram opposite.

115 Highland Fling 49 59 15N; 05 09 35W. The scattered steel plating, cast iron sections and anchor and chain are all that remains of the bow section of this large steamship. Of 4,088 tons, built as the *Morayshire* in 1890, she later became the *Duke of Portland* in 1906, and finally the *Highland Fling*.

After leaving the Thames in December 1906 a serious leak was discovered beneath one of her two boilers, and examination by a diver in Falmouth revealed a cracked bottom plate. Ordered to dry dock at Cardiff for repairs, she sailed in thick fog on 7 January, 1907, but was only a few miles from Falmouth when she stranded off Enys Head, near Cadgwith. Several unsuccessful attempts were

The wreck of the full-rigged sailing ship Gunvor (Site 113). Her bowsprit overhangs the rocks at Pedn Boar, where she was wrecked in April 1912, carrying a cargo of nitrates.

made to save her, but failed. With most of the ship from the boiler room bulkhead to her stern in deep water, it was decided to cut her in two, saving the greater part, to which might be fitted a new bow.

Explosive charges were laid around her bow, and with a little help from nature in the form of an easterly gale, the main section was re-floated on 20 January. Once in dry dock, Falmouth, it was found that the salvaged section was too badly damaged to justify the cost of rebuilding, and she was broken up on the stocks where she lay.

116 Socoa 49 59 30N; 05 10 00W. On her way from Szczecin to San Francisco carrying a cargo of cement in barrels – a gift from the French government to help rebuild the earthquake-shattered city – the steel, three-masted, full-rigged ship *Socoa* went aground in fog on 31 July, 1906. In order to lighten ship, 50,000 barrels of cement were thrown overboard, which hardened in the sea, and the remains of many of these can still be found in the shallows, among the rocks. While not very exciting, these are nevertheless a small piece of history.

117 Citrine 49 59 00N; 05 09 36W. The last large shipwreck to occur around the Lizard, this Glasgow registered motor coaster of 788 tons was carrying a cargo of limestone from Llanddulas (near Colwyn Bay) to London on 2 January, 1956, when her hatch covers were forced open during a gale and she sank.

All ten of her crew were saved in a daring rescue by the Lizard lifeboat, the only victim being the 70 years old ship's cook, who died later from the effects of exposure. The ship sank not far from Cadgwith, in 23m, the wreck being well broken with bow and stern section largely intact and upside down, the mid portion collapsed.

Transit marks for the *Citrine* are shown in the upper diagram opposite.

118 Bellucia 49 58 48N; 05 10 33W. Torpedoed by the German submarine *UB-31* on 7 July, 1917, the 4,368-ton British steamship *Bellucia* of Glasgow, owned by Bell Brothers and Company, was sailing from Montreal to London with a cargo of wheat and flour. Since she did not sink immediately, her captain got her as close in to the shore as possible, where she fell over on to her starboard side in 15m.

A salvage unit moved in, and since it was possible at low water to walk along her port side, access holes were cut in the plates and much of her cargo, which was bagged, was saved. Her engine, windlass, gun and part of the propeller shaft were later salvaged by the Western Marine Salvage Company. Today only her bottom plates, three boilers and the bow section remain, but make for an interesting dive. The wreck is owned by the author, who found her bell in 1972 – and you are requested to look, touch but not remove!

Transit marks for the *Bellucia* are shown in the lower diagram opposite.

119 Beaufighter aircraft 49 58 48N; 05 10 18W. A victim of World War Two, thought to have been stationed at Predannack airfield, overlooking Mullion Harbour, which was an emergency fighter field and is now used by the Naval Air Station at Culdrose for helicopter training. It is understood that this aircraft crashed during a training flight. Its two 30mm wing cannon have been recovered, as has one propeller.

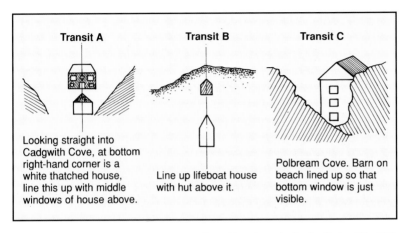

Above: Transit marks for the Citrine (Site 117).

Below: Transit marks for the Bellucia (Site 118).

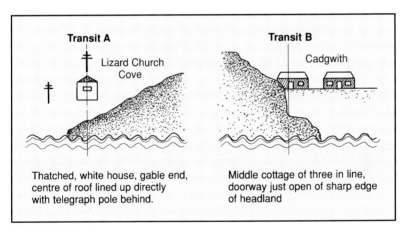

120 Brest 49 58 26N; 05 11 10W. On 6 September, 1879, although still summer, thick fog made it dark long before 8.30pm, so that when the duty Coastguards at the Lizard lookout heard an almighty crash followed by screaming, they had no idea of the source.

It took the Cadgwith lifeboat 30 minutes to locate the wreck, having gone as far as Bass Point and then worked back along the shore. Between Church Cove and The Chair, near Polbarrow, they found the 1,472-ton iron screw steamship *Brest*, of Glasgow, Captain Richard Elder, which was part of the Cunard Line. She had sailed from Le Havre the previous day for Liverpool with 134 passengers, mostly French, German, Swiss and Italian emigrants for the United States.

As the lifeboat went alongside, the panic stricken passengers hurled themselves over the rails into the lifeboat, fighting each other to gain a place. The situation forced the lifeboat coxswain to stand off for fear the boat would sink, and await the arrival of local fishing boats to assist in the rescue. Only five drowned in the accident, but they all lost their possessions, no small disaster to families carrying everything they owned. A tug was chartered to take them to Falmouth, but for many of the passengers this was their second shipwreck. They had been in a vessel bound for Le Havre that had sunk in the Mediterranean, and they all elected to walk the twenty miles rather than make another sea passage.

The wreck was sold on 25 October, 1879, when a great deal of her cargo was recovered, as well as the bodies of those drowned. Nothing much remains of the wreck, except a scattering of iron plate and frames, with small brass and copper bits wedged in among the rocks.

121 The Czar and the Vrogue Rock 49 57 33N; 05 10 25W. Built in Hull by Martin Samuelson in 1858, the *Czar* was a 1,100-ton, iron hulled barque rigged steamship, which left Woolwich Arsenal in the Thames on 16 January, 1859, for Malta, on what could only have been her third or fourth voyage. Her cargo consisted of 1,600 tons of government stores, which included fifty-one 68-pounder muzzle loading Lancaster guns, shot and shell of the same calibre, uniform clothing, hides, spirits, oil, sugar and cinnamon.

Fifty miles west of the Bishop Rock on 21 January, she developed boiler trouble, her steam pressure fell, and a decision was made to turn back for Falmouth. In worsening weather she closed the Lizard the next day, and while seeking some shelter from the high cliffs east of the Lizard, struck the Vrogue Rock, less than half a mile from Bass Point, and fell, badly holed, beam on to the sea. She then broke in two just behind the funnel, the two halves starting to sink as they drifted apart. One of her boats was swamped and went down, a second reached Parn Voose Cove with three survivors. Six men were taken off the bow

Transit marks for the Czar (Site 121).

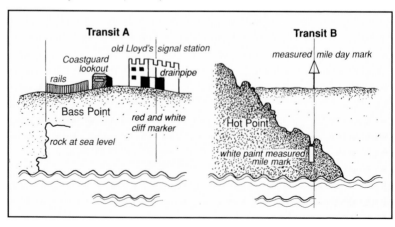

142

The auxiliary schooner Adolf Vinnen (Site 122) was on her maiden voyage when she was wrecked in 1923.

section by a Coastguard cutter, and an able seaman was saved from the sea. Everyone else was lost, 13 in all including her captain, his wife and son.

Diving the *Czar* is a unique experience, since in one part of the wreck the bottom is carpeted with 68-pounder round iron shot nearly seven inches in diameter. Many of her massive guns are still to be seen, and among the shattered plating and frames are brass uniform buttons, percussion caps, buckles and badges. Average depth of the wreck is 12 to 18m.

Within this relatively small area from Hot Point to Bass Point, the remains of no less than four ships are to be found, all of which have been heavily salvaged and broken by the sea.

Transit marks for the *Czar* are shown in the diagram opposite.

122 Adolf Vinnen 49 57 54N; 05 11 01W. When this fine German schooner went ashore here in 1923, she was brand new, only nine days out of her builders' hands. Owned by the renowned Vinnens of Bremen, she was a five masted, steel auxiliary sailing vessel, built by Krupps in 1922–23 and fitted with the same sort of diesel engine later used in German submarines. She left the builders' yard on 1 February, 1923, was fitted out, and sailed on her maiden voyage for Barry, to load coal.

By 23 February, the ship was dangerously close to the Lizard, and unable to work herself clear. She stranded only 61m off the cliffs, very close to where the German liner *Mosel* had sunk earlier. Seventeen of the crew were saved by breeches buoy from the cliff top that day, and the remaining five the day following. The wreck is broken up, very flat and in two pieces, but her diesel engine remains, as do a couple of her masts. The maximum depth is 12m.

123 Le Vieux Tigre 49 57 48N; 05 10 58W. A large steam trawler of Boulogne, which carried a crew of 29, two dogs and a cat. She went ashore just inside Bass Point in dense fog on 27 March, 1935. Her crew were all saved, and by morning only the top of her bridge, mast and funnel showed above the surface. The ship's cat refused to leave, going into hiding, but despite the accommodation having been under water, the tabby was finally coaxed off by a Cadgwith fisherman two days later.

Her remains have been driven up a deep gully in the shallows, with iron and pieces of brass concreted into the sea bed; her one boiler remains intact, lying in 7m.

Bass Point, showing the locations of the Adolf Vinnen (Site 122), Le Vieux Tigre (Site 123), Mosel (Site 124) and Clan Malcolm (Site125).

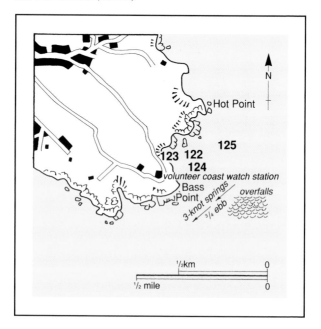

The Glasgow-registered steamship Clan Malcolm (Site 125) stranded in 10m on the Lizard in 1935. She was carrying a cargo of maize and when she was wrecked she broke in two.

124 Mosel 49 57 47N; 05 11 00W. This wreck lies right on Bass Point, on the same side as *Le Vieux Tigre*, and their remains are almost intermingled in one area. The *Mosel* was a fine German emigrant ship, a 3,200-ton vessel described by her owners Norddeutscher Lloyd as a liner. For almost nine years she had plied the emigrant route from Bremen via Southampton to New York and back. On 6 August, 1882, she sailed under Captain Julius Hesse with 100 crew, 20 saloon class passengers, 600 emigrants travelling steerage, plus a valuable general cargo including special mail and 400 tons of woollen material.

As with almost all the Lizard wrecks, fog was the basic cause, and on 9 August she ran into Bass Point at 14 knots. She was so close to the Lloyds Signal Station, which still stands on top of the cliffs here, that the duty signalman clambered down the rocks, got onto the bow and obtained her details from the captain.

The ship was aground in shallow water, and the passengers were asked to pack their luggage and embark on the Falmouth tug *Rosetta*, which also took off the mail and valuables. The cargo was transferred to other vessels over the next few days, then a fire broke out on board, and she was abandoned.

While no great amount of hull remains, deeply concreted into the sea bed in great patches are examples of her general cargo, including penknives, umbrellas, scissors, buttons, needles and mouth organs. The maximum depth is 11m, but the area is subject to a great deal of tide, and diving should coincide with low slack water. On a spring tide, it will be impossible to dive there during the ebb.

125 Clan Malcolm 49 57 52N; 05 11 00W. This large Clan Line steamship, 5,994 tons, was another victim of fog, this time during the evening of 26 September, 1935. The German salvage tug *Seefalke* was quickly on hand, but the *Clan Malcolm* had impaled herself on the rocks in the shallows, and never moved again. Three large boilers mark the centre of the wreck site, and the bottom is a mass of twisted steel plating and fittings. The wreck lies in only 12m, but is in the very centre of the worst tidal areas, where in excess of 5 knots flows on a spring ebb, and is best dived on a neap low water, when it is safe to stay down for the entire flood period.

126 Cromdale 49 57 45N; 05 11 00W. One of the magnificent full-rigged sailing ships of the period just before World War One and one of two such ships lost on the Lizard in 1913. The *Queen Margaret* (Site **129**) was lost in an unfortunate accident; the three-masted *Cromdale*, which had been at sea for 124 days after leaving Taltal in Chile with a cargo of guano, was lost in fog.

A week overdue at Falmouth for orders to discharge, she encountered fog close inshore. Her master had previously checked his position with a passing steamship, and was not overly concerned when after a number of hours nothing was heard of the Lizard or St Anthony foghorns. Without any warning, sheer black cliffs loomed up ahead, and the *Cromdale* sailed straight into the cliffs directly beneath the Lizard Coastguard Station. The first distress rocket fired exploded directly in front of the lookout position, which must have given the occupants a nasty shock! Next day, as the weather cleared, the ship presented a sorry sight, bow high up on the rocks, stern almost under water, her sails hanging

Housel Bay, showing the locations of the Cromdale (Site 126), Hansey (Site 127) and Robert (Site 128).

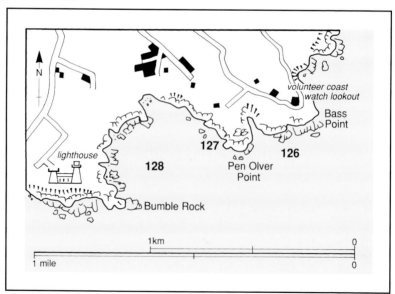

When the steel barque Cromdale (Site 126) went ashore under the Coastguard lookout on the Lizard point in 1913 her crew were saved by the Lizard lifeboat.

limply from the yards on all three masts. Her bottom frames and sections of mast and yards remain on the bottom in 11m, smashed and mangled by storm and ground seas.

Following on round from the Coastguard lookout, HOUSEL BAY is a small, deep bay on the south-eastern corner of the Lizard headland. A prominent feature of the whole area is the Bumble Rock, a distinctively bent looking outcrop on the western end of the bay, which is said locally to have been the wreck site of a treasure-laden Spanish galleon. Certainly a lot of diving took place here using diving bells – but if there ever was any truth in the story they did a good job, since there is nothing left today!

127 Hansy 50 57 45N; 05 11 28W. Launched at Dunbarton in 1885 as the square-rigger *Aberfoyle* and following a somewhat chequered career, she was sold

147

to Akties Hansy of Fredrikstad in 1910. She left Sweden for Melbourne on 3 October, 1911, with a full cargo of timber and pig iron, but was caught by a south-westerly gale off the Lizard and, while attempting to clear the land missed stays in going about, became trapped in Housel Bay and was wrecked on Carn Table. No lives were lost – the majority of her crew were rescued by breeches buoy from the cliff top, and the captain and mate were the last off, saved by the Lizard lifeboat.

For weeks after the wreck, large pieces of pine came ashore as she broke up, and many were put to good use in house repairs and boat building. Her broken hull lays hard against a rocky ledge, with a boulder strewn and sandy bottom in 12m. Some of the original pig iron ingots remain, concreted to the sea bed, a well-used source of ballast for local fishing boats over the years. Winter storms still turn up interesting finds, her brass pump in 1990 being an example.

The full-rigged ship Hansy (Site 127) was wrecked in Housel Bay in 1911. This photograph shows her deck cargo of timber spilling into the shallows. Much of her iron hull remains in position, as well as large numbers of iron ingots that also formed part of her cargo.

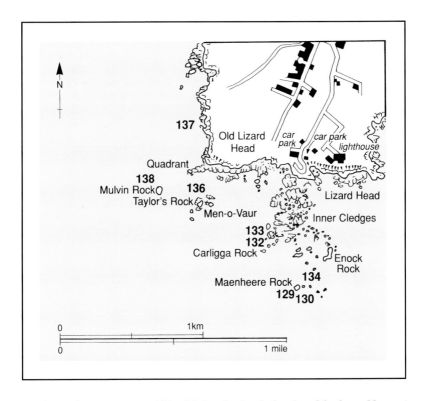

The treacherous area around Lizard Point, showing the location of the Queen Margaret (Site 129), Seagull (Site 130), Gloaming (Site 133), Skyjolaborg (Site 134), Suffolk (Site 137) and Rubaan (Site 138).

128 Robert 50 57 40N; 05 11 40W. While in Housel Bay, it is worth a general swim around the centre, since it is here that you will find at least traces of the cargo of this Caernarfon registered schooner. She sank on 19 July, 1887, on her way from Wales to London with cut slates, but having been blown into Housel Bay was unable to escape. No known fabric of the wreck has been found, but piles of slates (mainly broken) can be found buried in the bottom, or wedged between rocks.

The large rock outcrop that shows at all states of the tide south of the twin-tower lighthouse is MAENHEERE (marked Mên Hyr on many charts and maps). This rock marks the southernmost extremity of the Lizard reefs, which collectively are known as the Stags or OUTER CLEDGES. The Stags is the name you will find in guide books and old shipwreck accounts, but locally they are the Inner and Outer Cledges. Two wrecks lie alongside Maenheere.

Above: The Queen Margaret (Site 129), wrecked near Maenheere Rock in 1913.

Below: The Hamburg-registered Wandsbek (Site 131) on the Stags reef in 1900.

The reef extends parallel with the shore, westward from Maenheere for about half a mile, with an area inside often referred to by fishermen as the Shallow Ground. At low water there will only be 2 to 3m over the Outer Cledges, dropping off to 10m just off to the south, then shelving quickly to 30m. The sea bed overall is broken rock and reef, covered in dense weed, with plenty of wrasse, pollack, bass, mackerel and urchins. On a neap tide, the worst of the tide race runs outside the Outer Cledges, but on a spring tide, when the movement of water is very fierce, it covers the shallow ground as well. Among the crevices and gullies in this area there is an abundance of small artefacts from wrecks that have gone to pieces and been scattered. At least two ship's bells have been found here, as well as coins, brass and copper fittings and much more.

129 Queen Margaret 50 57 05N; 05 12 22W. This was the other steel barque lost in May 1913, along with the *Cromdale* (Site **98**). The four-masted *Queen Margaret* was only one of two British ships ever to carry three sky-sails, and had an almost legendary reputation among seafarers for her speed and grace. Of 2,144 tons, she left Sydney laden with wheat for Falmouth for orders on 17 January, 1913. One hundred and thirty days later, at 4am on 13 May, she was off the Lizard, close-hauled, and signalling to the Lloyds Station for instructions.

In the case of the *Queen Margaret*, Captain Bousfield received instructions, via code flags, that he was to proceed to Limerick and then Glasgow, where the crew were to be paid off. With only light and variable winds, and uncertain even that he could reach Land's End, he requested permission to hire a tug. The captain tacked back and forth as best he could, but the barque got closer and closer to Maenheere rock, the set of the tide pushing his ship nearer all the time, until without warning the ship struck the rock and shuddered to a halt.

Every effort to free her failed, and on the turn of the tide, she fell over on her port beam, her main yard touching the sea, it being so shallow. In no time the inrush of water saturated her cargo, it started to swell, and as was common with grain cargoes, the ship's deck bulged upward and then burst. At her auction, with none of the cargo left dry, and the hull already broken in two, she sold for just £10 as scrap metal.

Today, her remains include acres of steel plate, sections of masts and spars, and her windlass, all on the seaward side of Maenheere, in the shallows.

130 Seagull 49 57 04.5N; 05 12 26W. Between Maenheere and the next area of the Outer Cledges is a rocky gully, in which the sea has sculptured the granite into perfectly smooth surfaces. In the gap between this gully and the main rock can be found some wreckage including a single-ended boiler and a two-cylinder compound engine, which once powered the small paddle-tug *Seagull*. Exactly when or why this vessel was wrecked here is something of a mystery; the incident is supposed to have taken place in the early 1930s.

131 Wandsbek 50 57 13N; 05 12 00W. A three-masted steel sailing vessel of Hamburg, 1,783 tons register, on passage from Portland, Oregon to Liverpool via Falmouth with a cargo of grain. Because the wind was so light, she was assisted out to sea by the tug *Dragon*, which slipped her tow some six miles south-west of the Lizard on 26 May, 1900. The wind was so light, the sea was described as "a sheet of glass", and with no steerage way the *Wandsbek* was at the mercy of the tide.

She then drifted so close in towards the cliffs that despite excellent visibility and clear blue sky, the Coastguard requested the Lizard lighthouse to sound its foghorn. Apparently those on board did not hear this for some reason, so the Coastguards then flew a signal hoist instructing them to drop anchor. This too went unheeded, so as a last resort those on watch ashore started firing their signal gun to attract attention – but to no avail. The ship continued to drift, helpless it seems, although why it did not anchor is uncertain, and she ended up on The Dales, half a mile offshore.

Lloyds Signal Station telegraphed Falmouth for tugs, and the *Dragon, Victor* and *Eagle* all went to her rescue, the former taking her crew of 30 back to Falmouth. Built in 1898 and owned by Knohr and Burchard of Hamburg, like the *Queen Margaret*, her cargo swelled and burst her plates, and she was declared a constructive total loss. Her hull was sold for just £55, and within 33 days she had gone to pieces.

132 Suevic 50 57 10N; 05 12 30W. At the western end of the Outer Cledges is a large rock that just shows at low water, the last obstruction in a chain of rocks. Alongside this outcrop is where part of the remains of the *Suevic* are to be found. She left only her bow on the rocks when, carrying a 141 crew, 382 passengers and a stowaway, she went ashore in fog on 23 July, 1907.

The bow section of the Suevic (Site 132) on the Outer Cledges in 1907.

She was a 12,500-ton steamship of the White Star line, with frozen meat, butter and copper bars filling her holds. In a similar situation to that of the *Highland Fling*, which previously stranded near Cadgwith (Site **87**), her bow was blasted off using explosives and a new section added in Southampton dock, the main part of the ship having been towed clear.

She lived to sail again, and for a remarkably long time. In World War One she was requisitioned as a troopship, sold and renamed *Skyttern* in 1929 after conversion to a whale factory ship, and scuttled on 1 April, 1942, in the Skagerrak to prevent her falling into German hands. Nothing recognisable as a bow section remains, except a scatter of plates and double bottom, holding lengths of lead pipe. The maximum depth is 10m.

Between the Shallow Ground and the high cliffs of the Lizard is an area of many acres of rock and reef, the INNER CLEDGES, much of which dries at low water spring tides, in which there is much evidence of wreckage. At its western end, where there is a deep water channel leading out from the old lifeboat slipway, the remains of two wrecks are mixed together – possibly more.

133 HMS Gloaming This auxiliary steam wooden drifter of 94 tons, built by Forbes of Fraserburgh in 1919 for the Admiralty left Pembroke Dock on 3 March, 1921, as escort for the 1st Submarine Flotilla – the unfortunate "K" class of boats, the K.5, K.8, K.9, K.12 and K.15 – with two cruisers following astern. Well ahead of the small fleet, the *Gloaming* steamed straight into the Cledges. In heavy seas she went to pieces within one day, the only remains being her boiler and engine, her bell being found further inshore in 1965.

134 Skyjolaborg 50 52 10W; 05 12 22W. This small steel Norwegian steamship of 716 tons, registered at Haugesund, was sailing from Rouen to Swansea in ballast to load coal. She drove ashore inside the Maenheere rock, was lifted by ground seas onto the Shallow Ground on 18 January, 1920, and broke her back. Her crew took to their two boats, and rowed themselves round to Mullion, landing safely. The sea has long since pounded the wreck to pieces, but many souvenirs have been recovered by divers, including her bell, which bears the ship's name and port of register.

135 Men-o-Vaur This collection of outlying rocks make for an interesting dive, with lots of life and a fierce tide on the ebb; often misnamed 'Men of War', this has no connection with a warship wreck, but is an old Cornish name. At high water a channel becomes obvious through the rocks through which boats with shallow draughts can navigate in safety.

136 Royal Anne 50 57 25N; 05 12 55W. A King's galley bound for Barbados, which was wrecked at the back of Taylor's Rock, close to the Men-o-Vaur, in November 1720. There were only three survivors – 207 people died in the accident, in addition to her captain, all the lieutenants, twenty-four gentlemen and Lord Belhaven. The bodies are said to be buried on the cliff top, in Pistol meadow.

The *London Journal* reported that "the Henrietta yacht, and the Jolly Bachelor are going down to the Lizard with a newly invented diving engine, to fish upon the

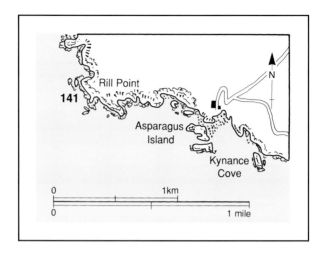

Kynance Cove, showing the location of the Abernyte (Site 141).

wreck of the Royal Anne." Unfortunately, history has not recorded exactly what they caught! Certainly you will find large iron cannon down there, some half dozen remaining, along with an intact anchor and another broken one, and numerous artefacts have been found in the concretion over the years. The site is now a protected wreck, and unauthorised diving is forbidden.

137 Suffolk 49 57 41N; 05 12 50W. The three-masted, 300ft schooner rigged steamship *Suffolk*, of 2,924 tons, left Baltimore for London on 14 September, 1886. On board were a crew of 38, two passengers and a cargo of tobacco in wooden casks, 8,000 bushels of wheat, 24,000 sacks and 500 casks of flour, barrels of resin and general Christmas fare. Her afterdeck was stacked high with walnut logs, while on the foredeck 161 prime New England steers were penned in stalls.

Fog was encountered as they approached the Lizard, and at the exact moment that Captain Williams went forward to join the lookouts on the bow, black cliffs loomed ahead, and the ship ran into the Old Lizard Head at six knots. A meeting of the officers revealed the worst, the boiler room was filling fast and the forepeak already flooded.

The Lizard and Cadgwith lifeboats were launched, who found 40 passengers and crew already in the lifeboats and afloat alongside. Many of the cattle died that night as heavy seas swept the wreck, although 26 were hauled up the cliff face. The wreck was finally purchased by Leans of Falmouth for scrapping. Very little remains for such a large vessel, what is there lies in concreted patches among the sand.

138 Rubaan 49 57 30N; 05 05 13.3W. Built as the *Tod Head* in 1921 by Cran and Somerville of Leith and registered at Glasgow, this was a small steam collier of 324 tons register, which struck the Dales in fog on 16 December, 1939, but got as far as the Mulvin before sinking. The wreck site still holds her single boiler, main and donkey steam engine, and is difficult to locate.

The wreck lies 500 yards to the west of the Mulvin, directly down the line of the tide. The main Lizard tide race flows directly over the wreck, which lies in 19m, so it is a slack water or neap flood tide dive.

139 Asparagus Island and Gull Rock Both are large islands off Kynance Cove, about half a mile from the beach. They both make attractive dive sites, being extremely sheltered from the north and east, with fairly deep water right up to the rocks. They have a wide choice of caves, deep gullies and a long underwater tunnel that passes right through from one side of Asparagus Island to the other. It is not recommended that you swim this feature in any sort of swell, since you may be thrown against the roof and injured. In calm weather with good visibility, it is an exciting and safe experience. The maximum depth around both islands is 14m, but on the south-west corner of Asparagus Island it can reach 23m with an all sand bottom.

At the approach to the tunnel, on the south-west side, there is evidence of a very old shipwreck. An iron cannon is concreted into the bottom at the tunnel entrance, and coins, sword guards, pewter bottle tops, brass and copper have

Transit marks for the Ilston (Site 142).

155

been found on the ledges to the left, offering evidence of a Dutch vessel around 1725, but still unidentified. It is not recommended that you dive here without boat cover, particularly on the ebb tide – you may find yourself unwillingly heading out into Mount's Bay.

The cliffs from Kynance Cove to the west are exceptionally steep and high, reaching over 200ft in places, but with very shallow water at its base. At its western extremity is THE RILL, a great granite bluff, from the top of which it is possible to see as far as Penzance on a clear day. There are the remains of a very old structure on the cliff top, possibly the site of the original Lizard light beacon when it was still an open wood or coal fire.

At sea level, on the very tip of The Rill, is a deep natural gully, going right up into the rocks. Within this can be found the remains of the *Abernyte* (Site **141**).

140 Rill Cove wreck 49 58 50N; 05 14 40W. The site of a designated and protected wreck of some antiquity, which was the subject of an order made by the Secretary of State dated 29 November, 1972. The wreck was found by accident.

Following the loss of a small fishing boat, the *Kerris Reed*, against the cliffs in September 1969, a party of divers including the author visited the wreck, recovered some equipment for the owners, and passed the information to Mike Hall of Ruan Minor. He and Ken Simpson visited the site, poked about in the sand and found a pile of silver pieces-of-eight! Subsequent to its designation, hundreds of coins have been excavated from the deep covering of sand over this old wreck, as well as an iron gun and other artefacts dating from around 1590.

141 Abernyte 50 58 30N; 05 14 05W. Fog was the cause of yet another victim of the Lizard area when the 700-ton Glasgow registered barque *Abernyte* was wrecked without loss of life. Under Captain Cardwell, she was on her way from Caleta Buena to Falmouth with a cargo of guano. The long gully is often full of drifting weed, but well worth the visit to see the broken remains of this fine vessel. The maximum depth is 7m.

142 Ilston 49 57 12N; 05 09 39W. The best of the deep water wrecks off the Lizard can be reached easily from Porthoustock, Coverack , Kennack or Cadgwith. An armed steamship of 2,426 tons, the *Ilston*, belonging to the Swansea Steamship Company, was on passage from Swansea to Falmouth and Rouen with railway material, when she was torpedoed by the submarine *UB-23*. Six of her crew were killed.

Although attacked well offshore, she managed to close the Lizard before sinking in 43m, the wreck standing 15m above the sea bed, which is all sand. The centre portion of the wreck is intact, but her bow and stern have collapsed, and was owned by the author until she was sold to a Plymouth company in 1976. At that stage her cargo of cast iron rolling stock bogies and wheels, plus railway lines and line chairs filled her holds, but most have been raised.

Because the wreck is well offshore, and in the shipping channel, you must maintain a good watch, and be able and prepared to move out of the way of larger craft that may not even have seen you on their radar. A slack water dive, since there is a lot of tide on the ebb.

Transit marks for the *Ilston* are shown in the diagram on page 155.

143 Eskdale 50 03 30N; 04 56 00W. Not an exact location, but very close if you wish to find this Norwegian Navy destroyer, No. L-36, which was one of the Hunt class Type III warships built for the Royal Navy in 1942. Of 1,087 tons, 264ft by 31.5ft., four 4ins. and two 20mm guns, plus two torpedo tubes, ships of this class were down-rated to frigates in 1947.

The *Eskdale* was loaned to Norway, but sunk by torpedoes fired by German E-boats on 14 April, 1943, while escorting a convoy. The maximum depth is 50m, with the wreck standing 10m above that.

144 Roche Bonne 49 54 54N; 05 10 24W. A World War Two Admiralty requisitioned trawler of 258 tons, built in 1913 and taken into Royal Navy service as a minesweeper in February, 1940. On 7 April, 1941, she was attacked by German aircraft three miles SSE of the Lizard and sunk with a direct hit by a bomb. The maximum depth is 55m.

145 Samlanes 49 55 35N; 05 12 02W. This 842-ton Norwegian steamship, 203ft by 30ft, detonated a mine two miles off the Lizard on 11 March, 1941, while sailing from Swansea to Shoreham with coal. She sank with all fifteen crew members, and lies in 67m.

146 Erato 49 55 40N; 05 06 40W. Another victim of a contact mine in World War One, this one laid by the submarine *UC-69*. The 2,041-ton *Erato*, built in 1911 for the Westcott and Lawrance Line, was sunk on 1 September, 1917 – in a position given at the time as four miles south-east of the Lizard Head – and lies in 50m.

147 Vav 49 55 40N; 05 13 30W. On passage from Glasgow to Le Havre in convoy, this 1,256-ton Norwegian steamship, built in 1919, was attacked and sunk by a torpedo fired by the submarine *UB-80*, while carrying 1,473 tons of steel. Being 235ft by 34ft, she makes a good fishing target, and is believed to be covered in nets in 47m depth.

148 Asaba 49 56 17N; 05 14 34W. Sunk two miles WSW of the Lizard in 56m on 6 December, 1917, by the German submarine *UC-17*, this 972-ton armed British steamship belonging to the Elder Dempster Line was on passage between Newport and Le Havre with an Admiralty cargo. Sixteen of her crew, including her master, were killed.

One of the many cannon remaining on the site of the Santo Christo de Castello. It has been so worn away by seabed material that over half the circumference of the gun has disappeared.

AREA 6:

Mount's Bay East

Only the eight-mile stretch of coastline between Cudden Point and Mousehole, centred on St Michael's Mount, is Mount's Bay – but in practice the entire area of sea between the Lizard and Lamorna Cove, which is some 27 miles long, is given this name. The area has been divided conveniently into two. The eastern portion runs from THE HORSE for a distance of fifteen miles to PRUSSIA COVE. The western area consists of twelve miles of coastline, as far as Lamorna Cove.

At least ten of the first fifteen miles in the eastern part of this area are sheer granite cliff with virtually no access to the sea, and no launching sites. Mullion Cove is therefore the first break in the cliffs to offer a decent slipway, but unfortunately has some restrictions. Three more possible launch sites follow, then the high ground prohibits access to the coast until Loe Bar, which is a 2¹/₂-mile shingle beach. More high ground follows Porthleven, with one mile of soft sand at Praa and only one additional access site to the end of the area.

Mount's Bay is very exposed to any wind from the prevailing south-westerlies through to north-west, and winds in excess of Force 3 or 4 will prohibit diving, bringing in a heavy swell and often ground seas. It is an area that is often deceptive as regards sea states. Even on hot sultry summer days, the bay can be influenced by strong winds way out in the Atlantic, bringing in a long, heavy swell that makes it difficult to launch and recover boats. Consequently, the summer can often be well advanced before Mount's Bay offers a glassy calm surface, which usually brings in the basking sharks.

On the other hand, winds from the northern quarter round to south-east do not affect the inshore area at all, and the sea off Mullion can be flat in a full easterly gale. There are no particular tidal problems in Mount's Bay, until you get about three miles offshore where you will find an average depth of 37m and you will encounter the full effect of the Lizard and Channel flow.

At the eastern end of this area there tends to be fairly deep water right up to the cliffs – 23m less than a quarter of a mile offshore, which slowly increases to about one mile off Loe Bar, and two miles off Cudden Point. The area is distinctive for its general lack of known offshore wreck and dive sites.

Similarly, while there are plenty of coastal wrecks, only four of these are relatively modern. Two older sites are licensed under the Protection of Wrecks Act, and the others are the remnants of 17th and 18th century sailing ships, with little left to see. However, this does not mean that there are no new sites to be found, since hundreds of ships have been lost in Mount's Bay, and it is reasonable to assume most wrecks leave some remains.

WARNING Monofilament nets are used extensively in this area, and trawl nets will be found on the deep wrecks at Sites **167** and **168**.

Coastal dive sites

Access to all the coastal dive sites in this area can be gained by taking the appropriate turning off the main Lizard to Helston road, the A3083, or the Helston to Penzance road, the A394.

There are three different routes to Mullion village from the A3083, but only one to MULLION COVE. The first of these is directly opposite the Mullion Holiday Park as you drive from the Lizard, the second is the turning at Cross Lanes, near the Wheel Inn, via Trewoon, and the third is a turning off via Poldhu Cove close to the Royal Naval Air Station workshop site.

Passing through Mullion, follow the signs for the Mullion Cove, which will bring you to a narrow, winding road. Continue past the official Mullion Cove car park, past the Quarry car park, Criggan Mill caravan and camp site, down to the cove itself.

WARNING There have been many problems at Mullion over the years with inconsiderate divers and groups blocking the slipway and endangering children playing in the shallows – but particularly through "diver saturation". As a consequence, the number of boats allowed to launch in one day is strictly limited, as is the number of divers per boat, plus the fact you will have to pay for both boat and occupants. There are ample notices advising you of the current situation (maximum of 20 divers out of harbour at any one time; no limit on number of boats, though there is a charge per boat and per diver; all boats must be out of the water by 7.30pm; no vehicles on slipway; boats must be manhandled in and out; no winches, ropes or towing lines). Do not attempt to launch without paying first, otherwise you will be banned.

The entire area is owned by the National Trust, including the cliffs, harbour and foreshore. Administration of the harbour and boat traffic is through the Mullion Harbour Master, Dennis Foster, who can often be found in his office, part of a fish store on the right hand side facing the sea (tel. 01326 240222) or can be contacted at his home, Island View, in the port. Vehicles are allowed into the immediate harbour area, but only to load and unload equipment or boats, but

Opposite: Dive Sites in Area 6, Mount's Bay East. This area is covered by Admiralty Charts 2565 (Trevose Head to Dodman Point); 777 (Land's End to Falmouth); 2345 (Penzance Bay); Ordnance Survey map 203.

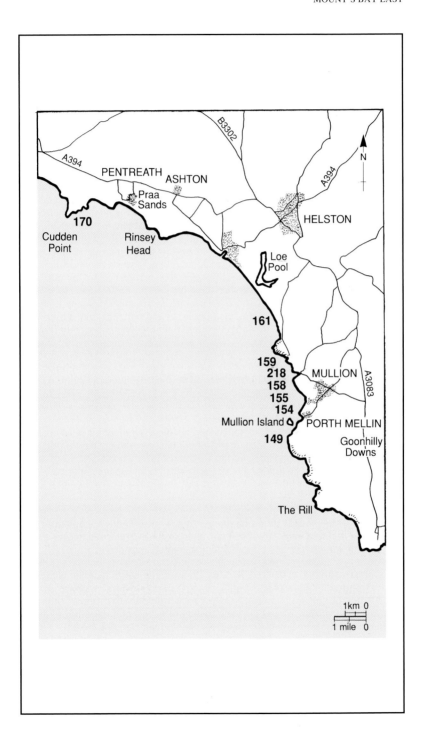

B3302

A394

N

PENTREATH ASHTON

Praa
Sands

HELSTON

170

Cudden
Point

Rinsey
Head

Loe
Pool

161

159
218
158
155
154

MULLION

A3083

Mullion Island ⬠

PORTH MELLIN

Goonhilly
Downs

149

The Rill

1km 0

1 mile 0

vehicles are not allowed on the slipway. Nor can you leave your trailer or vehicle here, but must return up the access road to one of the parking areas, the Quarry being the nearest.

Those intending to dive are advised to park, walk down to the cove, consult the Harbour Master as to what can be launched that day and how many divers accommodated, pay the necessary fee and abide by his instructions. The slipway is usually empty in the summer months, since the local wooden fishing boats will all be afloat in the harbour, but in spring and autumn these may be left part way up the slip, and in the winter right up at the top, possibly blocking all entry and exit.

If you can launch, then manoeuvre your trailer on to the slip and leave it standing across the width while you get ready, so that it will not run away. A runaway boat on the 25-degree slope could be disastrous if it struck anyone, so take great care leaving and returning. There is a power winch, but its use by visitors is forbidden. If you are in real trouble or some emergency arises then the fishermen may well help you – but do not expect it!

Mullion Cove has a sand and pebble foreshore that dries out completely at low water spring tides. At very low water take great care when leaving harbour in any boat with an outboard engine, keeping very close in to the end of the quay wall to avoid a rocky outcrop. There are also some nasty rocks just outside the harbour on the north side, only some 75ft from the quay. In the short distance between Mullion Harbour and Mullion Island, the bottom is sand with reefs and a maximum depth of 9m. There are a number of dive sites out of Mullion, none very far from the harbour.

149 Denise 50 00 14N; 05 16 00W. A French steamship of 1,598 tons with 25 crew, carrying coal from Swansea to Rouen, which ran aground south-west of Mullion on 6 June, 1918. She was a victim of fog, not hostile action, and after her cargo had been salvaged she was stripped of her gun, engine and heavy components, and abandoned to the sea.

The wreck can be found round the second headland south of the cove, inshore of a large rock that shows at most states of the tide except very high water. This stands about 78ft off the cliff, and the remains of the wreck, which include a boiler, plating and bits lie around the half-tide rock. The maximum depth inside the rock is 11m, outside 14m.

150 Mullion Island A large, irregular, uninhabited rocky outcrop, with shallow water on the Mullion side, but a bit deeper to seaward. There are vast areas of underwater reef and long sand-filled gullies to explore. The weed is very dense here in summer, but the site offers some exciting shallow diving.

151 Cannon site 50 00 45N; 05 16 07W. On the south-western corner of Mullion island, trapped inside a shallow gully running parallel with the shore, can be found a number of iron cannon, from an as yet unidentified wreck, probably around 1750. No real survey of these seems to have been carried out, and it would make an interesting club project to identify their size and weight.

152 Cannon site Part way along the high cliffs between Mullion Cove and Polurrian Cove, directly under where an area of cliff fall is obvious, lies a small

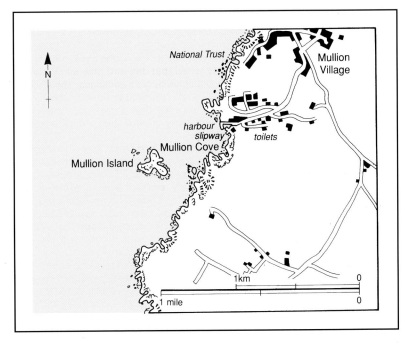

Mullion.

iron cannon site with just two guns. There is no identification as to their source as yet.

153 Cannon site Another small cannon site lies only a few hundred yards north-west of Site **151**. This is on the extreme south-eastern corner of Polurrian Cove (the right, looking towards the shore). The site is something of a mystery, since the guns are seen only after severe storms, when the sand levels drop, and the beach is stripped down to bedrock. Exactly how many guns there are, or how they came to be there, is not known.

154 Boyne 50 01 25N; 05 15 28W. This iron barque of 617 tons, registered at Scarborough, was on passage from Semarang to Falmouth with 900 tons of sugar. She became trapped here on 1 March, 1873, in a heavy south-west gale and was driven against the high cliffs just north of Polurrian Cove.

Only four men survived the wreck; they managed to get away in one of the ship's boats, the remaining fifteen drowning. Five of the dead were washed ashore at Mullion, all much mutilated by the sea, also a thigh and a hand were found among the rocks. She went to pieces very quickly, and all that survived when she was located in 1969 were her incomplete brass nameplate, a silver serving slice and a few brass ornamental pieces.

155 Santo Christo de Castello 50 01 30N; 05 15 42W. Probably best known as the "Mullion pin wreck" since the site when found in 1969 by Peter McBride was covered in thousands of hand-made brass domestic sewing pins. She was a Genoese merchant vessel of some 600 tons, on passage from Amsterdam to her home port. She had called in at Falmouth a few days earlier, was then forced to anchor off Polurrian by the wind, and finally blown ashore and wrecked in October 1667 in the small cove of Pol Glâs.

Ten years' work were put into this site, during which time it was surveyed and fully excavated, the results of which can be seen on display in the Charlestown Shipwreck Centre. Regrettably, a northern sub-aqua club used their newly found experience gained on a Bovisand explosives course, placed charges far too large for the task around a concreted cannon, and brought down about 100 tons of overhanging rock on part of the site. Whereas previously the sea washed shingle in at one end and out of the other, now blocked, the depth of shingle has greatly increased, denying everyone access to the many cannon on the site.

An unfortunate aspect of this site is that it lies directly beneath the Mullion area sewer discharge pipe! This makes it a quite disgusting dive and supposedly a health hazard, but in fact none of the original diving team between 1969 and 1979 was ever made ill as a consequence. The site is not difficult to find – round the first headland going north out of Polurrian Cove and you will smell it!

This stretch of coast is well worth exploring with a magnetometer, since the Angrouse Cliff here is a mass of rocks, gullies and crevices, and there have been more than ten recorded wrecks in the area, including a Dutch East Indiaman.

156 Jonkheer Meester van de Wall de Puttershock 50 02 22N; 05 16 15W. This Amsterdam-registered East Indiaman came to grief during the night of 24 March, 1867, on her way from Batavia (now Jakarta) to the Netherlands with passengers, and a cargo of coffee, arrowroot and tin worth £50,000. A Mousehole pilot boat had sen her tacking between the Lizard and Gunwalloe that afternoon, but had assumed she did not require assistance. Nothing more was heard from her until 2am, when distress rockets soared up into the night sky. A Coastguard on cliff

This vivid engraving shows the Dutch East Indiaman Jonkheer Meester van de Wall de Puttershock, which was stranded and wrecked under Angrouse Cliffs in 1867.

Poldhu Cove.

watch then found wreckage near Poldhu, the bodies of two women, a baby and several seamen.

A somewhat bedraggled and bruised sailor was then found among the rocks on the foreshore, but not even the local vicar could understand his tongue, learning only that he was Greek and had joined the ship at Batavia. At this stage the identity of the wreck was still in question, but the matter was settled when Captain Lammert's masonic membership diploma was washed ashore. Most of the 850 tons of coffee came on shore and was saved, together with baskets of sugar and a box containing gold coins, banknotes and jewellery. Local fishermen went to work on the site, and using glass-bottomed buckets known as "water-glasses" and wreckers' tongs, recovered most of the tin, receiving £15 per ton salvaged.

Halfway between Mullion village and Mullion Cove is a turning marked to the Polurrian Hotel. Vehicles may be parked at the end of this road, after which it is a 15-minute walk down to POLURRIAN COVE, a beautiful, clean, sandy beach facing south-west. It is not possible to get a boat down to here, but the effort to carry diving or snorkelling equipment down will be well worth while, if you do not have the use of a boat. There is no tide here, and it is no great distance to swim along to Pol Glâs or further. The maximum depth is less than 9m, the sea bed mostly sand and small boulders. The only facility is a public toilet.

Return to the main road leading through Mullion village, and just past the New Inn fork left where the signs indicate POLDHU COVE, which is only one mile from

Mullion. There are two spellings, Poldhu or Poldew, but both identify what was once Poljew – a small river estuary that silted up, now a pleasant sandy beach.

It is a very popular holiday beach, and while the sand at the edge of the surf line may be firm, the remainder of the beach can be a nightmare if you attempt to launch a heavy RIB on a trailer. Many vehicles have been bogged down here and had to be pulled out by tractor – though finding one is not easy. Launching here is possible, but not recommended, especially if there is any south-west wind.

The beach offers access to the Angrouse Cliffs, also Gunwalloe and Halzephron Cliff further west. The bottom is very shallow for some distance offshore with only moderate visibility.

157 Cannon site 50 02 00N; 05 16 00W. Facing out to sea, around the point from Poldhu Cove to the right, along a small reef with some inlets, there is at least one iron cannon and possibly the remnants of a wreck of the 17th century, the *San Salvador*. This French ship was on passage from the Baltic to Le Havre in 1669, carrying timber and provisions for the French fleet. Certainly a large number of silver Spanish pieces-of-one have been found in clefts in the rocks here, which suggests that there may be other coins buried in the sand, or artefacts of some antiquity.

Continue away from Poldhu Cove going north-west, up a steep hill, through the village of Cury, join the A3083 again near the Royal Naval Air Station, then turn off left again at the signposted turning to GUNWALLOE. The Naval Air Station, HMS *Seahawk*, is the largest military helicopter base in Europe, and provides the Westland Sea King and other helicopters that operate in a search-and-rescue role for the entire South West. The station, which was first opened in World War Two, is part of the long association that Naval aviation has with this part of Cornwall. In World War One the Navy maintained an anti-submarine airship patrol base at Mullion, and between the wars operated aircraft from Predannack airfield, which is still a satellite station for HMS *Seahawk*.

Continue on this minor road through Gunwalloe village, past the Halzephron Inn, and on to Church Cove. The last part of this route is very narrow indeed, but then widens out into the cove area. Gunwalloe is one of the most historic areas of south Cornwall, rich in legend and history, and has seen numerous shipwreck incidents and a great deal of smuggling activity. The area is in fact two coves, Church Cove (the more southerly) and Jangye-ryn (sometimes known as Dollar Cove). The two are separated by a headland that has a strong connection with the fabled Dollar Wreck.

At some time in the 1770s, a Spanish vessel is said to have been wrecked on the point of the headland, the site of an ancient cliff castle or fortification that shelters the little church of St Winwaloe. This vessel is said to have struck the rocks and been dashed to pieces with nothing saved, not even a record of her name.

On board was supposed to be a vast treasure in silver dollars, variously estimated according to legend at between 17 and 19 tons! Apart from stories of dollars being found on the beach, nothing developed until 1845, when a party of speculators decided to lay a watertight dam round the narrow rock gully in which the wreck was supposed to lay, so that they could pump the area dry. They cut away part of the headland to create an access passage and steps leading down to the base of the cliff and rocks. They set handrails stanchions in place with molten lead, the remnants of which can still be seen, and went to work on their dam, but a single gale destroyed their efforts and they pulled out.

A second attempt was made in the late 1880s, when the Dollar Wreck Recovery Company was formed. The public were invited to buy shares, and they went to work. The plan was to tunnel under the gully in which the wreck lay, first digging a vertical access shaft. It is uncertain how exactly the directors thought they would gain access to treasure by tunnelling beneath it without the sea flooding the tunnel – but tunnel they did.

The entrance to the circular access shaft can still be seen at low tide on the right hand side of the reef, looking down from the cliff. As they turned to go under the gully the sea broke in, and the workings flooded. A suction pump was then used to draw up anything that dropped into the tunnel – which perhaps was the intended plan, but without a single coin appearing. Gunpowder charges were then detonated in the tunnel, blowing it up, followed by more dredging, but no treasure.

There is still evidence of these attempts: the cliff cutting, remains of the handrails, square sockets in the rocks to hold the supports for the traction-engine driven belt for the pumps, and the shaft itself. The only evidence of dollars is to be found in the possession of the vicar of Cury and Gunwalloe, since the church estate includes two silver Pillar Dollars, said to have come from the site. The site still attracts attention to this day, and the subject has its annual airing in the local press when news is short and we hear of yet another attempt to find "the treasure of Dollar Cove".

It is most unlikely that such a vast sum of money, measured in tons of silver, would have been left in shallow water hard up against an accessible cliff face, waiting for some modern-day adventurer to just pick up, when our 18th century forebears were more skilled at wrecking than we are today! If you consider that a Pillar Dollar weighs one ounce, then 17 tons would amount to 609,280 coins

Gunwalloe, showing the location of the Grip (Site 158).

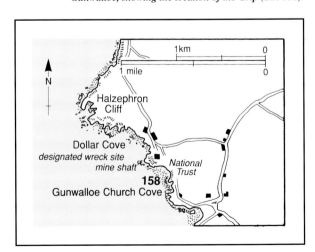

167

*The ship's bell from the wreck of the SS Grip (Site
158), which lies in Gunwalloe Church Cove in
10m. The bell is unusual as it carried the builder's
name plate, showing that the Grip was constructed
in Le Havre in 1874. The bell is on display at the
Charlestown Shipwreck Centre.*

and be worth about £15 million today. All the evidence is there and surely all
that effort was not some elaborate confidence trick – or was it? You will have
to judge for yourself, but many locals stand by the story, and claim they have
dollars themselves hidden away, but "sorry, I can't show you them right now" is a
standard reply to the obvious question.

With its large flat foreshore of sand and shingle, CHURCH COVE is popular with
holidaymakers and jealously guarded by the National Trust. There is a surf life-
saving post, and it is permitted to launch across the beach, but please move the
empty trailer back to the parking area and do not leave it on the sands.

It is very shallow for a long way out, with the depth never greater than 5m.
The depth of sand here can change dramatically overnight following a gale, the
depth of the sand dropping by as much as 6.5m. Following such a change you
may be lucky enough to swim into the only steamship wreck here, the *Grip*.

158 Grip 50 02 10N; 05 16 07W. This small Norwegian steamship is buried deep in sand for most of the time, but when uncovered the whole bottom of the ship, with single boiler, donkey engine and deck windlass, can be found lying level with the end of the church headland in only 4.5m depth. Of 566 tons, built in 1874 as the *Galilee* in Le Havre, she was wrecked in fog on 1 February, 1897, while carrying 700 tons of salt from Cadiz to Droutheim in Norway. Captain Falch and his crew of thirteen saved themselves in their own boats. The wreck is owned by the author, who raised her bell in 1965.

Trailed boats can be launched easily from JANGYE-RYN after being taken through the gap in the sand dunes, but the foreshore is rough, with relatively flat stones and uneven. Vehicles are not allowed on the beach. There is evidence of two shipwrecks within the cove – one, the *Schiedam*, is a designated site under the Protection of Wrecks Act, the other was the transport vessel *James and Rebecca* (Site **152**). There are also the remains of a crashed aircraft on the foreshore further round towards Halzephron Cliff. The cove is a little deeper than Church Cove, with many more rocks and reefs.

159 Schiedam 50 02 20N; 05 16 24W. Built as a fluyt, the precursor to the English flyboat, the *Schiedam* started life at Hoorn. Of 400 tons, she was a general trading ship, and in 1683 was carrying timber round the coast of Spain when she was taken by a Corsair frigate. Ten days later she was chased by the *James*, an armed galley of the Royal Navy, under the command of Clowdisley Shovell, later admiral aboard the ill-fated *Association* lost in the Isles of Scilly in 1707, and re-captured.

Taken into service with the Navy, she went to Tangier, was loaded with military stores, including several 18 and 32-pounder iron cannon placed in the hold, and sent home. On 4 April, 1684, she blundered into Jangye-ryn and was wrecked. Located and extensively excavated by Tony Randall and others over many years,

These brass and bronze cooking pots were found in the wreck of the Schiedam (Site 159).

Two 28-pounder iron cannon recovered from the
wreck of the Schiedam (Site 159).

their most recent find in 1991 was the ship's rudder almost intact, which has
been raised. Please remember this is a designated wreck, and that it is an offence
to dive here or interfere with the site in any way.

160 James and Rebecca No exact position can be given, since the actual
wreck has never been found, only remnants and coins on the foreshore of the right
date. This vessel was transport vessel No. 42 in Government service, under
Captain Rochester, on passage from Buenos Aires to Portsmouth carrying a
squadron of the 9th Light Dragoons.

She too blundered into Jangye-ryn in the dark on 6 November 1807, and went
ashore in a severe gale. A boat was launched but overturned, drowning five of the
six occupants. A line was eventually floated ashore, which was secured to create
a breeches buoy by which means most of those on board were saved. When the
ship went to pieces the remaining 80 men, women and children on board were
thrown into the sea – most of them were rescued, but 28 dragoons, 10 seamen
and 3 children lost their lives out of the 200 or so on board. The dead were
buried in a mass grave on the cliff overlooking the site, and its distinctive outline
of banked earth can still be seen. The victims of this transport ship were the last
to be buried without a proper Christian ceremony. Until that time, shipwreck

victims were always buried on unconsecrated ground but this was changed by a new law.

The remains of other wrecks lie buried beneath the sand in both bays, but finding a new site is a matter of luck and the vagaries of nature – it will not remain uncovered for long.

There is the strong tradition that the notorious pirate Captain Avery buried a vast hoard of personal treasure in the sand banks at Gunwalloe. In about 1770, a grant of treasure trove was obtained by John Knill, the Collector of Customs at St Ives, who had investigated and researched the subject. He spent many years searching, without success it seems. Before you are tempted to follow suit, remember that the National Trust are not too keen on people who go digging for treasure on their property.

The beauty of Gunwalloe is in its contrasts of scenery, with high cliffs, sandy beaches, the back drop of a spectacular golf course, and the tiny church tucked into the headland. Do not expect any facilities – there are none except for public toilets.

For all the long history of shipping losses hereabouts, there is very little remaining evidence, even around the notorious 200ft Halzephron Cliff, other than a single iron cannon at the north-west corner, and the remains of a radial engine from a fighter aircraft that lies on the foreshore to the right, along the cliff edge.

Return on the narrow lane to the vicinity of the Halzephron Inn, and a short distance past, turn off left down a track to GUNWALLOE FISHING COVE. Parking here is a problem, although access to the beach is not – provided you have a four wheel drive vehicle to cope with the difficult shingle beach when launching or recovering.

The cove is still in commercial use for concrete block making, so do not obstruct the lorries and diggers using the area. Trailers may have to be manhandled down the ramp, and surf often makes recovery difficult, so discretion is necessary. The site gives immediate access to the entire 2½-mile run of Loe Bar, right through to Porthleven and beyond to Rinsey Head. Immediately out from the beach you will find a lot of rock, but with sandy patches, depending on what nature has done over the winter. Depths will not exceed 15m until you are well away from the shore.

There is an interesting inlet on the south-western face of Halzephron Cliff called Pedngwinian, which is filled with rocks, gullies and cuts. This should have acted as a catchment area for wreckage driven south-east along the coast by gales over centuries. There is only one wreck site in the immediate area.

161 St Anthony 50 02 23N; 05 16 26.5W. The wreck lies 890ft north-west of the ramp leading to the beach. The ship was a large galleon that belonged personally to King John III of Portugal. Returning to Lisbon from Flanders, she was wrecked during a gale on 19 January, 1527. Her cargo was very rich indeed – copper cakes, jewels, cloth, silver, gold, jewellery, candlesticks, padlocks, musical instruments, horse harnesses, artillery and 18 blocks of silver bullion.

The wreck was located by the discovery of copper ingots in the beach, which led out to a site devoid of any evidence of shipwreck. Buried in the sand gullies were hundreds of fragments of candlesticks, over 40 copper ingots and one

Left: These copper "bun" ingots recovered from the carrack St Anthony (Site 161) are each about 8 inches across.

Below: Brass lion figures also recovered from the St Anthony. They are each about 2¹/₂ inches tall, and once formed supports at the base of large candlesticks.

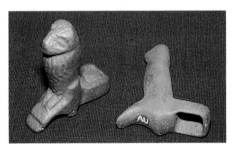

silver "melon" ingot, weighing 17lb, which is now in the British Museum collection of post-medieval ingots.

The site is a designated site and a Protected Wreck granted national protection in 1982. The author was the licensee for four years, handing over to Tony Randall, of Helston, in 1986.

162 Cannon site 50 03 15N; 05 17 00W. A cluster of perhaps six iron cannon on top of each other, which lies some 30m offshore, thought to be part of the prize vessel belonging to the Duke of Cumberland, described as Penrose's treasure ship, wrecked in the 16th century. Artefacts were found some years ago when a vessel with a prop-wash was put over the site, but no coin.

163 Brankelow 50 53 50N; 05 17 30W. A brigantine-rigged steamship of 1,661 tons, driven ashore on Loe Bar during a gale on 21 April, 1890. Carrying a cargo of coal, she stranded beam on to the coast, port side to, her bow towards Gunwalloe. The wreck was auctioned off on the beach, but went to pieces before anyone could make any money out of their purchase. Her wreckage lies scattered over a large area, partly buried in shingle only a short distance offshore.

Return to the main A3083 from Gunwalloe, turn left and proceed through the Naval Air Station that occupies both sides of the road. Immediately after passing under the road bridge linking the airfield with the administration area, turn off left on to a track and continue for about two miles, then take the second right hand fork for a further one mile. The going will be rough and narrow, possibly with farm animals and tractors. It is not recommended for large trailed boats.

This will eventually bring you to a point overlooking LOE BAR and LOE POOL, as well as the white memorial stone and cross to the victims of the wreck of HM man-of-war *Anson*. It is possible to leave a vehicle at the top of the track here, where it meets the shingle, and launch by carrying an inflatable to the water. Conditions are identical to Gunwalloe Fishing Cove.

It is possible to carry out a beach dive from here on the wreck of the *Anson*, but whether or not anything is showing is a matter of luck and Mother Nature. The wreck has been known to remain covered over for up to seven years at a time – in other years it may be uncovered and stay that way all season.

164 Anson 50 54 06N; 05 18 00W. In the days of sail, the wide sweep of Mount's Bay was a dreadful trap should a ship find itself caught there. No matter whether a vessel attempted to get clear to the north-west or south-east, the wind blew it closer and closer inshore, until eventually it struck. That is exactly what happened to the frigate *Anson* on 29 December 1807, a 44-gun fifth-rate ship of the Royal Navy on blockade duties off Brest. This still ranks as one of the major disasters in local history, brought about by bad weather.

The *Anson* was driven into Mount's Bay but managed to ride at anchor for a whole day. She then lost her best bower, after which Captain Lydiard deliberately ran her ashore in an effort to save the lives of his crew, though instead 120 drowned. What the captain did not know, and neither did many dozens of masters and captains over the centuries, that Loe Bar is deceptive in appearance. It is not

Loe Bar and Gunwalloe Fishing Cove, showing the location of the St Anthony (Site 161), which is a Protected Wreck Site.

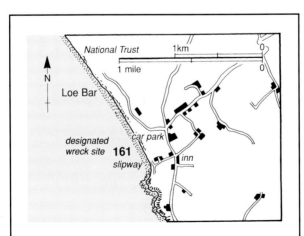

Left: This Portuguese astrolabe, 8 inches across, dates from around 1475. It was found on Loe Bar with a metal detector, after severe gales in 1981 that stripped over 5 metres of sand from the beach.

Right: The frigate Anson (Site 164) close inshore on Loe Bar, after being stranded in 1807.

Below: A 32-pounder canon from the Anson. Posing for the photographer are the captain of the salvage vessel (holding the lifting chain), his family and the crew.

a soft, yielding, sandy foreshore, with a gentle decrease in depth up to the water's edge, but a hard, stony beach, with a definite shelf just offshore, where the depth drops suddenly from around 3m to 8m and runs off into rock. Any hope of making a soft landing from where men could safely step ashore at low water, or a ship being re-floated, is out of the question. Any vessel coming in here in a heavy swell will strike the shelf a mighty blow, get thrown beam on and quickly pound itself to pieces in the shallows, with dry land only a tempting few yards away.

In the case of the *Anson*, since her progress had been monitored from the shore all that day, thousands of people lined the cliffs to watch as she got closer and was finally wrecked. Some good did come of the dreadful accident, since one of the spectators was Henry Trengrouse, son of a Helston cabinet maker. The sight of all those men drowning so close to shore made such an impression that he devoted the rest of his working life to the invention of a rocket-propelled life saving apparatus. This was to carry a light line across to a wreck from shore, which would then allow a heavier rope to be pulled out, and a breeches buoy rigged to bring people ashore above the waves. His invention was in competition with others – including Manby's mortar – but the rocket apparatus won through, eventually leading to the equipment that was still in use until 1987, and only discontinued in favour of search-and-rescue helicopters. Since Trengrouse was a Helston man, a chest holding a full set of his apparatus is held on display at the Helston Museum. There are also some relics from the *Anson* on display, and one of her 32-pounder cannon outside on a replica sea carriage.

Had the wreck of the *Anson* taken place some 500 years earlier, her captain would have seen an altogether different scene, since Loe Pool was at that time open to the sea, and ships could sail right up to Helston. Since then, as with Chesil Beach in Dorset, storms have thrown up millions of tons of shingle and changed the geography completely.

The entire length of Loe Bar is owned by the National Trust, who acquired it from the Penrose Estate. The remaining cannon and carronades from the *Anson*, when uncovered, are to be found in the very centre of the Bar, opposite the Pool, no more than 300ft clear of the surf.

Take the same track back to the A3083, turn left for Helston, following the signs through the town and bypass, to join the B3304 for PORTHLEVEN, a small, privately owned port that no longer accommodates the number or size of vessels it did in the past. It still supports a degree of fishing and fish processing, but is mainly concerned with the tourist trade.

The approach road from Helston will bring you down to the inner basin of the harbour, which has an excellent slipway, associated with a boat-builder's yard across the road. Permission from the Harbour Master is necessary to launch here, and a small fee is charged. On a spring tide the harbour dries out completely and stays that way for about 4 hours, so do not be caught out.

Parking is restricted within the village, but easier in the outskirts. There is an outer harbour, with jetties and a disused lifeboat station. The station housed a lifeboat from 1866 to 1929 and later a small shipwreck museum (now closed). No diving is allowed within the harbour confines.

Launching from Porthleven has the advantage that it gives immediate access to an otherwise remote stretch of coastline: Trewavas Head and the great offshore rock reef of which Trewavas is the eastern extremity. Within a mile of Porthleven

The Anson memorial. This photograph was taken looking to the north-west, along Loe Bar.

the maximum depth is 23m, with a sand and shingle bottom, broken by low reefs, the coast becoming high cliffs north-west of the port.

The sea bed is shallower between the *Anson* and Porthleven harbour entrance, and is a scattered mass of shipwreck debris from many centuries. Since everything is mixed up, there can be no identification of any one site, but a long drift dive of Loe Bar will reveal cannon, iron fittings, anchors, mill-stones, grinding-wheels and the odd souvenir.

More than sixty ships have come to grief on Loe Bar. Following storms, the beach level has been known to drop by 25ft in two days, which is the time to go beachcombing or metal detecting. The beach has yielded gold and silver coins and wreck artefacts – including a 15th century astrolabe in 1983.

165 Tye Rocks One of the larger buildings at Porthleven is the Tye Rock Hotel, named after the Tye Rocks, which lie a short distance out in the sea. This reef alone holds a number of iron cannon in 10m, but its origins are still unknown.

Facilities at Porthleven are excellent, with accommodation, camping and caravan sites, toilets, shops, cafés, restaurants, fuel and chandlers, as well as outboard repairs. Compressed air is unfortunately not available.

Approximately three miles east from where the B3304 joins the A394, a side road on the left will indicate Praa Sands, with an alternative circular route half a mile further on towards Penzance. Either route will take you to the one-mile stretch of clean, yellow sand beach, backed by sand dunes and shallow cliffs. It is a very popular holiday area facing south-west, gets very crowded and is therefore not recommended in summer.

Access to the beach to launch is available down a ramp, but no vehicles are allowed on the foreshore, neither must trailers be left on the sands. Praa is the last place in this area from which a boat can be launched (the next site is Perran Sands), so if you are contemplating a visit from seaward to Prussia Cove or the Cudden Point area the effort to launch here may be worthwhile.

Maximum depths off Praa Sands are around 14m, with a sand and rock-reef sea bed. There are no particular tidal problems but the beach can be unsafe in a heavy surf, and despite lifeguard supervision there have been a number of drownings here. Facilities are excellent – a great deal of accommodation of all types, camping and caravans, shops, toilets, pubs, cafés, restaurants and parking.

If you take the more easterly road away from the coast to join the A394 and turn left for Penzance, the signpost to PRUSSIA COVE is a little over one mile further on. The narrow tarmac road passes through the middle of a farm and ends in a field, where cars may be parked free of charge. The road continues off to the left, but is clearly marked "Private", since it leads to the Porthewalls estate. So from here on it will be necessary to carry everything down the track for about half a mile to the sea. It is not possible to launch a boat from here, although local boats are kept in the creek at Prussia Cove – and you may consider the effort to get diving gear all the way down unjustified.

Prussia Cove is best remembered for all its many smuggling activities, and its notorious "King of Prussia", a man named Carter who was head of a well

Porthleven.

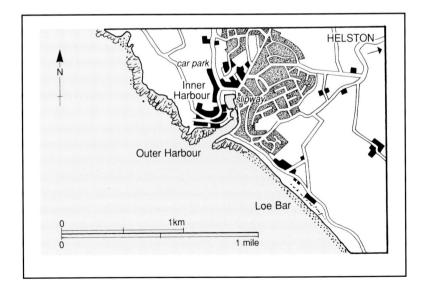

organised smuggling gang. The sheer isolation and suitability of the cove for this activity was ideal, and no doubt some of the proceeds went into building the large houses you will see here. The cove itself is a natural inlet, with surrounding cottages and a pebble beach. The immediately surrounding caves, gullies, reefs and shallows offer hours of underwater pleasure for photography or study of marine life.

There are no facilities other than cottages and flats to let (tel. 01326 315649 for details).

Offshore dive sites and wrecks

Other than Mullion island, already mentioned in detail, the only offshore dive site is the two-mile square of reef centred on Praa Sands, bounded by Cudden Point and Trewavas Head.

166 Reefs off Praa Sands A red navigational buoy marks Mountamopus Rock, which at low water may have only 3 to 4m of water over it. The Stone, half a mile away, is similarly situated. This area is infrequently dived, possibly due to its lack of wreck sites but the nature of the rocks and reefs make it well worth a visit. There is a good chance you will spot some of the very large conger eels that inhabit the miniature caves, and find a suitable shellfish for supper.

Some of the reefs have a considerable drop-off, going from 3 to 18m very quickly – almost a wall dive – and divers have reported ironwork from an unknown wreck. The offshore reef known as the Iron Gates is said to hold a cluster of iron cannon, and there is evidence to recommend two areas in which wreckage should be found.

All these rocks and reefs are marked on an Admiralty chart, and any of the local dive charter boat skippers will put you over the top of whichever one you want to dive. However, without Decca, GPS or an echo sounder only The Stone and Mountamopus Rock will be evident. Fish life across the reefs is prolific, with pollack and bass evident most of the year.

167 John R. Park 50 00 04N; 05 24 35W. This was a 7,194-ton American Liberty ship of World War Two built by the Luckenbach Steamship Company of New York and launched in March 1943. Part of convoy TBC-102, sailing from Southampton to the United States via Swansea in ballast, she was torpedoed by Oberleutnant Bushe in the German submarine *U-399* at 1.45pm on 21 March, 1945, about nine miles off the Lizard. Her complement consisted of 42 crew members, 28 Naval Armed Guard, and the convoy's Commodore and staff (six Royal Navy personnel), none of whom were killed or injured.

The *John R. Park* was leading the port column of ships when the torpedo struck her in No. 4 hold on the port side below the waterline. The entire breadth of that hatch ruptured, the crack extending from the port side across the main deck, over the bulwark and down the starboard side to the waterline. With her propeller shaft broken as well, the steering gear was destroyed, the mizzen topmast collapsed and the aft jumbo boom was blown overboard. She quickly settled by the stern, Nos. 3 and 4 holds filling quickly, and she sank at 7.35pm.

Five of her six lifeboats were picked up by the SS *American Press*, the next ship in the column; the sixth boat was towed to Newlyn by a crash boat stationed at Penzance.

The wreck lies in three pieces in a least depth of 40m (general depth 53m). The builder's name plate bearing the ship's number 466 has been recovered, also her many anti-aircraft guns from the mountings on the bridge and forward section. [Decca Position: SW Chain. Red (B) 7.89; Green (A) 44.42.]

168 Ibis 50 01 40N; 05 19 33W. Registered in London, this British steamship of 2,358 tons, bound from Bilbao to Glasgow with iron ore, was sailing alone when she was in collision with the Irish steamer *Whimbrel* on 12 May, 1918.

The accident happened at night, and in the ensuing confusion it was thought that the *Ibis* had been torpedoed. She went down with all 24 of her crew, in a position given at the time as six miles west of the Lizard. The wreck lies intact but collapsed on rock. The maximum depth is 31m. [Decca position: SW Chain. Red (B) 5.9; Green (A) 33.68.]

169 Speedwell II 50 05 25N; 05 25 00W. The much broken remains here are those of the SS *Speedwell II*, a British vessel registered in Hull, of 273 tons, which was said to have been one of the shadowy fleet of Q-ships of World War One. Previously named *Glendale*, she went ashore in dense fog on 15 July, 1918, carrying a cargo of Portuguese wine, since it was considered prudent for these ships to be genuinely employed while they waited for an opportunity to blast an unsuspecting German submarine out of the water with their concealed guns.

170 Warspite 50 07 10N; 05 29 20W. A well known old battleship built in 1915, the *Warspite* saw service in both world wars. Under tow to the breakers' yard in the Gareloch in 1947 she broke adrift and blew ashore. Her first resting place was in Prussia Cove, but after pumping out and re-floating she was towed to a position west of St Michael's Mount where she was broken up (Site **171**, next chapter).

Where the *Warspite* lay off Prussia, a little to the east of Piskies Cove, is a mass of debris from the grand old lady, since it was here that all the wire, cables, pumps, bridles and fittings were dumped in the shallows before she was towed away.

The wooden barque Noiseil, high and dry on Praa Sands in August 1905.

AREA 7:

Mount's Bay West

This area includes the coast from CUDDEN POINT to KEMYEL POINT. This western end of Mount's Bay is extremely beautiful on a clear summer's day. The clear blue sea, white sandy beaches, St Michael's Mount rising out of the depths like a fairytale castle, and the fishing ports of Mousehole and Newlyn huddled back against the high ground make a lasting visual impression.

From a diving point of view, it is certainly not the most exciting area of the south Cornwall coast. However, it does have the distinct advantage of a choice of launching sites and excellent shoreline diving, with shallow reefs and wrecks for trainees or snorkellers, and advanced interests for the more experienced. The more challenging diving lies in the west, nearer Land's End. Diving support based on Penzance is good, with a choice of air filling stations, charter dive boats and plenty of accommodation of all types.

This part of Mount's Bay is the site of a drowned forest, and St Michael's Mount, once the site of a monastery, is a huge rock outcrop that rose high above the trees that once surrounded it. When exceptionally low tides follow gales, petrified tree stumps sometimes uncover, and the whole area is rich in archaeological potential. A significant underwater find in 1974 was a quern (a stone hand mill for grinding corn), complete and dated at 2 BC, found in the Gwavas Lake area between Penzance and Newlyn.

The bay has a maritime history stretching back over many centuries, since this was the last place of refuge on leaving the English Channel, and the first on entering. Sailing vessels have sought shelter here for generations, since the high ground to the south-west protects them from the prevailing gales. With a maximum depth of 37m almost anywhere within the bay, a drift dive over the shingle and sand bottom in the shallower area could reveal anything.

There are quite a number of shipwreck sites. A number of World War One and World War Two losses are deep, two are of reasonable depth, and the remainder are shallow strandings. Penzance BSAC often find new evidence of wreckage in the line of shallow reefs just offshore from Eastern Green, the two-mile stretch of beach between Marazion and Penzance.

181

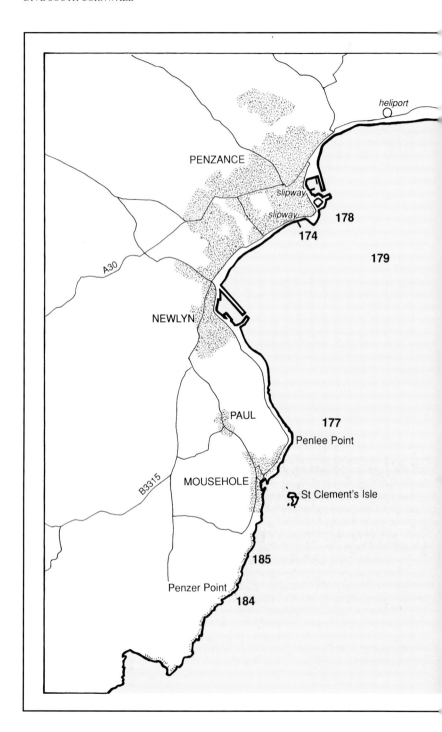

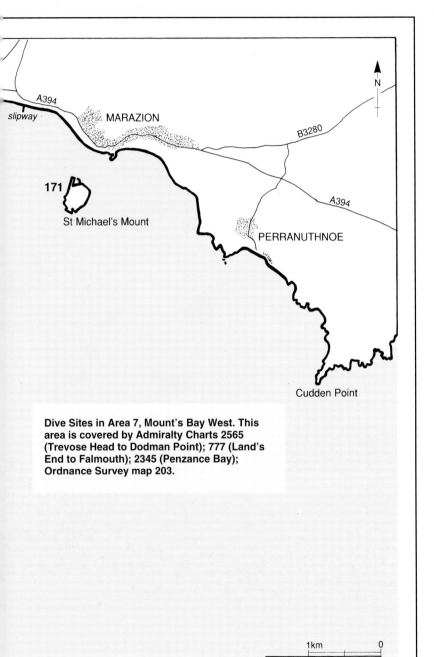

Dive Sites in Area 7, Mount's Bay West. This area is covered by Admiralty Charts 2565 (Trevose Head to Dodman Point); 777 (Land's End to Falmouth); 2345 (Penzance Bay); Ordnance Survey map 203.

Tide does not become a problem until you reach a position at least a mile offshore, or half a mile east of St Clement's Isle. At this point the full ebb of the English Channel begins to be felt – diving should be restricted to slack water where possible.

Warning If you are diving from an inflatable or small craft in Mount's Bay, the greatest hazard is damaging your propeller on the shallow reefs close inshore. The areas around Cudden Point and The Stone can be nasty on a spring ebb tide, and it is advisable to wait for slack water. Beware of commercial boat traffic, especially around St Michael's Mount, Penzance and Newlyn, and do not dive without flying the diving flag. Between March and October, the Isles of Scilly ferry RMS *Scillonian III* enters and leaves Penzance regularly, and the Scillies freighter *Gry Martha* comes and goes throughout the year, so keep clear of the main channel.

Coastal dive sites

Situated halfway between St Michael's Mount and Cudden Point, PERRAN SANDS can be reached via the signposted turning off the A394, through the village of Perranuthnoe, a distance of three-quarters of a mile to the sea. A concrete ramp gives access to the beach, and with a distance of less than 200 yards between the car park and head of the slipway, launching boats has been made easy.

The foreshore is soft, clean sand and is an excellent family beach, with extensive rock outcrops and loose boulders at the east and west extremities. For almost half a mile out from the shore, the sea bed is composed of rock and reef, with a maximum depth of no more than 12m, but when level with the tip of Cudden Point some tidal effects will be felt.

Local divers report evidence of wreckage strewn over a wide area, but all the pieces are small and probably the remains of some forgotten 19th century wooden vessels. The reefs are good shellfish country, with summer underwater visibility often better than 20m. It is not a particularly exciting area but excellent for the less experienced diver.

Within the village of Perranuthnoe can be found public toilets, a shop, café, post office, the Victoria Inn and a wide range of accommodation, including the Lyn Field camp site and St Piran's Holiday Cottages.

Inaccessible from the land, but only 1¼ miles from Perran Sands, is CUDDEN POINT. This large headland, with Prussia Cove on its southern edge, offers deeper water, around 14m, and a wide expanse of deep, sand-filled rock gullies that stretch out into the huge reefs off Praa Sands (Site **166**).

The A394 bypasses MARAZION, so turn off at the roundabout as you approach it. Marazion was not built for motor vehicles, and you will find the streets narrow. Just past the square and small shopping area, on the western side there is a large public car park, well signposted as the access point for those visiting St Michael's Mount. Beside the car park is a wide concrete slipway that can be used free of charge, and will allow the largest trailed boat to be taken onto the hard sandy foreshore complete with vehicle. The beach at Marazion (or Market Jew to use its old name) is the eastern end of a two-mile stretch of beach known as Eastern Green, which runs through to Penzance breakwater.

The most prominent feature of the area is ST MICHAEL'S MOUNT, a huge rocky outcrop owned by the National Trust. It is the permanent home of Lord and Lady St Levan, who reside among the turrets and battlements of the stronghold perched on top. At low tide a granite block causeway dries out to allow foot or vehicle passage. Visitors are welcome on Mondays, Wednesdays and Fridays in April to October between 10am and 4.45pm, or by special conducted tours in the winter. Visitors with no official business at the Mount should leave their vehicles in the Marazion car park and walk across.

Diving from or landing on the private jetty at St Michael's Mount is strictly forbidden, but its rocky base offers excellent and distinctive diving conditions, seldom over 10m, the bottom running off to sand. The small harbour to the landward side is used by fishing boats, and care should be taken not to impede their passage.

171 Warspite 50 07 05N; 05 28 51W. The main attraction for divers at Marazion is the remains of the battleship *Warspite*. For details of her initial stranding at Prussia Cove see Site **170** in the previous chapter.

After the *Warspite* was re-floated it was considered unsafe to continue to tow her to the Clyde. The 640ft warship was taken to a position just off St Michael's Mount and beached in shallow water. Here she was slowly broken up for scrap, a prolonged operation since all the metal removed had to be transported by vessel to the shore. The operation was not completed for several years.

The battleship Warspite (Sites 170 and 171) was on her way to the breakers in 1947 when she broke adrift from her tugs and drifted ashore. This photograph shows her on the rocks off Prussia Cove, before she was refloated and towed to the shallows west of St Michael's Mount.

Today all that is obvious on the sea bed (in 8m depth) are two boilers and a great mass of broken and half buried steel. A great deal of the ship's double bottom remains but has become buried. A good rummage around the area with a metal detector has shown up some excellent pieces, including brass tallies from gauges, controls, handles and cutlery.

Approximately a quarter of a mile west of Marazion, where the road swings away from the sea front and goes over a railway bridge, there are car parking facilities, public toilets and cafés at EASTERN GREEN. There are two free concrete slipways, both approximately 5ft wide and suitable for trailed boats, which give access to the same area as Marazion, and you may find it less crowded in summer. An additional launch site at Long Rock is no longer available.

Off Long Rock there is a beacon on the seaward end of the reef to aid location at high water. Numerous small wrecks have taken place all along Eastern Green – mostly fishing vessels – and pieces of iron, cannon balls and anchors are found regularly.

At Long Rock the A394 joins the main A30, which continues to PENZANCE, and on towards Land's End via a by-pass. Penzance is a busy town centred on the harbour, which has an outer quay used mainly by the Isles of Scilly Steamship Company's ferry *Scillonian III*. There is an inner basin with two slipways for small pleasure craft, and a floating or non-tidal inner dock used by commercial vessels, Penzance Ship Repairers and the Trinity House museum.

The road into Penzance will take you past the railway terminal and round to overlook the harbour and a large car park and coach station. Unless you want to carry on to the promenade, where there is a third slip, it is advisable to make use of this parking facility. It has the advantage that it is central, gives easy access to all amenities, including a dive shop, air charging, the Penzance BSAC club house and launching site.

The pier leading off to one side of the car park is Albert Pier and the best launching site is tucked away in the north-east corner; the alternative is across the harbour, opposite the dry dock at Penzance Ship Repairers. Both are controlled by the Penzance Harbour Commissioners – permission and the appropriate fee must be sorted out with the Harbour Master (tel. 01736 66113) before you launch. The Harbour Office is on the end of Albert Pier, overlooking the entire area.

No diving is allowed inside the harbour or in the fairways, and there is a maximum water speed limit of 4 knots. The Albert Pier slipway dries out completely at low water, so timing must be considered. The alternative slipway also dries out, and is more restrictive on movement that the larger car park site. Vehicles and trailers may not be left there and its use by visitors causes congestion in summer.

Part way along Albert Pier is Bill Bowen's compressor building, which houses the largest air compressor in Cornwall. A little further on you will find the Penzance BSAC club rooms, which are part of the sailing club building. Contact can be made via the club (tel. 01736 5226), or Bill Bowen (tel. 01736 752135).

A third slipway can be found along the promenade, past the outdoor swimming pool on the road to Newlyn. It is not much used, because a heavy growth of weed makes it slippery and the beach here is soft and mainly pebbles. Car

Above: Western End slipway, Penzance.

Below: The Trinity House museum is next to the harbour at Penzance.

parking (limited stay) is allowed along the sea front, and there is a car park on the opposite side of the road, within easy reach of local facilities.

There is little of diving interest along the western beach, despite the Chimney and Battery Reef rocks by the swimming pool, or the Wherry Rocks and Lariggan Rocks part way along. The promenade and harbour slipways give easy access to The Gear and the remains of the SS *Taycraig* (Site **174**) and HMS *Royallo* (Site **179**). Otherwise Gwavas Lake, the shallow bay off Newlyn Harbour, is very shallow, with sand and low outcrops on the bottom. This area was a freshwater lake when Mount's Bay was a forest.

A small town with an extremely busy harbour, NEWLYN is said to be the most active fishing port in the country. It offers no facilities for diving or the launching of small pleasure craft. There is a small slipway tucked away in one corner of the harbour, but it must be discounted.

The only coastal dive site between Penzance and Mousehole is on the coast road, half a mile south of Newlyn, opposite an abandoned quarry, known as Rôskilly. This is frequently used by the local sub-aqua clubs in bad weather, since it is extremely sheltered. There are a number of lay-by parking areas, but no facilities. Opposite a cave-like opening in the roadside cliff face is a narrow track leading to the foreshore and its flat rocks. It is not possible to launch a boat here, but a shallow shore dive is practical in the area known as Carn Gwavas, offering a maximum depth of 10m with a sand and gravel bottom and good visibility.

Take the B3315 south out of Newlyn; a turning off this road, via Paul, will bring you to MOUSEHOLE. Alternatively, an unclassified road to Mousehole runs parallel with the coast and past the Penlee Lifeboat Station.

Once a very active pilchard fishing port, and still strongly supportive of the fishing industry, Mousehole (pronounced "Mowzl") is one of the most attractive and charming of the Cornish ports, with narrow streets, blind turns and hidden courtyards. Historic in every sense, it was sacked by a fleet of Spanish galleons in 1595, which left just one building, the Keigwin Arms, standing among the smoking ruins.

The geography of the town makes it impossible to tow a trailed boat through, and while it would be perfectly feasible to launch from the slip on the northern side of the harbour, it cannot be recommended. An alternative slip leads off from the public car park, on the southern corner where there is a small sandy beach, but this too dries at low water, and it would be advisable to enquire before considering its use. It would be easier to charter a local diving boat as an alternative.

Diving is not allowed within the harbour or at its entrance – with the frequent boat traffic it is sensible to stay well clear for safety reasons.

Offshore dive sites and wrecks

Three offshore sites, which are not shipwrecks, can all be reached easily from Penzance, being roughly within one mile. From Marazion or Eastern Green the distance will be roughly 2½ miles.

You can launch a boat at Mousehole.

172 Cannon site In 1984 a new cannon site was discovered on the reef known as the Cressars, directly out from Eastern Green. Lying on a sandy bottom in less than 10m four or five iron guns were found, as well as cannonballs to fit. Nothing much seems to have come of the find, and it might well bear further investigation and excavation as a project. The location is approximately 50 07 08N; 05 31 05W.

173 The Gear An outcrop of rock due south of the harbour entrance at Penzance, The Gear is marked by a black beacon. The beacon is fixed at the shallowest part of the reef, which dries the best part of 2m at low water. This offers shallow areas over the reef, dropping off 14m on the eastern side and slightly less to the west. On the Penzance side, about 32ft from the beacon, can be found the scattered remains of the SS *Taycraig*.

174 Taycraig 50 56 38N; 05 31 36W. A British registered steamship built in 1901, of 407 tons, she struck the Gear Rock while working towards Newlyn at 1.30am on 27 January, 1936, and holed her engine room, which started to flood. She then foundered, leaving her bow sticking up at a steep angle. Despite having 5.5m of water under her stern she could not be moved, and before the end of the month had started to break up. Her crew were rescued by the Penzance lifeboat. The wreck lies scattered all round the reef, and much was salvaged at the time, but interesting items still turn up from time to time.

175 Carn Base 50 05 44N; 05 31 40W. A similar reef to The Gear, which is surrounded by deeper water, and never breaks the surface. Situated a quarter of a mile offshore from the Carn Gwavas area, there is a large, flat area, heavily weeded, with a wide range of starfish, urchins and fish life. The average depth over the reef is 10m, which drops off to a maximum of 16m. There are no known shipwrecks on Carn Base.

176 Low Lee Ledges Although marked by a lit navigational buoy anchored off to the north-east of the reef, the Low Lee Ledges are not easy to find without an echo-sounder. They are a crescent-shaped collection of reefs with the open mouth facing north. Average depth is 15m clear of the rock, with a minimum depth of 4 to 10m.

Heavily weeded and covered in marine life, Low Lee Ledges holds a secret that continues to defy solution. On the north and east sides there are two iron cannon, one close to the rocks the other well clear. There have also been large quantities of Friesland bricks found here – small, yellow Dutch bricks. Various additional evidence of a wreck survives: in 1961 and 1967 bronze cannon were raised from the area, one of which is on display outside the Morab Library in Penzance. The question is, from which wreck did they come? There is no evidence of a large, armed Dutch vessel being lost here, only a West Indiaman in December 1771, so the mystery remains unsolved.

Any other artefacts from this wreck are unfortunately mixed up with the remains of the small iron SS *Primrose*, which has been broken up by ground seas and well scattered over the reef.

177 Primrose 50.55.30N; 05.31.30W. After loading coal at her home port of Garston, the SS *Primrose*, 79 tons net, built in 1885, set off for Newlyn and was within a mile of her destination when Captain Lewis misjudged his distance offshore and struck Low Lee Ledges on 23 August, 1906. She flooded forward immediately and settled down, and was broken up by rough weather the following month before she could be salvaged.

The SS Primrose (Site 177) was carrying a cargo of coal when she drove ashore in August 1906.

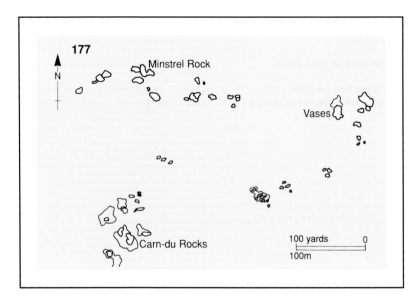

The SS Primrose (Site 177) lies on Low Lee Ledge.

178 Ransome 50 06 55N; 05 31 17W. A small steam collier, which struck the Low Lee Ledges while carrying coal for Newlyn on 17 April, 1885. With a great hole in her bows and leaking badly she ran for Penzance, hoping to be able to beach inside in the shallows. Unfortunately, she foundered a few yards short of the entrance, in 4.5m.

Although almost nothing remains of the *Ransome*, it was marked on Chart No. 2345 before it was redrawn to meet the new metric standard. Since the site lies directly in the path of any craft using Penzance Harbour diving here is not recommended.

179 Royallo 50 06 46N; 05 30 56W. A much dived and popular wreck site, unfortunately widely scattered and largely dispersed by explosives, so that little shows above the sandy bottom. Launched in 1916 at Goole as a steel ketch-rigged trawler of 248 tons, she was requisitioned by the Navy as a minesweeper in 1939, and armed with two small guns.

While attempting to locate mines dropped by aircraft on 1 September, 1940, she detonated one of them in a shattering explosion that echoed around Mount's Bay. The ship was obscured by a huge column of water, and disappeared. After she sank, her wheelhouse and top of her funnel showed, and a concession was given to the British Iron and Steel Corporation to scrap her, but very little was removed. The wreck lies in 10m, about a quarter of a mile south-east of where the *Ransome* sank. Her bow, boilers and stern areas are intact, the remainder flattened. The remains are liberally covered in sea squirts, sea anemones and dead man's fingers.

180 Alice Marie 50 06 11N; 05 29 21W. Formerly a well dived wreck lying in 26m, three-quarters of a mile from St Michael's Mount, almost nothing remains of this steel barque that sank in 1908, since a salvage company lifted huge sections of her for scrap metal during 1986.

181 Hellopes 50 04 32N; 05 29 33W. It was very much a case of "so near, and yet so far" when the 2,774-ton screw steamship *Hellopes* sank 1½ miles east of Mousehole, about 4 miles out in Mount's Bay, on 21 December, 1911. Launched in 1899 and operated by the British and South African Steamship Company, she traded until 1911 when, after stranding at the Cape, it was decided she should be scrapped.

She was on her last voyage, from the Mersey to Falmouth, carrying her last cargo of coal, when she started to leak in a howling gale off Land's End. She

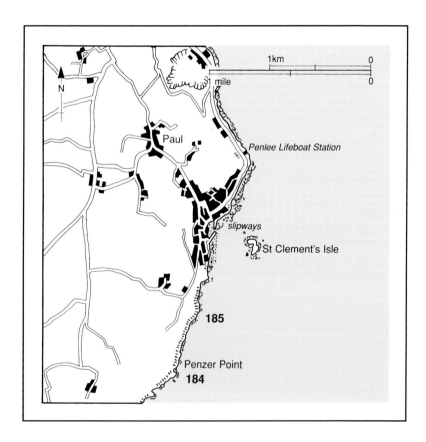

Above: The 9,500-ton Ansgir on the rocks near Penzer Point after going ashore during a gale in December 1920.

Opposite: The area near Mousehole, showing the locations of the Ansgir (Site 184) and the Conqueror (Site 185).

Below: The trawler Conqueror ashore near Penzer Point in December 1977.

reached Mount's Bay almost on her beam ends and full of water, to sink so close to her destination. The wreck lies in 33m with a least depth of 24m, and is in three parts. She lies north-west to south-east with her stern lying on its starboard side, the mid section and boilers stand upright about 4.5m, her bow is at an angle, and both masts lie off to one side. [Decca position: SW Chain. Red (B) 3.12; Green (B) 33.61; Purple (C) 52.51.]

182 St Clement's Isle Some 200 yards off Mousehole is the low rocky mass of St Clement's Isle, an extension of the deep rocky gullies that stretch out from the shore. This is an excellent dive site but, with the risk of local boats choosing to use the southern channel to reach Mousehole and the depth of water, it is not a shore dive.

Beyond the island, depths drop quickly to 37m with a fine sand bottom once clear of the reef. The area is subject to quite a lot of tide, particularly on a spring ebb.

183 Penzer Point The site of a Coastguard lookout, now unmanned, and the disused Lloyds Signal Station, Penzer Point is the western boundary of this area. From Mousehole to Lamorna Cove, high cliffs dominate the coastline, so there is no access from the land and a boat is needed to visit the remaining wreck sites in the western part of Mount's Bay. Penzer Point is an interesting dive in itself, with water deeper than one would expect close to the headland, and a profusion of reefs and gullies in the 14m range.

184 Ansgir 50 04 12N; 05 35 24W. One of the largest vessels ever wrecked on the coast of Cornwall, the *Ansgir* had a deadweight capacity of 9,500 tons and was surrendered to Britain as a prize of war in 1918. Her German crew brought her over to Leith, where she was handed over into the management of Gow, Harrison and Company of Glasgow. She sailed in ballast to Hampton, Virginia and returned with a cargo of coal for Rotterdam.

A second similar voyage for coal was successfully completed, then her ownership was awarded to Japan as part of their war reparation. She sailed from France to Barry to load bunker coal, but in hazy weather, with a full gale blowing, she struck the rocks a little to the west of Penzer Point on 1 December, 1920, and became a total wreck. Her boilers still remain close to the shark's-fin shaped rock, close inshore in 7 to 10m, and plate and wreckage is jammed in almost every crevice.

185 Conqueror 50 04 21N; 05 32 15W. The most recent wreck of any size in Mount's Bay, the *Conqueror*, a fairly new 1,157-ton Hull registered freeze-trawler, ran aground in clear, calm conditions on the morning of Boxing Day, 1977. Her mate was held responsible for leaving the bridge unattended with the ship on automatic pilot while he went below for breakfast.

Attempts to re-float her failed, and she was sold to Eurosalve of Folkestone, who were unsuccessful in saving her. By January, 1979 there was almost nothing left showing above the surface. A small amount of salvage work took place, but she was abandoned with most of her equipment still fitted until the sea broke her into three parts, which lie in an average depth of 17m.

186 Reidar 50 00 02N; 05 27 25W. Although lost on 22 February, 1918, the 1,353-ton London registered *Reidar* was not a war loss. Carrying a cargo of coal between Newport and St Nazaire, she struck the Runnel Stone off Land's End and started to take in water. Struggling to get to shallow water before she sank, her master managed to reach Mount's Bay, where she sank in 56m, the least depth over the wreck being 43m. Only one man lost his life when she foundered, the remainder reaching Penzance in their own boats.

The wreck has been dived, and is sitting upright, with her bow collapsed. [Decca position: SW Chain. Red (B) 7.89; Green (B) 32.1.]

187 Ocean Foam 50 05 12N; 05 30 47W. A steam drifter of 90 tons, built in 1911, the *Ocean Foam* was requisitioned by the Admiralty in November 1914, armed with a single 3-pounder gun and given the prefix HMS. On 7 October, 1918, she was involved in a collision and sank off Penzance. All the details are available, but her wreck seems not to have been found, although reports of the period say she sank in 22m.

188 Pursuit 50 03 55N; 05 30 41W. A similar steam drifter to the *Ocean Foam*, 79 tons, built in 1903, and taken into Royal Navy service in 1916. She too was sunk following collision, and went down in 39m, least depth over the wreck being 30m. There are no reports of conditions on the bottom.

189 Antwerpen 50 06 55N; 05 31 19W. Built in 1887, and operated by the Shipping Controller on behalf of Foster, Hain and Read, this 1,637-ton steel steamship was carrying coal from Barry to Rouen, when she was attacked by the German submarine *UC-77* on 18 November, 1917.

At the time she was about two miles south-west of the Runnel Stone, but managed to remain afloat long enough to reach the shallows of Mount's Bay, where she sank in 4m. There are very few remains, since she was dispersed almost to sea bed level.

*The Minack Theatre at Porthcurno.
There is a launch site nearby.*

AREA 8:

Land's End

To most people, almost anywhere west of Penzance is vaguely "Land's End", so this last area starts at Penzer Point, just east of LAMORNA COVE, and follows the coast for some 12 miles west to GRIBBA POINT, north of Whitesand Bay. This part of the coast offers some of the best diving in south Cornwall. While such expressions as "fantastic" or "outstanding" might seem extravagant, and more in keeping with Truk Lagoon or Scapa Flow, generations of divers continue to visit here for "the big one". Perhaps the isolation of the area is part of the attraction.

Land's End itself is but a very small pimple on the map of Penwith District Council's responsibility, perhaps less than a two-mile stretch of sheer granite cliffs and tourist-worn turf. It is looked after by a Jersey-based company, which owns and operates the Land's End Visitors Centre and attracts some 1½ million tourists each year.

Probably less than a fifth of the area has been explored under water; until the early 1960s no one dived here at all. There was then a short period when a lot of young men made a lot of money diving for crayfish, until they fished them out. They were the pioneers, most of whom lived or lodged around Penzance, who went to impossible depths, broke every rule in the book, ignored decompression tables, and still turned up every night in the Dolphin Inn at Penzance to talk about it! The majority, unfortunately, did not do too well for their efforts, but they did pass on what they had seen.

Their particular activity, geared to making as much money as possible in the shortest possible amount of time, relied heavily on making perhaps just one deep drop each day. That way they found the crayfish on the reefs that lay between 36 and 61m, which did not give them sufficient time for shipwreck sightseeing. Like all divers, though, they appreciated what they had seen, and told tales of sheer rock faces, dark drop-offs, tides that pinned them to a rock wall at 50m, incredible scenery and good visibility.

When the crayfish vanished, some of the divers stayed on in Cornwall or the Isle of Scilly, offering dive charter trips, and so others slowly took the opportunity to explore the shallower depths around Land's End. Much of it is still virgin territory, apart from the better known sites such as the Runnel Stone. There are still only a few divers who have intimate knowledge of the area – and those that do tend to hang on to it! With limited access to the coast due to the high cliffs, it is essentially an area for boat diving only, and the best way to gain local knowledge would be to make your first couple of visits on a dive charter boat. Get to know the area and some sites before planning your own visits.

There are some six miles of almost vertical rock, with only a few sandy coves, between Penzer Point and Gwennap. Offshore from Gwennap are to the Runnel Stone, Lee Ore and Poldew Rocks, then a further four miles of high cliffs broken only at Mill Bay, before reaching Whitsand Bay, Sennen Cove and Gribba Point.

Off Land's End itself is a great mass of reef known as the Longships, marked by a lighthouse, while eight miles south-west is the Wolf Rock, a lonely, isolated pinnacle rising sheer from over 90m.

WARNING The dangers in this area are tide and depth, regrettably proven over and over again by avoidable fatalities. One of the worst cases was a young German couple who have not been seen since they dived together on a deep wreck off Gwennap Head.

Coastal dive sites

All the following turnings are off the B3315, which runs from Newlyn to just outside Sennen village, where it joins the A30.

A turning off the B3315 at Trewoofe, down a well made and well signposted road – through very pretty countryside well known for its daffodils in spring and later bluebells – will bring you to LAMORNA COVE. Here there are two vehicle parking areas, both right on the waterfront, with an excellent wide concrete slipway right alongside. In fact, it is almost the only dive site in Cornwall where you can get changed by your vehicle, with the boat bobbing almost alongside. Protected by a huge granite pier, the area and harbour are privately owned, and launching and parking fees are payable to the owner, usually found in his office or in the café next to the gift shop. Very popular with visitors and divers, though there can be a degree of saturation, Lamorna Cove continues to be a favourite launch site, offering good easy access to the entire peninsula.

190 Lamorna Cove Diving is permitted inside the breakwater, and many visiting groups take the opportunity to carry out training or night dives. It is advisable to use SMBs and have boat cover, since fishing boats may appear around the corner without warning and may not see a diving flag stuck in a crack in the blocks.

Opposite: Dive Sites in Area 8, Land's End. This area is covered by Admiralty Charts 2565 (Trevose Head to Dodman Point); 777 (Land's End to Falmouth); Ordnance Survey map 203.

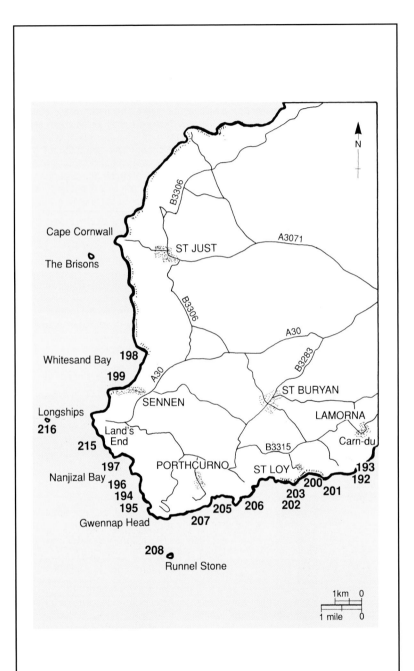

Cape Cornwall

The Brisons

B3306

ST JUST

A3071

B3306

A30

B3283

Whitesand Bay **198**

199

A30

SENNEN

ST BURYAN

LAMORNA

Longships

216

Land's
End

Carn-du

215

B3315

197

PORTHCURNO

ST LOY

193
192

Nanjizal Bay **196**

200

194

203 **201**

195

205 **206** **202**

Gwennap Head

207

208

Runnel Stone

1km   0

1 mile   0

Lamorna Cove is an ideal site for a wide range of diver experience. Depths range from 8m just outside the granite pier to over 18m in the centre of the cove, with loose rock and sandy bottom, heavily weeded. The area was once the site of a granite quarry, and towards the end of the 19th century sailing ships loaded great blocks stone from the tiny pier, built expressly for this purpose.

Facilities at Lamorna Cove include a café, shop, public toilets, the Lamorna Wink Inn, some accommodation and a camp site. The freshwater stream discharging on to the beach can be put to good use, offering a free wash-off for your gear after diving.

A plinth over 20ft tall and weighing 20 tons was sent to the Great Exhibition of 1851 by sea from Lamorna Cove quarry but, in later years the problems of loading caused the stone to be taken to Penzance by road. The business declined, and other quarries nearer the port were started. In its wake, the quarry left the eastern side of the cove a huge rock-slide, and each winter gale tears loose new material and deposits it on the sea bed.

Part way along this eastern cliff, towards the headland of CARN-DU, the coast curves to form a bay.

191 Unidentified wreck 50 53 35N; 05 33 21W. Directly level with a prominent patch of bright green lichen on the cliff, a number of iron cannon are to be found in 15m – from a wreck yet to be identified. Five cannon were on the bottom at the last count; one has been lifted and found its way to Stoney Cove in Leicestershire, where in shallow water it forms part of an underwater archaeological training area. From local records it has been established that a privateer was frequently moored at Lamorna Cove by the local lord to whom it belonged. It was blown ashore in a gale and wrecked at the time of the Civil War, and a number of silver coins of the period found on site in 1984 and 1985 confirm the period.

Penzer Point and the wrecks mentioned in the previous area are only a 15-minute boat ride away to the east, while going westward, the loose rock and sand patches continue with increasing depth of 11 to 15m as you approach the Bucks Rocks, an offshore reef with two pinnacles that dry out at low tide. On the seaward side it is possible to find 28m, while on the inshore side you can see the remains of a steamship wreck, the *Garonne*.

192 Garonne 50 03 05N; 05 34 25W. A small error in dead-reckoning, brought about by seaweed wrapped around the "fish" of the patent log towed astern to measure distance covered, contributed to one of the worst shipwreck disasters along this coast. The ship was the two-masted iron screw steamship *Garonne*, built by Earle's of Hull in 1866, the same company that built the ill-fated *Mohegan*. Her owners were William Miles Moss of Liverpool whose line of steamships operated between the Mersey and the Continent.

A comparatively small ship of only 638 tons and 215ft length, the *Garonne* was divided by four watertight bulkheads, and her compound engine of 90hp gave a maximum speed of 12 knots.

She sailed from Bordeaux on 21 May, 1868, with 600 tons of general cargo and sixteen passengers including four women and eight young children. On 22 May, with the Ushant light dead astern, Captain Drew set course for the Longships

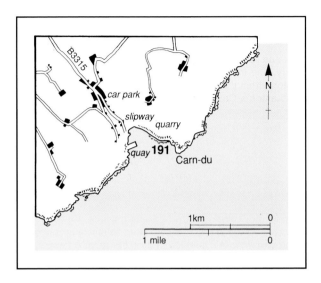

Above: Lamorna Cove, showing the unidentified wreck site (Site 191). The wreck is believed to have belonged to a member of the Penrose family. They kept a privateer in the cove, which was wrecked in a storm.

Below: These three silver shillings, the top one clearly showing the date 1653, were found in concretion close inshore to the stone quarry at Lamorna Cove.

light. Drizzle then set in, visibility dropped, and when sent to read the patent log, the seaman reported it fouled with weed and not reading. At 11.25pm land was sighted dead ahead, but they could not stop her in time and she crashed onto the Bucks Rocks. Holed beneath her engine and boiler room, she filled and settled down. Flares were ignited, boats lowered, but there was confusion in the darkness. Twenty minutes after she struck, the *Garonne* heeled over and sank, drowning 14 of the passengers and three of the crew.

There is no structure left, only scattered corroded ironwork, with many fragments of pottery, tile and bottles. Nick Baker, a Midlands diver, has made a study of the wreck, recovering many artefacts over the years, which he is pleased to show people.

193 Avebury Between the Bucks Rocks and Lamorna Cove, past a prominent cave in the cliff-face and directly opposite an obvious indentation, can be found the remains of this Cardiff collier. On 4 November, 1884, the *Avebury*, homeward bound in ballast from Lisbon, got off course towards the Wolf Rock, missed Land's End completely in the fog, and continued steaming until she plunged onto the rocks about a quarter of a mile from Lamorna Cove. Attempts were made to re-float her, but very few ships ever escape once they go aground around Land's End. All that remains today is the usual scattering of broken iron (at approximately 50 03 15N; 05W); almost nothing recognisable as part of a ship.

The entire coastline from Lamorna Cove to Sennen Cove is littered with shipwrecks and interesting rocks and reefs on which to dive, but there are no

Lamorna Cove, one of the best places in Cornwall for diving groups and families, has good beachside facilities.

other launch sites for a further 4¹/₂ miles until Porthcurno or Porthgwarra, both of which have limitations. The coast itself is 10 miles of almost unbroken cliff, except at Mill Bay, which is suitable for shore diving but not launching. PENBERTH COVE is owned by the National Trust, who prohibit diving boats and divers, and notices make this quite clear.

The village of PORTHCURNO was best known for its Cable and Wireless station and college, which closed in 1992. The road into the village continues down to a large public car park, or over the top of the hill on the western side to the high cliff face and the open air theatre near Minack Point. From the car park it is only a short distance down to the sandy beach and access is excellent. The beach is the landing place for numerous submarine telephone cables to France, Spain and Portugal – heavy plant is needed on the foreshore when new cables are being pulled in from the cable-laying ships. It is also very popular with holidaymakers, and parking attendants may stop you taking trailers and vehicles on to the beach at peak periods. There is now a small wireless and cable museum.

Offshore the bottom continues as clean sand for some distance, with a maximum depth of around 14m. Three coastal wreck sites can be reached from here by boat: the *Granite State* (Site **205**), *St Guenole* (Site **206**) and *Vert Priarial* (Site **207**).

A miniature cove with a small, steep slipway and half a dozen houses, PORTHGWARRA is reached via a very narrow winding road almost two miles long. The entire area is private property, owned by the St Aubyn estate, and is totally unsuitable for anything but a small group of two or three divers at one time.

In the past there has been a considerable amount of friction over large groups who have turned up without making enquiries first, and become abusive when they were told that they were not welcome. This is private property, and the owner has no obligation to let anyone dive here.

The size of the cove is the main limitation, so contact the Harbour Master, Mr Rawlins (tel. 01736 87698) in advance. Give him your party size, type of boat, the time you would like to arrive, and so on, but do not be disappointed if you are refused. There is a daily fee; camping or overnight sleeping are not permitted. Facilities include public toilets, and a shop selling drinks and ice-cream. Out from Porthgwarra, the sea is shallow with a very rough bottom, entirely rock and weed.

Beyond Hella Point the coast is subject to a very strong tide. To the west lies GWENNAP HEAD, around which there are three shipwreck sites, all within Pendower Coves, in a maximum depth of 10m.

194 Wimborne 50 02 32N; 05 41 28W. A Cardiff registered steamship of 3,466 tons, in ballast from Rotterdam to Barry, the *Wimborne* was driven inshore by bad weather on 7 November, 1910, and wrecked close to Carn Guthensbrâs. Her two boilers, engine block and bottom plating remain outside the reef in 15m.

195 J. Duncan 50 02 21N; 05 41 06W. Built by the Ailsa Craig Shipping Company in 1905, the Cardiff collier *J. Duncan*, 1,939 tons, was under charter by the Admiralty to carry coal to Devonport Dockyard.

The SS City of Cardiff (Site 197) was on passage from
Dartmouth to Barry Roads to load coal. She drove ashore in
Mill Bay on 21 March, 1912; one of her boilers still shows
above the surface at low water.

Naval tugs and HMS *Liffey*, plus the lifeboat and local boats all did their best to re-float her after she ran ashore on the north side of Pendower Coves on 14 August, 1913 – but to no avail, and she was abandoned. A single boiler, propeller shaft and cellular double bottom remain on the outside face of a large rock in 15m.

196 Sardius II 50 02 20N; 05 41 05W. A 206-ton steam trawler, wrecked on 13 February, 1918. She too was abandoned complete, but little remains today in a gully between the innermost rocks and the cliff face.

At the point on the B3315 indicating the turning for Porthgwarra, there is a second turning on the same side, leading into a long straight road, with a house on your immediate right hand side. This is a private toll road leading to Bosistow, and it is necessary to stop at the private house to pay. Beware of speed bumps in the three-quarters of a mile made up section of road, which then becomes a very rough track for a similar distance, eventually bringing you to a free parking area overlooking MILL BAY (also known as Nanjizal).

Launching a boat here is not possible; facilities are non-existent, and one must commune with nature when nature calls!

The bays offers a water depth no greater than 11m, with a rock and sand patch bottom, excellent underwater visibility and a great deal of marine life. To the northern side of the bay are the boilers and plates of another steamship wreck.

197 City of Cardiff 50 03 14N; 05 41 48W. Under Captain Storey, the *City of Cardiff* sailed from Le Havre to Cardiff in ballast, bunkered at Dartmouth, and on the 21 March, 1912, was trying to round Land's End in a gale. Only six years old, of 3,089 tons, at 11am she anchored one mile south of Land's End, but slowly dragged inshore. She finally went ashore in Mill Bay, and the crew were

Above: Porthcurno beach.

Below: You can launch at Porthgwarra.

rescued by breeches buoy. The steamer became a broken hulk within 24 hours; one of her boilers remains among the wreckage, and dries at low water.

Today SENNEN COVE supports a modest fishing industry, a lifeboat station, and the tourist industry, being popular with holidaymakers who flock to Whitesand Bay in the summer. The nearby bay has a large sweep of flat sand, from which it is possible to see Land's End to the south, and Cape Cornwall to the north.

Further offshore the twin humps of The Brisons can be seen and, to the south-west, the Longships reef and lighthouse. At low water, vast expanses of offshore rock are exposed, with little more than 6m of water in which to dive, but it is ideal for the less experienced or those wishing to snorkel.

There are three main car park areas, one at the top of the hill before dropping down to sea level, a second at the bottom of the hill, and a third at the far end of Sennen Cove, past the lifeboat station. Of these, the latter is recommended for divers, since it is alongside the wide concrete slipway, on which vehicles can be used to assist launching or recovery. At low water, an expanse of firm sand is exposed leading off into 3m of water alongside the granite quay. Facilities at Sennen Cove are good, with the Old Success Inn, public toilets, cafés and shops, but there is limited accommodation. Outside the village, at the top of the hill, can be found a large food store, a garage, hotel and restaurant, as well as the Mayon Farm self-catering cottages (tel. 01736 87477).

Of the three slipways at Sennen Cove, one is used exclusively by local fishermen and has a power winch. The second is pretty steep with difficult access, but the third (by the harbour wall) is ideal. Permission to launch should be sought from the Harbour Master, and care taken not to obstruct or damage local boats.

To the north of Whitesand Bay, on Gwynver beach, sections of the wreck of the barque *Trifolium* can still be seen at certain states of the tide. The remains of the steamship *Beaumaris* are off the end of the slipway.

Sennen Cove, at the south end of Whitesand Bay.

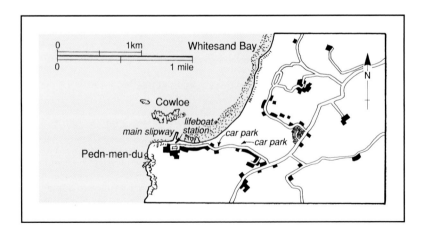

The slipway at Sennen Cove by the lifeboat station is restricted to local use only. Visiting divers should use the slipway further to the north, which runs down onto a sandy beach.

198 Trifolium 50 55 25N; 05 41 48W. Five lives were lost when this 519-ton iron barque of Gothenburg, Sweden, built in 1875, was thrown ashore on Gwenver beach, close to Aire Point on 15 March, 1914. Already 16 days on passage from Cardiff to Brazil with coal and well out into the Atlantic, she started to leak, and had to put back to Falmouth for repairs. She sailed again, straight into the teeth of a dreadful gale, and spent all that Saturday night and Sunday morning beating back and forth around Land's End. During the hours of darkness both her captain and mate were washed overboard and lost.

She blew ashore at 5.30am. The Sennen Cove lifeboat was launched, but was unable to get close to her. A rocket fired at 6.30am to illuminate the wreck showed men in the rigging, but they were too afraid and weak to brave the gale-swept main deck to get hold of the rocket line and rig a breeches buoy. One man did at last jump into the sea and was saved by the lifeboat; three more followed and were rescued, but the rest remained where they were, and drowned when the wreck broke up during the morning.

199 Beaumaris 50 04 50N; 05 42 00W. This was a British steamship of 2,372 tons, armed with a stern-chaser gun and belonging to the Furness Withy Line. On 7 February, 1918, 2½ miles off the Longships, she was in convoy from Cardiff to St Nazaire with coal when she was torpedoed by the German submarine *U-53*. Taken in tow by a warship, she was beached in Whitesand Bay. Her remains – stern post, stern gland, plating and frames – are only a short distance out from the slipway by the car park, opposite the inn. The maximum depth is 3m.

Offshore dive sites and wrecks

The Land's End peninsula offers such a wide range of diving – with vast areas still unexplored, almost anything can still be found on the bottom. In 1992 four new steamship wrecks – one a very old steam paddle tug – were located and identified, either by a nameplate, crockery or a bell.

The two-mile stretch of coast from Tater-du to Merthen Point is essentially a boat dive, since there is no shore access. This stretch of high and rugged cliffs saw the end of at least four identifiable ships, as well as the Penlee lifeboat *Solomon Browne*, lost with all hands in such tragic circumstances. The RNLI and the new lifeboat crew request that it should not be touched.

200 Vierge Marie 50 03 08N; 05 34 50W. Four Belgian fishermen lost their lives when this steel trawler went ashore in heavy seas and bad visibility on 11 January, 1937. She stranded at 7am after having engine trouble off Land's End and drifting out of control. Her skipper, Emil Lus, and a deck hand started to climb the cliffs, but were rescued by breeches buoy. The bodies of the other four crew were found by the lifeboat near Lamorna Cove.

201 Union Star 50 03 00N; 05 35 30W. Perhaps the worst shipwreck incident in Cornwall this century, and one that is still alive in the minds of local people to this day. It was 19 December, 1981, when the Penlee lifeboat was called to assist the brand new Dublin registered coaster *Union Star*, on her maiden voyage from IJmuiden to Arklow in conditions that could not have been worse. Winds were gusting over 115mph, so the sea conditions off Land's End can hardly be imagined.

Exactly what happened that night is still not clear, and never will be, although there is some evidence from the crew of a search-and-rescue helicopter crew and salvaged sections of the lifeboat. The skipper of the *Union Star* delayed in seeking the assistance of a salvage tug that was on site, and the *Solomon Browne* somehow managed to get alongside and save four of those aboard, including a woman.

It was probably during a second attempt to save the remainder that she was lifted high on the crest of a mountainous sea, perhaps 60ft high, dropped like a stone into the trough directly on top of a submerged rock, and was shattered. Next morning, all that could be seen was the upturned hull of the coaster on the rocks in a small cove, and masses of floating wreckage. The lifeboat was completely gone, along with its eight-man crew, plus all eight on board the *Union Star* – an unbelievable tragedy in this modern age. The *Union Star* was torn to pieces long ago by the sea, but her remains are still there, in 10m depth, some 165ft from the cliffs, jammed into the rocks.

The impact on the Mousehole community just before Christmas 1981 of losing not only its lifeboat but its entire crew – not all of whose bodies were found – was traumatic in the extreme. Only part of the boat was recovered for examination, and you are requested not to open old wounds locally by bringing up pieces as souvenirs.

202 Juan Ferrer 50 02 59N; 05 35 24W. During the early hours of 23 October, 1963, in thick fog, the 32-year-old captain of this 700-ton coaster registered in Valencia, Luis Ruiz, was in radio contact with Land's End Radio to check his position. Seconds later a lookout called out "Rocks ahead!", but his call for "Full astern" was never heard or acted on, since she crashed into a wall of granite below Carn Boscawen. At 3am the radio station picked up a second message from her, "Juan Ferrer; am ashore vicinity of Mount's Bay". It was the last signal they could make before the sea drowned the generator.

Lifeboats and cliff rescue teams scoured the cliffs from Marazion to Land's End to find the casualty, and the Penlee lifeboat saved the captain from the sea. Eleven of her crew drowned. Her wreck lies between Boscawen Point and a large rock to the west, in 12 to 18m, very broken and dispersed.

203 South America 50 03 00N; 05 36 00W. There are two shipwrecks at this location. On 13 March, 1912, residents living on the cliffs overlooking St Loy Bay, near Merthen Point, were woken up by the crack of distress rockets. Through the rain and fog they could just make out the square outline of a large steamship ashore. She was the 4,197-ton *South America* of London, on her way from Hamburg to Cardiff in ballast, and she had gone aground while attempting to avoid fishing vessels in the area.

Shouts led the onlookers to two ship's lifeboats holding fifteen men and a woman. The cliff rescue unit was summoned, set up their gear, and in their haste

In the most tragic shipwreck on the south coast of Cornwall in modern times, the MV Union Star was driven ashore near Boscawen Point on 19 December, 1981. In a rescue attempt to save the people on board, the Penlee lifeboat Solomon Browne went out in hurricane conditions and was lost with all her crew.

In a remarkable coincidence, the wreck of the SS South America (Site 203), which went ashore near Merthen Point in March 1912, was joined by the smaller Abertay seven months later. Both ships grounded in fog.

fired a line across the wreck without bothering to ask if there was anyone on board! There was no one there, and their efforts were wasted.

204 Abertay Seven months later, on 14 October, the residents were again disturbed by strange noises coming from the sea. Reaching the foreshore they were amazed to see a second steamship tight up against the port side of the *South America*. This turned out to be the 599-ton steel *Abertay* of Lorient, bound for Barry with pit wood. She too had got lost in the fog, and crashed into the side of the existing wreck.

Both wrecks were partially dismantled where they lay, but when winter gales tore the remains to pieces, they were abandoned. Today all you will find are bent steel plates half buried under boulders.

205 Granite State 50 02 30N; 05 38 50W. At dawn on 4 November, 1895, the residents of Porthcurno woke to find the American clipper *Granite State* lying very close inshore with all sail set. Built at Kittery, Maine, in 1877, she had called at Falmouth for orders and had been instructed to proceed to Swansea to unload her cargo of wheat from Buenos Aires. Rounding Land's End she struck the Lee Ore rocks – an outcrop of inside the Runnel Stone, but just as lethal – and it was fortunate that the Cardiff tug *Elliott and Jeffry* was on hand to get her off, and tow her into Porthcurno.

Water entering her hold swelled the cargo, and she was abandoned a total wreck. Wreckage came ashore in large quantities, but her hull remains where she sank in the bay.

206 St Guenole 50 02 36N; 05 37 42W. It was at 1am on 1 November, 1948, when the duty Coastguard at Treen saw the lights of a vessel appear out of the rain squalls and head directly for Pedn-e-Vounder sands. His Aldis lamp flashed out an instruction, and the mystery vessel vanished eastward around the Logan Rock.

In Penberth Cove there was no sign of wreckage, but then the Coastguard smelt diesel fuel in the wind, and called out the Treen Coastguard Cliff Rescue Company. A man seen in the surf was rescued, a life-jacket marked "St Guenole – Rouen" was found, and at dawn a 500-ton vessel was sighted upside down beneath Gribba Point. A steel tar tanker, the *St Guenole* she was in ballast from Nantes to Irvine (on the Clyde) to load. Twenty-three-year-old André Fourcin, the sailor saved from the sea, was the only survivor. The only remains are in shallow water, the steel plates and fittings part buried under boulders.

207 Vert Priarial 50 02 18N; 05 39 25W. On 13 March, 1956, a faint SOS signal, prefixed by the call sign "Dieppe 1517", was picked by the Isles of Scilly steamer *Peninnis*. A search of the sea revealed nothing, and extensive enquiries were made to determine which vessel this was. It proved to be the 250-ton Dieppe trawler *Vert Priarial*, which had been heading for the fishing grounds off Trevose Head.

Next morning at 5.30, a man searching for driftwood at Porth Chapel found a large steel trawler wrecked in the shallows. Of her 17 crew there were no survivors. Only her engine block and some plating remains on the rocks under Wireless Point today in shallow water.

It is said, though not meant to be taken literally, that the shallow water around the RUNNEL STONE is due to the vast number of wrecks piled one on top of the other. Between 1880 and 1923 over 30 identified steamships were wrecked, stranded or sank in the area, and another – believed lost near the French coast in 1918 – was found there recently. Until 1923, the top of the reef always showed above the surface at low water, but that year a steamship struck it fair and square, and knocked the top clean off!

208 City of Westminster 50 01 26.5N; 05 40 17.9W. This was a 6,173-ton steamer operated by the Ellerman Line after being taken over by the Shipping Controller at the end of World War One and having her name changed from *Rudelsburg*. Bound from Belfast to Rotterdam with a cargo of South African maize, she struck the Runnel Stone rock at 3pm on 8 October, 1923. A total of 72 people were taken off by the Sennen and Penlee lifeboats, which were towed by a Penzance steam drifter to Newlyn. The ship broke its back, and became a total loss.

Today her remains lie in 30 to 36m depth, her bow jammed into the eastern side of a gully, almost touching the eastern face of the Runnel Stone, with a great depth of packed steel and plates, at least 2.5m in places. Her stern is more intact and is in slightly deeper water. The wreck is upright, with some of the superstructure intact, and lies north-north-west to south-south-east, her stern towards the south. The sea bed is strewn with her masts, derricks and fittings.

209 Moorview 50 01 21N: 05 40 18W. A Royal Fleet Auxiliary vessel, this 177-ton ship bound from Belfast to Devonport also struck the Runnel Stone. She went headlong into it at 2.30am on 4 March, 1920 in dense fog, sinking at once, but her crew of 28 managed to get clear in their own boats.

If the SS Bluejacket (Site 216) had struck the rocks some 300 yards to the north when she went ashore in 1898, she could well have damaged the Longships lighthouse.

Less than three months old, having been launched at Paisley that December, 1919, the *Moorview* went down in 30m and her remains are mixed up with other wreckage.

210 Febrero 50 01 26N; 05 40 17W. On the eastern face of the Runnel Stone, between 20 and 25m deep, with her bow towards Porthgwarra Cove, lies the Spanish 1,863-ton steamship *Febrero*, lost with a cargo of iron ore on 20 June, 1910. She saw the worst loss of life in any modern wreck here, only the cook being saved out of a crew of 28 and four passengers.

211 HMS Wild Boar 50 01 21N; 05 40 18W. A 238-ton British 10-gun brig-sloop of the Indian Cherokee class, built by Pelham at Frindsbury (near Rochester) in 1808. She blundered into the Runnel Stone on 15 February, 1810, when bound for the West Indies from Falmouth. No reports have been made of her location, and her ten iron cannon may well still be on the bottom.

212 Unidentified Admiralty store ship 50 01 21N; 05 40 26W. Still with no name – if ever she had one in the first place – this stores hulk was under escort of the 14-gun sloop HMS *Caroline*, bound for Milford Haven from Portsmouth, when she too hit the Runnel Stone, on 7 March, 1806. Lieutenant Derby of the escort ship managed to take off all the crew, but the ship went to the bottom, taking with it a prodigious quantity of copper bolts, brass and gunmetal fittings, spars and yards, all destined for use on men-of-war under repair.

In September 1969 some three-quarters of a ton of copper hull pins from this ship were declared to the Receiver of Wreck at Penzance, and over the next few months the wreck was stripped clean of non-ferrous metal.

213 Lake Grafton 50 01 45N: 05 40 10W. Another steamship, a 1,609-ton Chicago vessel, which struck the Lee Ore rocks. If you can locate the wreck of the *Febrero* (Site **210**) you will find that her bow almost touches the *Lake Grafton*, which was wrecked on 14 May, 1920, carrying coal.

214 Joshua Nicholson 50 01 47N; 05 40 10W. If you continue along the length of the *Lake Grafton*, going north and inshore, you will encounter the mid section of yet another steamship – the *Joshua Nicholson*, which lies in only 15m.

Attacked by the German submarine *U-70* off the Wolf Rock on 18 March, 1917, this 1,853-ton British steamship, built in 1880 by the Tyne Iron Shipbuilding Company, was on passage from London to Alexandria with a general cargo. A single torpedo struck her, killing 26 crew including her master, but she did not sink. Taken in tow, she broke adrift off Land's End and drifted ashore inside Lee Ore rocks, where she sank. The wreck was identified by her bell, which was located in the 1970s.

Words cannot adequately describe diving on the Runnel Stone, since there is wreck after wreck everywhere, and more yet to be found. A drift dive across the reef will guarantee you see the remains of at least five ships, if not more, with masses of fish, sponges, cup-corals, urchins and shellfish.

WARNING The times of slack water on the Runnel Stone are not easy to calculate, the main slack being 1½ hours before high water slack at Newlyn, then another brief slack 2 hours after Newlyn. The same goes for the Lee Ore rocks, where great caution is necessary. As the tide ebbs out of Mount's Bay, the last of the ebb flows in towards Tol-Pedn headland, and then follows the coast close in, going north-west.

The offshore outcrop of rock beneath Land's End known as the Armed Knight has an average depth of 12m, is scoured by tide and, despite being close to the land, can only be dived at slack water.

215 Dieppois 50 03 40N; 05 43 05W. A French steamship on her maiden voyage, which struck the Armed Knight on 28 March, 1890. Homeward bound for Dieppe from Swansea with coal, she would not have been so close inshore but for the dense fog. Two boilers, propeller shaft and plating survives.

Outside the usual dive boat charter area for licensed boats, the LONGSHIPS is a reef running north–south, and supports a lighthouse. It is also described as excellent diving country – in fact some of the best there is. The tide here is extremely fast, and a huge area of overfalls show into the ebb, as the great mass of water from the Bristol Channel and the English Channel empties out into the same area.

The best diving is to be found on the north and north-west side drop-offs down to a sandy sea bed at 42m, and in one place there is a wall of at least 24m. As with the Runnel Stone, there are pinnacles and gullies, some 3m deep, others bare, but everywhere abundant life. Near the lighthouse, on the western side, in 12m will be found ironwork from the SS *Bluejacket*.

216 Bluejacket 50 03 55N; 05 44 42W. The most spectacular shipwreck on the Longships, this Cardiff tramp steamer struck the rocks less than twenty yards from the entrance to the lighthouse, and could well have knocked it down! This happened on 9 November, 1898, while the *Bluejacket* was in ballast between Plymouth Sound and Cardiff to load coal.

The weather was thick, but since shore lights were visible, she maintained her top speed of 10 knots. She went ashore during the second mate's watch, even though the captain had asked to be called as they approached Land's End so that he could be on the bridge. Of 2,205 tons, built in 1883, the *Bluejacket* became a total wreck.

217 Chase While the *Bluejacket* was being salvaged, the small steam tug *Chase* dragged her anchors, and in a strong westerly gale, was wrecked beneath the windows of the Land's End Hotel.

Directly beneath the Visitors' Centre at Land's End are a number of deep gullies, including Dollar (or Dorlor) Cove.

218 Dollar Cove 50 53 50N; 05 42 54W. This cove between Carn Kez and the Armed Knight is worth a visit when perfectly flat diving conditions exist. Within this gully at least four steel ships have been lost in recent years, including the Cypriot motor vessel *Nefeli* on 5 November, 1972, and the French trawler *Jean Gougy* on 3 November, 1962.

On passage from Garston to Antwerp in ballast, the MV Nefeli (see Site 218) went aground in fog on the Longships, and then drifted off to be wrecked in Dollar Cove, under the cliffs at Land's End.

*The French Trawler Jeanne
Gougy (see Site 218) aground
near Land's End in November
1962. As the tide fell, five of the
crew were plucked to safety.*

219 Gamper Bay In the adjacent Gamper Bay, the trawler *Laverenne* was
wrecked on 20 September, 1973.

The SHARK'S FIN ROCK is another isolated rock offshore north-east of the
Longships, which shows some 3m at low water and offers spectacular diving (at
slack water only, due to the heavy tide). The rock drops off to 30m at one place,
and wreckage has been reported at the base.

The WOLF ROCK is well outside the range of usual dive charter boats, but some of
the larger craft from Falmouth can operate in the area. It is seven miles offshore
and has been described as perfect diving. Due to its isolation and position it
offers almost gin-clear water at times – when it can be reached.
   The rock holds a lighthouse, now automatic, and derived its name from a rock
feature that used to cause the wind to howl like a wolf. An isolated pinnacle, it
has up to 61m depth all round. It is seldom dived, and no positive sightings of
wreckage have been reported, although many have taken place in the area after
striking the rock itself. There is a story that a World War Two German U-boat
drove straight into the rock and was lost, but the wreck has never been found.

APPENDIX 1:

Dive Services

Boats for charter or hire

The following boats are available from Plymouth:

Catch 22 (diver skipper Dick Linford), 6 divers, 22ft, all electronic equipment (tel. 01752 862488).

Cee-King (diver skipper Richard Kings), all electronic equipment (tel. 01752 663247).

Deepwater, 65ft, 8.5 knots, twelve divers, all electronic equipment, lifting hoist. Contact Fort Bovisand (tel. 01752 48021).

Excalibur (diver skipper Roger Webber), 10 divers, 30ft, all electronic equipment fitted (tel. 01752 405403 or 0891 222762).

Plymouth Beatrice (diver skipper John Holman), 35ft, twelve divers (tel. 01752 790605).

Ranelagh (diver skipper Ted Cavanah), twelve divers, 36ft, electronic equipment, lifting bags and sledge available (tel. 01752 670674).

Sapphire (skipper Ernie Palmer), twelve divers, 33ft, all electronic equipment fitted (tel. 01752 266248).

Storm (diver skipper Rod Davies), 31ft, all electronic equipment, 10 divers (tel. 01752 862165).

Boats are also available for charter from the Plymouth Boatman's Association (tel. 01752 862488 or 0860 463233).

At Millendreath a charter boat for up to twelve people is available for hire with a skipper. Contact Millendreath Marine (tel. 015036 263281).

At Looe there is only one licensed diving charter boat:

Ibis (skipper Paul Greenwood), twelve divers, 32ft (tel. 01503 263311).

No boats are available for hire for diving at Portwrinkle.

Very few dive boats are available for hire at Fowey. Dennis Rose at Fowey Marine Services, 21–27 Station Road, Fowey (tel. 01726 833236) has at least one hard boat and one inflatable for hire. Dive Charter have a fully equipped Mitchell 31 hard boat – contact Rob Crayton (tel. 01726 817790).

Names and details of other fishing vessels available for hire can be obtained through the Fowey Harbour Master, Captain M.J. Sutherland (tel. 01726 832471, fax 01726 833738).

The slipway at Albert Pier, Penzance. Alongside are the BSAC branch headquarters and compressor station.

The following boats are available in the Falmouth area:

Patrice II, licensed for twelve divers, diver skipper. Echo-sounder, Decca, toilet. For hire evening, day or weekend. Contact Mike Tuffrey (tel. 01326 313265).

Seaquest, 33ft, Lochin, diesel engine, licensed for twelve divers, all electronics, diver skipper, tows 16ft inflatable. Contact John Ellis, Seaways Dive Shop, Commercial Road, Penryn (tel. 01326 375544; fax 01326 375401).

Mentor, 23m former Naval tender, fully equipped cabins, shower, galley. Will take 10 divers to Scillies, Channel Islands, Brittany, Southern Ireland from Mylor or Penzance. Contact Ken Dunstan (tel. 01872 862080).

Rum-Tum, Helford River based diving boat, 8 divers, Decca, sounder, air. Contact Bruce Vicars (tel. 01326 231224).

Duchess of Cornwall, 54ft former Watson Class lifeboat *Sir Godfrey Baring* stationed at Bangor. Licensed for twelve divers, fitted with all electronics. Contact John Bolitho, Ruan Minor, the Lizard (tel. 01326 290623).

RIBs and hard boats are available for charter from Dive Action Watersports, Predannack Holiday Village, The Lizard (tel. 01326 240042).

These boats are available from Penzance:

War Lord of Pentargon, 36ft, licensed for twelve divers but prefers groups of eight to ten, fitted with all electronics and toilet. Contact Peter Uterhark, 2 Pendarves Road, Penzance (tel. 01736 68859).

Son Caliou, 36ft, licensed for twelve divers, fitted with all electronics and professional magnetometer, toilet and cooking facilities. Contact Bill Bowen, Monrovia, 17 Hayle Terrace, Hayle (tel. 01736 752135).

Chalutier, 65ft live-aboard charter boat, fully equipped, all electronics. Cornwall, Devon, Scillies, Channel Islands, Brittany. Contact CDF Charters (tel. 01329 431841).

Air supplies

Fort Bovisand, Plymouth (tel. 01752 408021). Also diving equipment, repairs, cylinder testing, inflatables and equipment hire.

Sandford and Down, 24 Pier Street, The Hoe, Plymouth (tel. 01752 266248). Also diving equipment, repairs, equipment hire.

Sound Diving, Queen Anne's Battery Marina, Plymouth (tel. 01752 670674). Also diving equipment, repairs, equipment hire.

Millendreath Marine (summer season only), Millendreath Holiday Centre, near Looe (tel. 015036 263281). Also diving equipment, equipment hire.

Fowey Marine Services, Caffa Mill Car Park, Fowey (tel. 01726 833236).

Oceansports, 17 West End, Pentewan, St Austell (tel. 01726 842817).

Cornish Diving Centre, Bar Road, Falmouth (tel. 01326 311265).

Falmouth Underwater Centre, Maenporth Beach, Falmouth (tel. 01326 250852). Seaways Diving Shop, Commercial Road, Penryn (tel. 01326 375544).

Polkerris Divers, St Keverne (tel. 01326 280620).

Sea Acres Holiday Park, Kennack (tel. 01326 290064).

Dive Action Watersports, Predannack Holiday Village, The Lizard (tel. 01326 240042).

Francis's Holidays, Cury Cross Lanes, Mullion (tel. 01326 240301).

Bill Bowen, Albert Pier, Penzance (tel. 01736 752135).

St Hilary, Trevenegge Farm, St Hilary, Goldsithney.

Outboard motor servicing

Below Decks, Queen Anne's Battery, Plymouth (tel. 01752 222546).

International Marine Sales, Coxside, Plymouth (tel. 01752 221802).

Boating World, Landrake (tel. 01752 851515).

Robin Curnow, Commercial Road, Penryn (tel. 01326 373438).

Gus Cashmore, Commercial Road, Penryn (tel. 01326 372353).

Norgar Engineering, Newquay Road, Truro (tel. 01872 71997).

Malpas Marine, Malpas, Truro (tel. 01872 71260).

Polkerris Divers, St Keverne (tel. 01326 280620).

Penzance Outboard Motor Centre, Longrock Industrial Estate, Penzance (tel. 01736 68798).

Inflatable boat repairs and spare parts

Penryn Marine, Freeman's Wharf, Penryn (tel. 01326 76201).

BSAC and SAA branches

Just Divin' (1501). Contact S. Shelley, 20 Westfield Avenue, Hooe, Plymouth.

Plymouth Sound (164) meet on Wednesdays at 8pm. Contact P. Martin (tel. 01752 405771).

BSAC special branches in the Plymouth area: Greenbank (1612); Joint Services SAC (872); Plymouth Armada (1418); Plymouth Command SAC (1418); Plymouth Diving School (1703); Plymouth Polytechnic (474); RNAD (627); Sound Diving Instruction School (1704); Tamar (1233).

Bovisand Sport Divers (1550) meet on Wednesdays at 8pm. Contact E. Rudge (tel. 01752 872656).

Fort Bovisand BSAC School (1047).

Looe BSAC (1631) meets at the Jolly Sailor at West Looe on Wednesdays at 8pm. Contact E. Whitley, The Old Chapel, Minard Cross, Downderry PL11 3HE (tel. 01503 5605).

Mid Cornwall BSAC (885) meets at Polkyth Recreation Centre on Wednesdays. Contact P. McDermott, 29 Carlyon Road, St Austell, Cornwall PL25 4LJ.

Fowey SAA meet on Thursdays, 9pm at the Fowey Hotel. Contact D.J. Rose, Fowey Diving Services (tel. 01726 833236).

Falmouth Dolphins (1402) meet on Wednesdays at the Odd Fellows Inn, 8pm. Contact Steve McEwan, Cornish Diving Services, Barr Road, Falmouth.

Truro Divers (1541) meet Mondays at 9pm at Truro Swimming Pool. Contact R. Pritchard, 5 The Parade, Truro. TR1 1QE (tel. 01872 78701).

Truro Diving Services BSAC School (1327). Contact John Ellis, Seaways Diving Shop, Commercial Road, Penryn (tel. 01326 375544).

Mullion SAC. Contact Richard Harris, 38 Church Hill, Helston (tel. 01326 561087). Camborne Tolgus BSAC (778) meet at Carn Brea Leisure Centre on Thursdays at 7.30pm. Contact Paul Roberts.

Penzance and District BSAC (116) meet at the club house on Albert Pier on Thursdays.

You can launch a boat at Flushing.

APPENDIX 2:

The Diver's Code of Conduct

Divers must at all times adhere to the BSAC code of conduct. It is reproduced here with the kind permission of the British Sub-Aqua Club, and has been extracted from the BSAC *Safe Diving Practices* booklet, available from BSAC Headquarters.

THE DIVER'S CODE OF CONDUCT

More and more people are taking to the water. Some for recreation; some to earn their living. This code is designed to ensure that divers do not come into conflict with other water users. It is vital that you observe it at all times.

Before leaving home

Contact the nearest British Sub-Aqua Club Branch or the dive operator local to the dive site for their advice. Seek advice from them about the local conditions and regulations.

On the beach, river bank or lakeside

1. Obtain permission, before diving in a harbour or estuary or in private water. Thank those responsible before you leave. Pay harbour dues.

2. Try to avoid overcrowding one site, consider other people on the beach.

3. Park sensibly. Avoid obstructing narrow approach roads. Keep off verges. Pay parking fees and use proper car parks.

4. Don't spread yourselves and your equipment since you may upset other people. Keep launching ramps and slipways clear.

5. Please keep the peace. Don't operate a compressor within earshot of other people – or late at night.

6. Pick up litter. Close gates. Be careful about fires. Avoid any damage to land or crops.

7. Obey special instructions such as National Trust rules, local bye-laws and regulations about camping and caravanning.

8. Remember divers in wetsuits are conspicuous and bad behaviour could ban us from beaches.

In and on the water

1. Mark your dive boats so that your Club can be identified easily. Unmarked boats may become suspect.

2. Ask the harbour-master or local officials where to launch your boat – and do as they say. Tell the Coastguard, or responsible person, where you are going and tell them when you are back.

3. Stay away from buoys, pots, and pot markers. Ask local fishermen where not to dive. Offer to help them recover lost gear.

4. Remember ships have not got brakes, so avoid diving in fairways or areas of heavy surface traffic and observe the "International Regulations for the Prevention of Collisions at Sea".

5. Always fly the diving flag when diving, but not when on the way to, or from, the dive site. Never leave a boat unattended.

6. Do not come in to bathing beaches under power. Use any special approach lanes. Do not disturb any seal or bird colonies with your boats. Watch your wash in crowded anchorages.

7. Whenever possible, divers should use a surface marker buoy.

On conservation

1. Never use a speargun with an aqualung. Never use a speargun in fresh water.

2. Shellfish, such as crabs and lobsters, take several years to grow to maturity; over-collecting in an area soon depletes stocks. Only take mature fish or shellfish and then only what you need for yourself. Never sell your catch or clean it in public or on the beach. Don't display your trophies.

3. Be conservation conscious. Avoid damage to weeds and the sea bed. Do not bring up sea-fans, corals, starfish or sea urchins – in one moment you can destroy years of growth.

4. Take photographs and notes – not specimens. Shoot with a camera not a speargun – spearfishing makes fish shy of divers. Never spearfish wrasse or other inshore species since once an area is depleted of such fish, it may take a long time for them to re-colonise.

On wrecks

1. Do not dive on a designated wreck site. These are indicated on Admiralty Charts and marked by buoys or warning notices on the shore nearby.

2. Do not lift anything which appears to be of historical importance.

3. If you do discover a wreck, do not talk about it. Pinpoint the site, do a rough survey and report it to the BSAC Archaeology Adviser and the Council for Nautical Archaeology who will advise you.

4. If you do not lift anything from the wreck, it is not necessary to report your discovery to the Receiver of Wreck. If you do lift, you must report.

5. If your find is important, you may apply for it to be designated a protected site. Then you can build up a well qualified team with the right credentials and proceed with a systematic survey or excavation under licence without outside interference.

Don't Let Divers Down – Keep To The Diver's Code

This monument in St Keverne churchyard is to the victims of the Mohegan.

APPENDIX 3:

Reference Books on Cornish Shipwrecks

British Merchant Ships sunk by U-Boats in the 1914–1918 War. Tennent, A. J. 1990. The Starling Press Ltd, Newport. ISBN 0 9516314 0 3.

British Vessels Lost at Sea 1914–8. (HMSO, reprint). 1977. Patrick Stephens, Cambridge. ISBN 0 85059 291 7.

British Vessels Lost at Sea 1939–45. (HMSO, reprint). 1977. Patrick Stephens, Cambridge. ISBN 0 85059 267 4.

British Warship Losses in the Age of Sail. Hepper, D. J. 1994. Jean Boudriot Publications, Rotherfield. ISBN 0 948864 30 3.

Castaway & Wrecked. Cowan, R. 1978. Duckworth & Co. ISBN 0 71561145 3.

Cornish Lights & Shipwrecks. Noall, C. 1968. D. Bradford Barton, Truro.

Cornish Shipwrecks – the South Coast. Larn, R. & Carter, C. 1969. David & Charles. ISBN 7153 4289 4.

Cornwall's Lighthouse Heritage. Tarrant, M. 1990. Twelveheads Press, Truro. ISBN 0 906294 20 7.

Cornwall's Maritime Heritage. Kittridge, A. 1989. Twelveheads Press, Truro. ISBN 0 906294 15 0.

Dive South Devon. McDonald, K. 1995 edition. Underwater World Publications Ltd. ISBN 0 946020 24 8.

The harbour at Coverack.

Don't Forget the Diver. Chard, C. A. Chambers. 1958.

Guide to Historic Wreck Sites. Archaeological Diving Unit. University of St Andrew's. 1994.

Lloyd's War Losses, the First World War. Lloyd's of London Press Ltd. 1989. ISBN 1 85044 314 9.

Lloyd's War Losses, the Second World War. Lloyd's of London Press Ltd. 1989. ISBN 1 85044 217 7.

Mullyon, its History, Scenery & Antiquities. Harvey, Rev. E. G. 1875. W. Lake, Truro.

Shipwreck. Fowles, J. & Gibson, F. 1974. Jonathan Cape. ISBN 0 224 01053 0.

Shipwreck Index of the British Isles, Volume 1. Larn, R. & B. 1995. Lloyd's Register of Shipping, ISBN 0 980528 88 5.

Shipwrecks around Land's End. Larn, R. & B. 1992. Tor Mark Press, Penryn. ISBN 0 85025 307 1.

Shipwrecks around Mount's Bay. Larn, R. & B. 1991. Tor Mark Press, Penryn. ISBN 0 85025 326 8.

Shipwrecks around the Lizard. Larn, R. & B. 1989. Tor Mark Press, Penryn. ISBN 0 85025 306 3.

Shipwrecks – Falmouth to Looe. Larn, R. & B. 1993. Tor Mark Press, Penryn. ISBN 0 85025 338 1.

The Cruel Cornish Sea. Mudd, D. 1981. Bossiney Books, Bodmin. ISBN 0 906456 09 6.

The Treasure Ship of Gunwalloe. Whitley, H. Royal Institute of Cornwall Journal, No. 10, Part 1.

The Wreck of the St. Anthony. Chynoweth, J. Royal Institute of Cornwall Journal, 1968. Vol. 4, Part 4.

West Country Shipwrecks. Behenna, J. 1974. David & Charles. ISBN 0 7153 6569 X.

Acknowledgements

So many divers, non-divers, companies, organisations and authorities have assisted the author and publishers in the preparation of this guide, that it is impossible to list them all. Many will recognise their contribution immediately, particularly:

- John Ellis of Seaways, Penryn

- Kevin Heath of St Keverne

- Steve McEwan of Cornish Diving Services

- Ken Bazeley of Maenporth

- John Davies of Truro

- Dennis Rose of Fowey Diving Services

- Mike Hall of Ruan Minor, The Lizard

Many others who have assisted with information or suggested improvements to the content of this guide. Their time, co-operation and expert knowledge of local waters is acknowledged with sincere appreciation. Hopefully they will take some pleasure from having helped to provide the diving fraternity with what can only be described as the most comprehensive underwater publication concerning south Cornwall ever published.

All the colour photographs – except those on pages ii, 87, 120, 158, 170, 172 (both), 174 (top and bottom) and 209 – were taken by Roy Smallpage and the photograph on the front cover was taken by David McBride, Isles of Scilly. The photograph on page 30 was taken by Mike Milman of Plymouth. The photographs on pages 45 and 57 were supplied by Harry & Billie Graeme and the photograph on page 72 was supplied by George Ellis of Bodmin. All the other photographs were taken by the author or are from his collection.

Index

The bold numbers in parentheses are dive site numbers.